PEARSON

Communication in Everyday Life

Fifth Edition

Dalton A. Kehoe

Cover art and design and all figures and illustrations by Monica E. Venditto.

This special edition published in cooperation with Pearson Learning Solutions.

Pearson Learning Solutions, 501 Boylston Street, Suite 900, Boston, MA 02116
A Pearson Education Company
www.pearsoned.com

Printed in Canada

6 17

000200010271749951

LF

ISBN 10: 1-269-15107-X
ISBN 13: 978-1-269-15107-8

COMMUNICATION IN EVERYDAY LIFE

FIFTH EDITION

BRIEF TABLE OF CONTENTS

COMMUNICATION IN EVERYDAY LIFE

FIFTH EDITION

TABLE OF CONTENTS

PREFACE

In this book I have done three things that are not usually done in most introductory communication texts. First, I have placed the social scientific model of interpersonal communication (outlined in Chapter 1) in opposition to what I believe is a widely shared view of talk as an important, but mostly automatic, process of reaction to others' behaviors. By doing this, I am not simply taking the role of the dispassionate reporter of research theory and data as much as I am attempting to arouse the students' interest in seeing their behavior from a different perspective. I want to awaken them to the complexity of the communication behavior that lies beneath the surface of their "natural" — deeply enculturated — patterns of responses to others' talk.

Second, my approach emphasizes the shaping power of the cognitive unconscious in everyday life and talk. It is the storehouse of our deep cultural learning, and as recent research has indicated, it acts as an irresistible shaping force in our feeling, perception and thinking processes and thus on our talk. Moreover, it produces instantaneous and continuous emotional reactions to the people we encounter and to situations in which we find ourselves. I argue that these reactions not only affect the meanings of our words and the nature of our relationships with others while we are talking with them, but also before we have exchanged a word with them. They act as a third level in the communication of meaning in our model of face-to-face talk.

The cognitive unconscious is always influencing our thoughts and words to some degree, and in difficult conversations, it can create dramatic shifts in our behavior unless we notice the "somatic markers" of change in our body and consciously intervene. With practice, we can learn to use our conscious mind to slow down our reaction processes in these situations. Effective practice requires two things: (1) a change of mindset about our communication — a view of talk based on mindfulness and appreciation; and (2) a choice of skills — including what to say, when — that allow us to express ourselves as consciously self-managed communicators.

The third and perhaps most distinctive contribution of this text is the "Three Mode" model of interpersonal talk. It is here that I distinguish between the types of talk we automatically use and those situations where we can learn "what to say, when" to be more effective. I have divided all face-to-face talk into three general categories — C.O.N.N.E.C.T., C.O.N.T.R.O.L. and D.I.A.L.O.G.U.E. talk. The names of the first two types of talk reflect their intention and purpose. These two categories cover the mostly automatic responses we make in two general contexts — talk in predictable, orderly situations where people agree that connection is the central purpose — and talk in problematic situations where problems develop or already exist and disconnection looms. The third type of talk represents a mindful and appreciative way of speaking consciously when faced with problems. The D.I.A.L.O.G.U.E. acronym guides readers through a set of conversational choices, named by each of its letters, toward a more satisfying solution to whatever problems they encounter. Unlike other texts where good advice seems to be "added on" to theory in order to help the reader, here it flows directly from the model of talk itself.

The effectiveness of this approach is demonstrated every year when I am told by many of my students, and participants in my communications training workshops, that this way of thinking about and changing their talk has helped them alter some key relationship in their life for the better. As a communicational pragmatist I am even more pleased when they sum up their experience by asserting, "This stuff really works!"

Dalton Kehoe, Ph.D.
Senior Scholar
Communication Studies
Faculty of Liberal and Professional Studies
York University

CHAPTER ONE

THE NATURE OF FACE-TO-FACE COMMUNICATION

The Perfect Communicator

You and I know that we suffer through communication breakdowns a lot in our lives. One of the reasons we get by without questioning our own communication when this happens is the fact that we unwittingly think of ourselves as perfect communicators.

Take a moment and think about your initial reaction when someone you're talking to just doesn't seem to get it. You think you've explained things as clearly as you can and they just don't understand. How do you react?

If you're like the thousands of people who've answered this question in my classes and workshops over the years, you'll say that your first reaction is usually frustration or anger, and your first thought is, "What's wrong with them?" If we believe something is wrong with them then we don't have to understand what's really happening — we already know — it's their fault. This is what organizational communication theorist Chris Argyris[1] calls a "self-sealing belief" — we don't have to learn anything about ourselves, or our communication, if a problem occurs, because we automatically deny any responsibility for it. An opening for awareness and learning is automatically sealed and we don't have to think about it. How easy. How safe.

The Vain Brain

Neuroscientists believe our brain is hardwired to reinforce the "I am an effective communicator — you're a dunce" model of explaining communication problems. In her funny and informative book *A Mind of Its Own*, neuropsychologist Cordelia Fine[2] reviews the experimental literature and concludes that whenever challenged, our brain enhances and aggrandizes us. She reviews survey data that says, when asked, we will "modestly and reluctantly confess" that we are simply better than most other people on most dimensions of human behavior. Social psychologists call this the "self-serving bias." She calls it our "vain brain." It excuses our faults and failures and lets us take credit when things go well, and blame circumstances when they don't. When dealing with communication problems, it tells us that it must be their fault since we are "way better than average." In fact, we're perfect.

What Is Effective Communication?

Effective communication happens when we try to understand what we're doing, not just from our own point of view, but also from the point of view of the receiver of our messages. Blaming the other doesn't teach us very much; understanding the effect of our talk on them does.

Effectiveness in communication means three things have to happen:

1) We get what we want:

- This can be a moment of positive emotional connection, or
- A tangible result — i.e., some kind of deal or exchange has occurred.
- Ideally, both of these events will have transpired. Even when we're creating tangible results, we want to make a positive emotional connection.

2) We've been understood — from our point of view.

- We know this because the other person has communicated this to us.

3) The other person seems fine with the exchange.

- They gave no indication of uncertainty, frustration, or anger. If asked, they would probably say they got what they wanted, too.

If our daily lives were no more than a string of simple and successful exchanges, there would be little point in looking more deeply into the process of face-to-face talk. But sometimes, instead of feeling that we got what we expected, our interaction leaves us confused and upset. Suddenly our effortless talk becomes complicated and difficult.

In everyday talk, we assume that everyone else uses words the same way we do, attaches the same meaning to them, speaks and gestures as we do — while holding firmly to the belief that we, of course, are unique and have our own distinct experiences, and that people should recognize this when they talk to us. We just don't have to remember it when we talk to them.

We ignore this contradiction because, most of the time, talk works. Social life *is* highly structured and to deal with it, we learn ritual habits of speech and thought. You don't need to think much about your talk in the purchasing ritual:

"Hi, how much is this top? I don't see a tag."
"$16.99."
"Great. Here's a twenty."
"Thanks. Here's your change. Have a good day."
"You too."

Our mind is built for exactly this kind of unthinking success. Early in life we struggle to be heard and to understand others, but over the years we lose our awareness of these efforts. We can talk without thought because we "overlearn" our responses and they become automatic habits. Not having to think about what to do next makes our talk fluid and smooth. In fact, without this ability to forget what we've learned, we could barely function in our daily lives, let alone do something as complicated as maintain lasting relationships and raise children while making world-class deals or doing quantum physics.

To illustrate this, put yourself in a situation where you don't share the deeply learned patterns of talk and interaction familiar to everyone else in the situation. The first time I visited my wife's family in Italy, I was essentially mute for two days. My wife is fluent in Italian but I didn't speak the language, so I couldn't participate. We don't notice all of the background structuring that makes our talk so easily understood until it's not there.

Why Do People Talk?

The answer to this question lies in the fact that as human beings we don't come equipped with very much information in our genes and in our neural systems when we're born. We are the most open-ended animals on the face of the earth at birth. We spend longer in our parent's tutelage and that of the institutions in our society focused on making us "human" than any other creature on the planet. We also work at a much higher level of complexity than other creatures. To do this we have to work out conversational relationships to take care of our most fundamental human needs, virtually from the moment we're born.

Basic Human Needs: We Talk to Discover Ourselves

Abraham Maslow's model of **basic human needs**[3] offers insight into why people talk (Figure 1 on page 4). From the beginning, we need to negotiate with others to ensure our physical and our psychological safety. Early on in our lives we have to work out a communication relationship with those people who protect us and take care of us. Without this, we don't do well. We may become psychologically distorted or even die. Living is a complex process, so once born, we learn the habit of communicating to get others to provide the essentials of life — food, warmth, dryness, shelter, and safety from psychological abuse or physical attack — then we keep on doing it forever.

From the beginning, we bring our needs to every conversation — to connect, to belong and to enjoy the company of other people. We need to share information in order to belong, because, generally speaking, human beings do not function well outside of social groups. When human beings have their physical and safety needs taken care of, when they realize that they are an accepted member of a group, Maslow argued that they also need to be recognized as individuals within that group and valued for their **individuality**. Self-recognition and self-esteem issues come to the fore at this point. Somewhat paradoxically, human beings need to belong to groups so they can be recognized and positively valued as individuals.

Figure 1

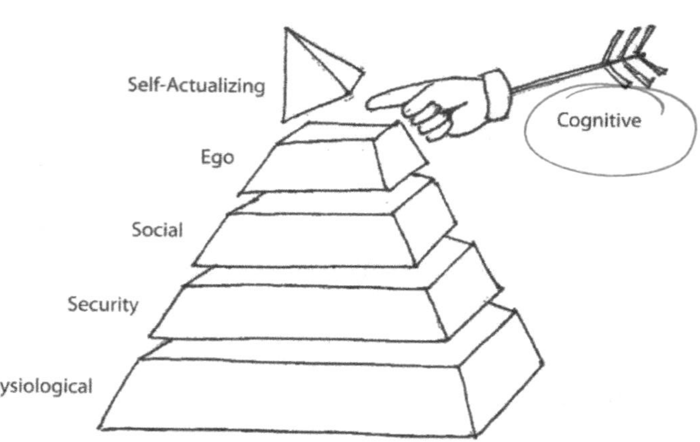

Finally, when we have our basic needs taken care of, when we belong, when others recognize us as a unique entity, and when we feel good about that, we allow something else to happen to us. We grow internally — psychologically, emotionally and spiritually. Maslow calls this **self-actualizing**. We strive to find or become our authentic selves — the self that is argued to lie within but hidden behind the socially acceptable self (or false self) we developed in order to belong and to be recognized in the first place.

Cognitive Needs: We Talk to Know

Along with the aesthetic needs, Maslow added **"cognitive needs"** — the need to know — to his later versions of the self-actualization process. We become conscious of unanswered questions about our lives. We feel the need to ask, learn and discover, in order to know and understand our version of being fully human. I think that this idea speaks to a deeper need than that which is expressed in the maturing cycle of self-actualization. Unlike Maslow's suggestion that it arrives at a later stage in our personal development, I am arguing that it is the one need that is present in all stages of our growth in both conscious and nonconscious forms. This "need to know" lies behind all the other needs already described. Human beings talk because they need to reduce their fundamental uncertainty about the world around them.

Our Need to Reduce Uncertainty

Neuroscientist Gregory Berns[4] argues that the fear of uncertainty is one of the deepest we have. Experiments about "choice making" repeatedly show that when we must make one of two choices in an ambiguous situation and are given a little information about one choice and none about the other, we seem to be driven to take the option where we think we know more — even though logically, knowing more doesn't improve our chances of making the right choice. We are averse to ambiguity, so even a little information seems to reduce the risk involved in choosing. As Berns[5] asserts:

> Ambiguity stems from a lack of knowledge. It looms over the psyche like a dark cloud on the horizon. The brain constantly tries to predict what's going to happen next, and when it can't, a sense of foreboding ensues . . . when fear of ambiguity bubbles to the surface, it is universally experienced the same way.

We simply hate uncertainty. Behind the fundamental truth that human beings are driven "to know things" lays the complementary notion that uncertainty in any situation makes us uncomfortable and sometimes deeply fearful. The human mind has deeply learned mechanisms that can be used to "make sense" of situations overall, but we still need to know what the others in it are thinking or feeling. The only way to reduce this uncertainty is to talk.

We also have to talk to each other to discover who we are and whether who we are is acceptable to others. We do this to avoid what Berns calls the other great fear we all share, the fear of social ridicule. Maslow may argue for the positive necessity of developing a fully functioning self, but the shadow side of this is our drive to protect whatever sense of self we have developed, particularly in our earliest relationships.

Talk and the Three Fundamental Questions

Everyday talk is meant to answer three persistent and interconnected questions that arise in every situation. They are:

1) What's going on?

2) Who am I to you in this situation?

3) What's going to happen next?

What's going on?

More precisely, this question asks about what is expected in this situation and whether we can get through it with as little disagreement as possible. Every conversation exists for a reason, even if the reason is "we're just kidding around" or "we're not really talking." Discovering the overt topic of the talk gives an important clue to what's going on but also to the way one should participate in terms of "how to say" what might be said. It seems that we are always purposeful in our talk, even when we share the unspoken agreement that there is no overt purpose to this particular talk. In fact, communication theorists create lists of purposes for talk — to discover self and the world, to help, to control, to entertain, to play, etc. There is no such thing as purposeless talk. When we begin a conversation, our job is to find out what the purpose is for this talk, in this situation, so we know how to respond next.

Each person tries to enter into the spirit of the moment with what they perceive to be the appropriate style: playful connection talk, or serious discussion and debate, or mutual problem solving. Having entered the situation, well-socialized speakers (most of us) try to create a workable level of agreement about the topic and about the nature of the talk ("only kidding" or "very serious") so that the conversation will flow reasonably well without forcing one or more of the parties to "lose face," that is, to endure some level of social ridicule — damage to the self they are presenting to others while talking. This necessitates the next question.

Who am I to you and who are you to me, *in this situation*?

In everyday life this question is phrased more simply: "How am I being treated here?" And no matter how it's phrased, it's always answered by three other questions we carry around in the back of our head. They are answered by the way we are treated in that conversational moment. They represent our sense of self-worth or self-esteem:

- Do I matter in this situation?
- Am I competent in your eyes?
- Do I have any influence in this situation?

Despite the fact that we come into every interaction with our own answers to these questions based on our previous life experiences, they are always open to being supported, rejected or renegotiated in the moment. It just depends on how others respond to us and how we perceive their responses.

For example, in a disagreement between a child and a parent or between two colleagues in the office, one person may have the right answer but the other simply won't see it or agree to it because of the way the first person spoke. If there is even a hint of condescension in the speaker's voice, the listener may ignore what is said (even when they see its truth) because they feel forced to defend their self-worth or "face" in the situation.

If someone comes to a conversation with a negative sense of self-worth ("I'm worthless, incompetent and never get my way"), they will present a face in the conversation — in the way they speak and act — that is quite different from those who see themselves as worthy, effective and powerful. Each is looking for cues to support their self-worth in the talk of the other and will respond differently to the same cues. Even if a person enters a situation with a positive sense of self, they can still be undermined by persistently treating them as if they have nothing of value to say (more on self-esteem in Chapter 7).

What's going to happen next (after the conversation)?

The last major concern we have in a conversation concerns the need to do something as a result of the talk. Is there an **instrumental** reason for the talk? Can we achieve outward agreement on how the topic is to be perceived or acted on in the future? Will our behaviors be aligned enough to take concerted action, if that is called for? The topic can be anything from "whose team will lead the hostile takeover?" to "whose turn is it to pay for the pizza?"

Or is this purely **relational** talk — simply about making a connection? If so, can we carry on by speaking in such a way that others will listen: showing respect and care; listening to the other's story; acknowledging their humanity?

Although the need for agreement on goals and actions is not essential for every conversation, it acts like the operating system on our computer. It's always there, always working in the background. We may be talking for "no real reason" at this moment but the talk itself can create connections that could be called upon in the future for joint action.

One Final Need: We Talk to Influence

We also need to influence the world around us. We need to talk to people to get them to change so that we will have what we need. We may need to get them to change their minds or their hearts. We make efforts to **control** the world, so we'll feel better. Control is a critical part of our lives and we exercise it all the time. But we all exercise it differently and at different levels or in different ways in the same situation.

In their hearts, human beings know that they can't get everything they want without the help of others, so connection building is the fundamental purpose of all talk. Moreover, no matter what the outcome of the talk is, and whether or not there was some degree of disagreement in the conversation, at some level all talk is about connecting to the other. Connecting means at least achieving shared understanding and creating shared meaning (including agreeing to disagree about the topic).

Shared Meaning and the Three Questions

Face-to-face talk is a great deal more than it appears to be. It is a complex, interlocked system of simultaneously occurring mental processes and expressed behaviors, to which we, and our listener(s), are constantly responding in an attempt to reduce our uncertainty.

To answer the questions — "What's going on?" "How are you treating me?" and "What's going to happen next?" — we are not just exchanging words. We're doing something much more important: creating shared meaning. If we don't have the same pictures pop up in our heads while we are talking, we haven't communicated. It's not what I say that matters, it's what you "get" that matters. If you don't seem to get what I said, then I'm compelled to say it again or say it another way. Shared meanings emerge as we talk to each other and as we try to figure out, from each other's words and nonverbal gestures, whether or not we share the same mental picture of the situation. We also talk to be certain about who we are to each other and about what's going on here, so we can get through this without embarrassing each other. When we start to talk, we share two opposing beliefs: this exchange will be orderly and predictable and it can crumble into disorder any moment (because we just don't know exactly what's going to happen next). The way we manage this paradox is to keep on talking.

How We Manage the Paradox

To manage life we make the most amazing collection of assumptions about the orderliness of interpersonal communication. To demonstrate — a stranger stops you and asks for directions. In order to respond:

- You have to quickly pull together a collection of verbal symbols — words — whose single, clear meaning will describe that image, and
- Assemble those words into a recognizably ordered message to communicate this image.
- You then utter the sounds representing these symbols in a way that you assume the other person will recognize.
- But along with these sounds, you also transmit a set of nonverbal gestures — most of them automatic and unintentional, such as facial movements and tone of voice.
- All this flies through the air in a context where (you assume) there is no distracting interference from external sources.
- You send the information to the ears and eyes of the other person in the certain belief that they will:

- Physically hear and see everything you said, and
- Stay mentally focused while you said it, and
- Decode (translate) your message correctly, i.e., they will pick your meanings — not their own — from the archive of meanings they have accumulated based on their previous experiences — not yours — while
- Avoiding misinterpreting any number of your words because of the unintended and unconscious nonverbals that were displayed at the same time as you spoke them, and then
- Translate this verbal message into the same picture in their mind as you had in yours (without any distracting internal thoughts, feelings or beliefs of their own).

All this has to happen for them to simply "get" your message and indicate they did, so we can feel effective. Given the uncertainties hidden in these assumptions, the odds of this happening successfully are not high the first time. That's why we have to repeat ourselves.

Wiio's Laws

In fact, our simplistic assumptions about face-to-face talk are so disconnected from the underlying realities of communication that communications experts often resort to humor to get their point across. One of my favorite efforts comes from Professor Osmo A. Wiio[6] — described on the Web as a famous Finnish researcher and professor of communication — who wrote seven "laws of communication." These are Murphy's Laws of talk — if anything can go wrong it will. Here are three of my favorites:

1. Communication usually fails, except by accident.
2. If a message can be interpreted in several ways, it will be interpreted in a manner that maximizes damage.
3. There is always someone who knows *better than you* what you meant by your message.

Thinking about the Process of Communicating: Talk as Tennis Match

Since we need to communicate in order to discover how to survive physically and psychologically, one would think that our basic everyday, commonsense model of interpersonal communication would focus on creating a shared reality out of interwoven exchanges of words and gestures. It doesn't. How we think about things shapes how we respond to them in the real world. We all have models in our head about how life ought to be and how it works, including fairly detailed models of the behavior and intentions of good and bad parents, teachers, friends, and people in general. Our mental life is full of these "pictures" and they work in exactly the same way that scientific models do — as collections of elements that go together in predictable ways to help us understand the world. So it is with face-to-face communication.

We seem to share an unspoken model that conversation is like a **tennis match.** We assume that words, whose meanings other people already share with us, are the ball. The physical and psychological distance between us is the court and any perceived differences represent the net and the "foul" lines of that court (potential disruptions or conversational "noise"). We serve (speak) to start a conversation and we volley (hit the ball, in this case, the words) back and forth between us until we reach some sort of agreement about the situation (i.e., discover the answers to the three questions described above) or, in the case of a disagreement, until the other person can't reply effectively (by then we've "made our point").

Notice the assumptions built into this tennis-match view of face-to-face talk:

- If I say something to you, I will say it in the way that I think it ought to be understood, using the "right words."
- You will automatically get it, the way I meant it (because we both speak the same language and words have the same meanings).
- You will respond appropriately (the way I expect you to).
- If you don't get it the first time, I will say it again pretty much the same way I said it before, with a little more intensity (created by the "righteous" feeling that the meaning of what I've just said should be obvious to anyone).
- If we get to three repetitions, and you still don't "get it," the problem doesn't have anything to do with me. It's your problem because I did all the "right" things. The model provides me with a default explanation for what happened: "It's not my fault. I'm a better than average communicator."

Talk as Contest

When we disagree with someone, the game in our unspoken model simply gets more intense. It becomes a contest rather than a pleasant exchange. The assumptions behind this model of talk are outlined by Flick.[7] She argues that we start by assuming there is a right answer and we have it, or if we don't have it now, we'll find it by proving the other side wrong by:

- Listening to find flaws in their argument and build counterarguments

- Defending our assumptions as if they were objective facts or truths
- Critiquing their position, and
- Seeking a conclusion that justifies our position.

We know we're right because we're "better than average." Finding "truth" through contest can work in formal debates where participants are compelled by the rules to present coherent arguments and supporting data. It doesn't work well for everyday disagreements.

Things Do Go Wrong: The 3 D's

Difficult situations can and do emerge when talk doesn't happen predictably or produce expected results. What are some of these moments?

- When we're resisting another's attempt to take something we don't want to give.
- When we're trying to get a loved one or family member to see something important from our perspective and they seem to neither understand nor care.
- When we're trying to keep our cool when others are angry, critical, frightened, distracted, or worse, when they are demanding or demeaning in the way they talk to us.

These and many other situations involve the same elements — what I call the 3 D's:

1) **Differences:**
    - When others display differences in behavior, opinions or values that seem beyond our immediate understanding, and
    - These differences suddenly emerge in conversations where we thought we were talking with people "just like us."
2) **Disagreements:**
    - When we are faced with outright, perhaps even expected, disagreements that represent differences which have hardened into positions about:
        - How to think about or what to believe about something.
        - What to do, or when to act.

- A shared history of not being able to find a common position on perceived differences.

3) **Disorder:**

- When intense emotions disrupt an exchange.
- When the other person says things that seem inappropriate or just plain crazy.

The 3 D's and Good Information

All of these situations undermine our sense of the ease and simplicity of talk because they arouse the negative emotions attached to uncertainty or unpredictability: surprise, anger or fear. As Berns said earlier we are "uncertainty averse." Whether we realize it or not, we yearn for good information about each other and the situation we are in. "Good information" is information that is accurate, relevant, truthful, and clear, so that when we talk, we:

1. Can make automatic predictions about others.
2. Don't have to work too hard at it. When it comes to everyday talk we are "energy misers," and
3. Can feel "normal" or "effective" in the moment we have to make conscious choices. Whether we are on the talking or receiving end, we don't want to be taken by surprise or feel coerced or manipulated.

How People Feel as Communicators: Comfort versus Effectiveness

A national survey by the National Communication Association, called "How Americans Communicate," found that, in general,

- 62% of Americans felt they were comfortable communicators
- 87% rated themselves very comfortable as communicators in personal relationships with significant others, but
- Only 42% said they were *very effective* when communicating.

In other words, people felt good saying what they said — they thought they spoke easily, clearly — but they weren't sure whether their message was getting across. Interestingly, those surveyed understood the consequences of ineffective communication. For instance, when asked to choose the most frequent cause of marriage breakup:

- 53% said a lack of effective communication between partners was the most frequent cause.
- 29% said money problems were the most frequent cause.
- All other causes were chosen by less than one person out of ten.

The problem is that our sense of ourselves as "very comfortable" talkers doesn't give us much insight into the reasons for our feelings of ineffectiveness as communicators. We focus on communication as the "comfortable delivery of words" but when others don't get our messages, the problem lies with them, not us. We lobbed the ball over the net; the return is their problem . . . not ours. In fact, to become better communicators, we need *to know more* and *blame less*.

A More Complex View of Interpersonal Communication

This simplistic view of interpersonal communication — lobbing words back and forth — can lead to a great deal of frustration in our relationships. In fact, it leaves out most of what social scientists have discovered in their research on face-to-face talk.

Decades of study indicate that when we are talking with someone, we don't just exchange words about a particular topic — we also exchange definitions of our "selves." Moreover, these "definitions of self" (our conversational "face") deliver complex emotional messages to the other person. We have also found that in most situations people's choice of words is likely to have much less impact on others than *the way* those words are said (our nonverbal behavior). Moreover, unlike our "common sense" belief, words have many meanings and these will vary depending on the context in which they are spoken.

Our theory suggests that people talk because they don't know the answers to basic questions, not because they do. Moreover, in typical conversations the answers to the three critical questions are constructed out of a mutual exchange of messages, not imposed by one person on another. DeVito[8] outlines the accepted theoretical model of interpersonal communication talk as a complex exchange of words *and* nonverbal behavior — a **transaction** happening on several levels at once. It's not a game but a **complex dance** between two or more people — a flow of anticipations and simultaneous reactions aimed at achieving some level of mutual understanding.

Communication theorists realized that our everyday model of talk needed to be replaced by a model that reflected these interconnected fundamental needs. We had to move away from our 2,000-year-old model of talk-as-persuasion (rhetoric) focused only on senders and their manipulation of words to change the minds of an audience (essentially one-way communication) to a model of talk that is face-to-face and two-way.

By the 1950s we had put together a basic model that described a **sender** in every face-to-face moment, and **a message** — and that message is sent down **channels** to a **receiver** of the message. Not surprisingly, it was called the SMCR (Sender — Message — Channel — Receiver) model. Now, unlike rhetoric, we have two people to study — sender and receiver. This was reinforced by the addition of the concept of **feedback** — describing the receiver's immediate verbal response to whatever the sender said.

On the surface, the SMCR model doesn't look much different from the everyday "tennis match" model. Analysis is still focused on the sender's **word messages** (intended to "inoculate" others with our ideas or transfer information directly into their heads) and the receiver's **feedback** (see Figure 2 below.)

Figure 2 The Everyday "Tennis Match" Model of Talk

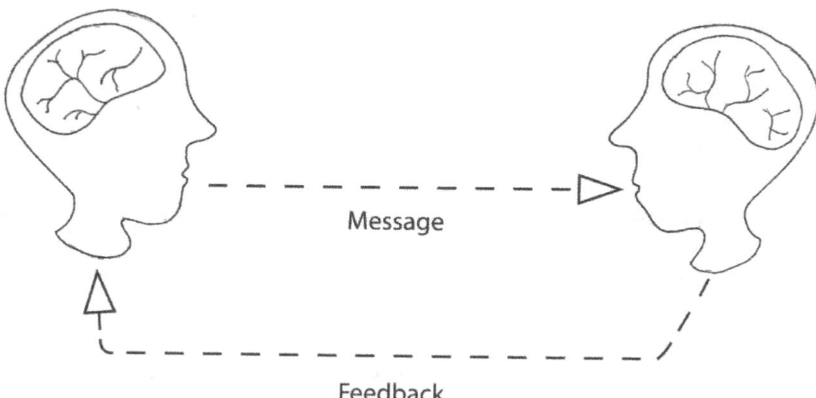

Below the surface, however, researchers were concerned about more than the words being exchanged. The person on the left isn't just talking and sending a message; they first have to encode it. They have to take the ideas in their head and put together a string of word symbols, to create a recognizable message that they predict the other will understand. They're going to send this message to the person on the other side of the model, not just by uttering a few organized grunts, but down the channels of the body's sensory perception systems: sight, hearing, touch, smell and taste. For most of our communication we use sight and hearing — occasionally we use touch, depending on whom the conversation is with, and how well we know them. And in this model, before the other person can "hear" the message they need to decode it.

And how does the receiver of the message decode it? They have to assign meaning to the incoming symbols that have been strung together in the sender's head and uttered as words in order for them to receive it. This more complicated set of concepts allowed researchers to study the communication process in far more detail. They gained insight into both the intrapersonal (in the head) and interpersonal (between sender and receiver) factors that could enhance or diminish the quality of the communication being exchanged.

To be clearer about the quality of the sender's encoding and sending processes and the receiver's decoding processes, the concept of noise was added to the model. There are three categories of noise that can interfere with face-to-face communication: physical, semantic and psychological.

- **Physical noise** is anything that can get in between two people and interrupt the message. This can be anything from the sound of a truck going by while you're trying to talk with someone on the sidewalk or the shadow of an overpass that interrupts a cell phone signal in the car. Physical interruption of the sender's message can cause the receiver to miss the message or get a different message.

- **Semantic noise** is the noise in the sender's head. One example is if the sender picked the wrong set of symbols, used words that were too abstract or too complicated or required a different level of education in the receiver.

- **Psychological noise** is in the head of the receiver. They don't unpack our message the way we meant it because they have biases, prejudices, preconceptions — any number of things that can get in the way of their thoughts — as they try to figure out what we said.

The concept of noise added a whole new series of insights and layers of understanding to why messages do or do not get through.

As scientific understanding of interpersonal communication grew in the 1950s, scientists eventually came to recognize that what's in people's heads isn't, in fact, noise but their personal experience. What they get from the sent words may not be the sender's intended meanings but the meanings they put into the words as they received them. This idea was summed up in a now-famous comment by David Berlo[9] in the 1960s, when he wrote, "Meanings are in people, not in words."

Words are empty vessels with multiple written-down meanings that can be chosen by a sender. What we began to recognize is that they also have additional meanings that are specific to the receiver's experience. After several thousand years of analyzing talk, research had essentially shifted from focusing on the sender to the receiver.

As our thinking and research progressed over the decades, we came to realize that to truly understand interpersonal exchanges, research needed to move away from the traditional emphasis on words and focus on the relationship between words and nonverbal displays in the continuous and simultaneous flow of messages — on both the sending and receiving ends. It turned out that people were not just talking about topics — they were entering into a kind of continuous transaction and exchange, not just of words but of definitions of themselves — and definitions of the others — *while* they were talking about something else.

The Interpersonal (IP) model of communication, shown below in Figure 3, offers a more realistic and complex picture of talk. Besides adding the realistic notion that a variety of forces (i.e., "noise") can interfere with delivering our meaning through our words, the IP model of communication reframes our interaction as a transaction in nonverbal messages that do three things at the same time: (1) add meaning to our words; (2) provide information about the nature of our relationship — how we feel about each other while we are talking; and (3) tells us how we feel about ourselves in the moment. In effect, the IP model argues that face-to-face talk represents more than an exchange of words but a transaction in "selves."

Figure 3 The Interpersonal (IP) Model of Talk

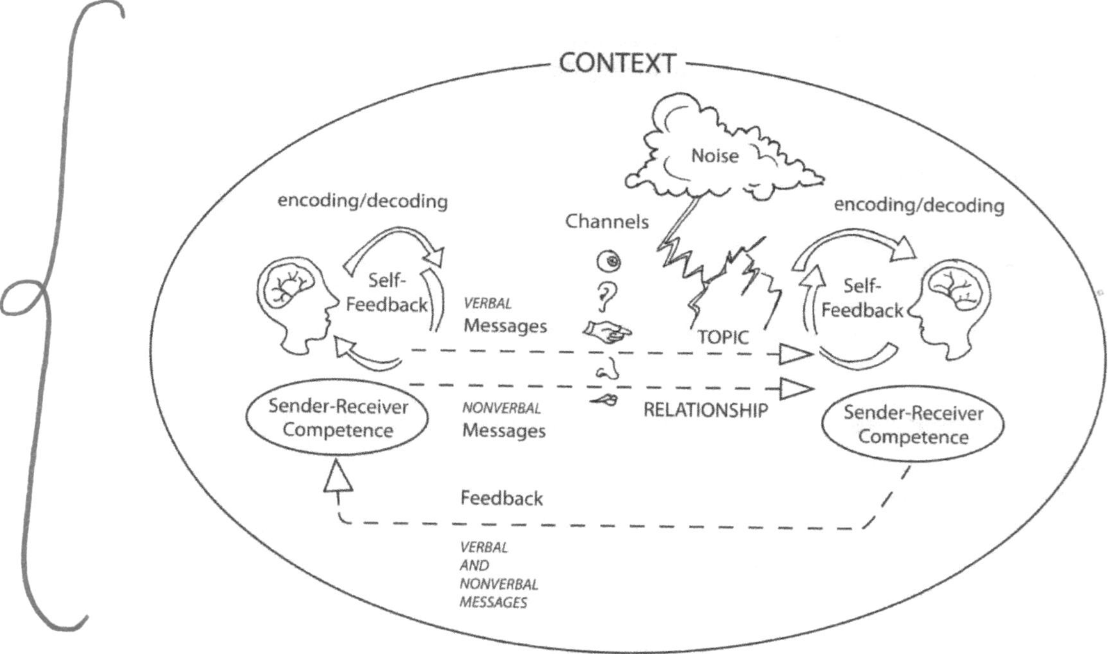

When we see talk as a "transaction in selves," we are compelled to notice the internal feedback loops that are only implied in the simple "tennis match" model. These key processes are shown by adding the concepts of **relationship messages** and **self-feedback loops** to the "common sense" model of talk.

The IP model portrays the true complexity of communication. It shows that we communicate through a variety of channels (our five senses) and that "noise" can alter the messages we are sending (first level of complexity). It also shows that while we are exchanging messages about topics and providing feedback to each other with our words, we are exchanging relational messages through our nonverbal responses (second level of complexity). Finally, it also portrays the reality that we respond emotionally to ourselves while we're talking with another through a process of "self-feedback" (third level of complexity). This internal communication process affects how we respond to the other person.

In a nutshell: we have external communication happening between people as well as internal feedback. There are messages working at two levels — topic and relationship — happening instantaneously also at two levels — verbal and nonverbal. People are senders and receivers at the same time — simultaneously encoding and decoding — and talking to themselves while they're talking to somebody else. If it seems complicated, it is!

But rather than focus on the complexity, through this text we will look at what this model does. It gives us many more ways of understanding how talk works. And perhaps more importantly, it gives us explanations for why talk doesn't always work. We can learn something from each of the elements.

Key Elements of the IP Model

In addition to adding the practical concept of "noise" or interference that can make conversation more complicated, communication theorists agree that seven additional elements are needed to understand how face-to-face talk works. They are summarized as follows:

Table 1

Messages	Any symbols or actions to which people pay attention. People create (words) and display (nonverbals) messages.
Source-Receivers	In the IP model both people create and display messages (as sources of messages) and perceive and interpret messages (as receivers) and so are referred to as source-receivers.
Encoding-Decoding	Terms that describe the mental processes of creating messages and interpreting messages. They are hyphenated because each communicator is both a speaker and a listener in a conversation.

Encoding	The process of turning our images — thoughts and feelings — into a "code" of socially recognizable sounds — spoken words.
Decoding	The process of translating that sound code into thoughts and images and assigning it meaning.
Channels	The sensory systems of the body through which we receive data. They are the visual (sight), auditory (hearing), olfactory (smell), gustatory (taste), and tactile (touch) systems.
Noise	Anything that distorts or interferes with message reception.
Physical	Example — Loud sounds that block hearing a message.
Psychological	"In the head" interference from competing thoughts, schemas, prejudices.
Semantic	Source-receivers don't share language base of word meanings.
Feedforward	Messages from the speaker that give the listener an idea about the kind of message the speaker is about to send verbally.
Feedback	Messages created, displayed and sent back by the receiver, in response to a message already sent. These give the speaker some sense of the effect on the receiver of their sent messages.
Competence	Each participant's abilities to effectively communicate.
Language	Knowledge of the sound system: the meaning and the order of words (syntax).
Communication	Knowledge of the rules of interaction (particularly nonverbal rules for appropriate facial vocal gestures, turn taking, etc.).
Emotional	Ability to recognize your own and others' emotions and to express them appropriately.

Context	This is the environment in which communication occurs. Often ignored, context influences the content and form of communication. It refers to **where** (the physical) and **when** (temporal) the talk occurs, and most importantly, **with whom it is occurring** (the social-psychological context — the relationship between participants).

As communication research has revealed the complexity of interpersonal communication, our individual abilities (competencies) to manage the process have become an important focus of current research and a key element of the IP model. Our competencies include: (1) our "in-the-head" self-feedback loops — how we manage our emotional responses to others, and (2) how we recognize the effect of context (the "where, when, with whom") on the other person's interpretation of the meaning of our words and nonverbal gestures. Communication is now seen as a continual process of adjustment of thought, feeling, and response actions and reactions between people as they attempt to reach an agreement on what they are talking about.

The Six People in Every Two-Person Exchange[10]

This mutual adjustment is easily understood if we remember that in the IP model of talk there is a transaction in "selves" not just words, and, considering the self-feedback loops, there are always more than two "selves" involved.

When we're talking to someone, we have an image in our head of ourselves talking to them. Erving Goffman[11] argued persuasively that we are always presenting ourselves to another while talking. We literally put little bits of ourselves into our talk. There are emotional messages intertwined with our words. As the conversation goes on, we hope that the other person's nonverbal responses to us will support the aspect of ourself that we are presenting with our words — he called this our "face." This self-image, or "face," is our positive image of us taking a particular position in a conversation in order to express our views of the situation, of ourselves and of the others involved. This self-image is never neutral. We invest it with emotion and our hope is that others will respond to it in ways that support our face — make us look good — or at least not do or say anything to make us look bad. Essentially, we want people to support more than our words — we want their support for us — as we've presented ourselves. If they support us, we feel enhanced; if they don't, we can feel diminished, even threatened.

We also have an image of the receiver — their "face" and their "face work" in the discussion — and the efforts they seem to be making to maintain their face and ours. And finally, we have an image in our head of how the receiver must be thinking about us while we're talking to them. When you add in the fact that the receiver shares the same views — their own "face," their image of us responding to them, and a projected self-image of how we must be thinking about them while they're talking to us — "six people" come into the moment. The way we talk to each other tells the other person how we feel about them as well as *how that person should feel about themselves*. These in-the-head self-feedback loops of interpretation are based on our emotional reactions to the relational aspect of others' messages.

The Six Axioms of Communication Process

Over many years of observation and controlled research, communication theorists developed both the descriptive details of the IP model of talk outlined above, and a series of essential propositions or axioms that attempt to explain the processes of the model, that is, the ways the key elements work together to help or hinder our ability to talk together and develop shared understanding of both the topics we are discussing and each other. DeVito[12] states the axioms in the following table and reframes each of them as advice we might follow to be more effective communicators.

Table 2

Axiom	Advice
1. Interpersonal Communication Is a Transactional Process Interpersonal communication is a process, an ongoing event, in which the elements are interdependent; communication is constantly occurring and changing.	Don't expect clear-cut beginnings or endings or sameness from one time to another.
2. Interpersonal Relationships May Be Viewed as Symmetrical or Complementary Interpersonal interactions may stimulate similar or different behavior patterns, and relationships may be described as basically symmetrical or complementary.	Develop an awareness of symmetrical and complementary relationships. Avoid clinging rigidly to behavioral patterns that are no longer useful and mirror another's destructive behaviors.
3. Interpersonal Communications Have Content and Relationship Dimensions All communications refer both to content and to the relationships between the participants.	Seek out and respond to relationship messages as well as content messages.

4. Interpersonal Communication Is a Process of Adjustment Communication depends on participants sharing the same system of signals and meaning; generally, people move in the direction of imitating or echoing the interpersonal behavior of the other.	Expand common areas, and learn each other's system of signals to increase interpersonal effectiveness; share your own system of signals with significant others.
5. Interpersonal Communication Is a Series of Punctuated Events Everyone separates communication sequences into stimuli and responses on the basis of his or her own perspective.	View punctuation as arbitrary, and adopt the other's point of view to increase empathy and understanding.
6. Interpersonal Communication Is Inevitable, Irreversible, and Unrepeatable In a face-to-face situation, you cannot not communicate. You can't un-communicate and you cannot repeat exactly a specific message.	Seek to control as many aspects of your behavior as possible. In listening, seek out nonobvious messages. Beware of messages you may later wish to take back, for example, conflict and commitment messages.

What's interesting, from our point of view, is that after each restatement DeVito also gives advice to the reader based on the meaning of each axiom. In his overview, he follows the established view in the field by focusing on improving our communication competence by suggesting that we consciously manage what he calls the "systems of signals" — what we deliver to each other via words and nonverbal gestures. What he doesn't note, however, is that many of our nonverbal gestures are "overlearned" or automatic responses to others. Moreover, as we will point out in the next chapter, one of the critical functions of our nonverbal behavior is the unthinking expression of our evaluations about the other and ourselves, while we are consciously talking about something else. Such evaluative messaging represents fundamental emotional reactions that lie outside of our conscious control — unless we choose to learn the skills of emotional self-management, that is, to consciously interrupt our inner dialogue and "think before we talk."

In fact, it is this automatic evaluative messaging between people that makes the concept of "self-feedback loops" so vital to understanding why people respond the way they do in any conversation. Self-feedback loops are rooted in evaluations of ourselves and others that are so deeply learned we've "forgotten" them and can't quickly bring them into our consciousness. Our inability to consciously control all levels of our communication can explain why some conversations can start out as easy exchanges and suddenly "go wrong"; or start out not being easy at all "for no apparent reason"; or why we end up feeling unhappy and disconcerted about our own reactions when others disagree with us or criticize our views. Thus, when DeVito gives us quite reasonable advice to "Seek to control as many aspects of your behavior as possible" or "Avoid clinging rigidly to behavioral patterns that are no longer useful" — *we often can't*. And when he suggests: "Don't expect clear-cut beginnings or endings or sameness from one time to another" — *we do anyway*. Why is that?

Talk Is a Complex Three-Level Experience

I have found that the IP model of communication, as currently developed, isn't complete. It describes the first two layers of interaction with great clarity — they are summarized below as the first and second level of complexity — but has not yet adequately dealt with the third level of information exchange that goes on in face-to-face talk and that explains why we often can't easily enact the rational or reasonable advice that communication theorists and practitioners offer us. This third level of complexity is described below.

First Level of Complexity

We communicate through a variety of channels (our five senses) and "noise" (situational or mental interference) can alter the messages we are sending and receiving in unintended ways. So can the context of our exchange. Thus, despite our naïve assumption that words "mean what they mean," they actually have multiple meanings. The processes of encoding, sending and decoding of messages can shape their meanings for our receivers in ways that we, as speakers, may not notice until they react. In fact, until two communicators create shared meaning out of the words being spoken and mutually agree to the answers for our three essential questions, effective communication hasn't really happened.

Second Level of Complexity

While we are exchanging word messages about topics and providing verbal feedback to each other, we are also telling each other what kind of relationship we have in this moment. Through our nonverbal responses — facial and body gestures, tone of voice — we provide each other with guidance about how we see ourselves in our social relationship to them — for example, as an equal to a friend, as a son or daughter to a parent, or an employee to a manager. And as our nonverbals tell them, and us, what kind of relationship we have, they also say how our words are to be interpreted in that moment. Essentially, we rarely speak about it directly but we are always talking about our relationship to another while we're talking with them.

Third Level of Complexity

Finally, before we speak, we are already responding emotionally to the other, and to ourselves, and these first reactions shape what will happen next. As we talk, we continue this parallel *automatic and wordless* process, which we earlier described as "self-feedback." This internal communication is based on our moment-to-moment emotional reactions to *the way* the other is communicating with us (the overall tone or "feel" of their nonverbal reactions) and we use this to indicate to ourselves how they are evaluating us as we talk (answering the question: "How am I being treated here?") as well as developing an answer to the question: "What's going to happen next?" Will this relationship continue past this moment or not? These emotional reactions automatically affect how we respond to them at the first two levels and, in turn, shape their automatic responses to us. This parallel conversation of emotional reactions is carried out constantly and without words in the cognitive unconscious of each person in the conversation. We will discuss this in much more detail in Chapter 3.

Layers within Layers

All this makes talk really interesting and complex. Communication research has revealed the unspoken side of communication — the shaping power of nonverbal behavior. In many situations, our choice of words is likely to have less impact on others than the way those words are spoken and the context (the "when and where") in which we say them. Chapter 2 will review the research on this effect.

This "layers within layers" approach is my attempt to distinguish this book from other communication texts by clarifying the limits to our rational choices — our competence — as we talk with others. These limits appear dramatically in difficult communication situations and they recur so regularly that I believe we should add an additional axiom — a fundamental truth — to the six axioms that support IP model of communication. This seventh axiom explains why we sometimes can't — and sometimes don't want to — do the rational thing in face-to-face talk.

The Seventh Axiom: Problem-Solving in Interpersonal Communication and "Rightness"

We have already argued that much of interpersonal communication is a nonconscious process. But when conversations "go wrong" — when the three questions don't get answered in the way we predicted — when we are confronted with uncertainty and our "face" is called into question, we *do* become conscious about our talk — for a moment.

The only problem is that in this moment of clarity we also notice the potential for feeling the emotional pain that might ensue if we don't get what we expect — i.e., if we're not being treated as the person we feel we are, or if, instead of knowing more about what's going on, we realize we know less. We hate that possibility so we quickly slip back into an automatic, reactive mode of talk (C.O.N.T.R.O.L. talk) that will instantly reduce our uncertainty and fear in any situation and also prevent us from learning how we could have done things differently (another variation on the "above average communicator" fallback).

As can be seen in the summary above, the IP model of communication suggests there are six fundamental qualities or processes (represented by the six axioms) we have to be aware of if we are truly going to understand how talk works in general. I have also described the key elements of an additional fundamental process that explains why people talk the way they do when a situation changes from **predictable and supportive** to **unpredictable and threatening.** We respond to behavior that might undermine our certainty about who we are and how the world is. To explain this recurrent pattern and to strengthen the analysis of face-to-face talk by recognizing the role of emotions around our sense of self, I have created a seventh (pragmatic) axiom of the IP model (which will be discussed in more detail with C.O.N.T.R.O.L. talk):

> **7. In interpersonal communication, when faced with difference, disagreement or disorder, human beings need to be or feel *right* and respond accordingly.**

Face-to-Face Communication: The Pragmatics

The IP model and its axioms describe the universal processes that are essential to face-to-face talk in all situations and every time one person talks with another. The model of talk discussed in the later chapters of this text derives from the IP model but is about the **pragmatics** of communication — the behavioral effects of our communication on each other. It builds on the model of universal processes that make talk work but argues that people also make conscious or nonconscious choices about what to say and how to say it in particular situations.

The model is called the "Three Mode" model of interpersonal communication because it describes three ways of talking to each other and the effects each has on people when they find themselves in one of two types of situations. First, when they are simply trying to make a relational connection with another person (start, build or maintain a communication relationship) — C.O.N.N.E.C.T. talk — and second, when they are trying to handle a "problem" with another person. Whether the problem is:

(1) An issue that both parties recognize is "at arm's length" from the conversation itself because they think they are communicating quite effectively in the situation, or is

(2) An issue about the talk itself — a "communication breakdown" — where one or both of the speakers feels misunderstood or unappreciated by the other.

In either case, they are dealing with a difference that one or both of them feels needs to be resolved so they can reconnect. In this case, we use two other modes of talk. The first mode, based on our *nonconscious reactions* to "problems," is C.O.N.T.R.O.L. talk. The second mode, based on making *conscious choices* about our responses in a problem-solving situation, is called D.I.A.L.O.G.U.E. talk. Both words are acronyms where every letter describes a particular behavior that is part of the overall mode. These models will be clarified in Chapters 9, 10 and 11.

Summary and Definition

In this chapter we have seen that communication as understood through the eyes of communication theorists and researchers is far more complicated than our "common sense" version. We have attempted to shift the word-centered simplicity and certainty of our everyday model of communication to a more complex and complete way of understanding talk. This includes describing the general purpose of communication as one of reducing our uncertainty through the creation of shared meaning with others about several key questions and presenting the interpersonal communication model, its key concepts, and the seven axioms.

What remains is to provide a straightforward definition of interpersonal communication that captures all of the above in a few statements. Interpersonal communication is:

- Two or more people, within a particular context
- Who are aware of each other
- Acting together to create, sustain, and manage shared meanings
- Through simultaneously sending and receiving messages
- About both themselves and the topic of conversation
- Using socially shared verbal symbols and socially defined, biologically shared nonverbal symptoms and symbols
- In an ongoing process of mutual adjustment.

Where We're Going Next

People may talk together and in the process create shared meaning as they go, but they have to begin somewhere. They must have something in common before they can create something in common. We all begin our conversations with a database of "socially shared verbal symbols and socially defined, biologically shared nonverbal symptoms and symbols" in our head. This is a result of our being socialized into the culture of our family and society. How we do this and how it shapes our ability to communicate is the subject of Chapter 2.

End Notes

---

[1] Argyris, C. (1990) *Overcoming Organizational Defenses: Facilitating Organizational Learning.* Boston: Allyn and Bacon.

[2] Fine, C. (2006) *A Mind of Its Own: How the Brain Distorts and Deceives*. New York: W. W. Norton and Company.

[3] Maslow, A. (1970) *Motivation and Personality* (2nd ed.) New York: Harper and Row.

[4] Berns, G. (2010) *Iconoclast*. Boston: Harvard Business Press.

[5] Berns, p. 74.

[6] Found on http://www.cs.tut.fi/~jkorpela/wiio.html

[7] Flick, D. (1998) *From Debate to Dialogue: Using the Understanding Process to Transform Our Conversations.* Boulder, CO: Orchid Publications.

[8] DeVito, J. (2001) *The Interpersonal Communication Book* (9th ed.) Toronto: Addison Wesley, Longman, Inc.

[9] Berlo, D. (1964) *The Process of Communication: An Introduction to Theory and Practice*. New York: Holt, Rinehart and Winston.

[10] These ideas emerge out of one of the earliest articles in Interpersonal Communication by Barnlund, D. (1962) "Towards a Meaning-Centered Philosophy of Communication," *Journal of Communication,* 12, pp. 197–211.

[11] Goffman, E. (1967) *Interaction Ritual: Essays on Face-to-Face Behavior*. Garden City, NY: Anchor Books.

[12] DeVito, pp. 8–15.

CHAPTER TWO

CULTURE IN COMMUNICATION

Culture as Context

In Chapter 1 we discussed the importance of the concept of context in interpersonal communication for defining the meaning of words and actions. In this chapter we'll look at "the mother of all other contexts," the culture. It is both the societal storehouse of meanings for the words, actions and events that are poured into the mind and body of every new member of a society, and also the largest symbolic environment within which all these meanings make any sense. Without some understanding of the communication "tools" provided by each culture (the verbal language and the repertoire of symbols for shared, nonverbal behaviors) and how we acquire them through socialization, we can't answer an essential question about interpersonal communication: "How can so many, do so much with something they seem to know so little about?"

Cultural learning, often called enculturation or socialization, gives us enough "stuff" to create common meanings at some level with everyone we talk to in the same culture. Moreover, when we understand how learning within a shared context impacts our communication, we can also see why and how we have a hard time communicating with people from other cultures. In addition, we will discover that, even within the same group, not everyone learns exactly the same content or the same communication techniques in the same way. Thus, we can begin to recognize how "subcultural" learning occurs and how that can contribute to misunderstanding and communication breakdowns.

In general, people can talk together and in the process create shared meaning but they have to begin somewhere — and they do — with an "in the head" database of "socially shared verbal symbols and socially defined, biologically shared nonverbal symptoms and symbols," as well as shared perspectives (the larger context) on what is or isn't appropriate to communicate. If we don't share at least some of these basics with others, we can't communicate. Speakers from different language backgrounds and cultures can't speak to each other and those from within the same culture and language base, with radically different perspectives on a topic, can't listen to each other.

Culture as a Storehouse of Meanings

Our culture stores the meanings that comprise our way of life. It contains both the tools for our communication (the languages we use), verbal and nonverbal, and just as importantly, the meanings we attach to our words and to our nonverbal behavior in order to make sense of our own and of other peoples' communication. It provides the basis for the "shared meaning" that we strive to create every time we talk with someone. Like the air we breathe, culture is invisible but essential to life.

It also permeates every pore of our minds and bodies, shapes every action we take and sound that we make. In the process of revealing the power of culture we will also answer two key questions:

1) "Why are those people like that?" and

2) "Why do North American tourists always whisper in the cathedrals of Europe?"

Culture as a "Way of Seeing"

We could also think of culture as the contact lenses through which a group of people sees the world and lives in the world it sees. When contact lenses fit well we don't even notice we have them on. It is only when we are not wearing them that we discover that we can't "see." In fact, we take our cultural lenses — view of the world — so much for granted that when we have to travel to another part of the world that is very different from our own, we may suffer something called "culture shock." This occurs when we enter a society whose culture seems so completely unfamiliar that we can't "see" anything familiar. When we're not even sure what's real or normal, we can feel uncertain, fearful, even depressed. At first sight, we may feel surprise or shock ("Why are those people like that?") but if the behavior seems radically different from that which our own culture supports, we may react with a mixture of anger and disgust — "What's wrong with those people?" Less intense versions of these reactions may also happen when we observe the behavior of people from other societies who have recently arrived in our communities as immigrants.

We don't have to say or do anything about these internal reactions — we have a choice not to react outwardly. Moreover, we can learn more about the people and the meaning of the behavior we are experiencing and, like most international diplomats, business people, students, aid workers and experienced travelers, move beyond first reactions to understanding the larger context in which others' behavior occurs. We are pointing out this first "gut reaction" to cultural differences only to remind ourselves that: (1) something we are unaware of in our everyday lives (our culture) is the "background" against which everything we think, feel and say is processed, and that (2) enculturation is never neutral. Our deepest learning is intertwined with our deepest emotions.

Culture: A More Specific Definition[1]

We can broadly define culture as a way of living that is learned and shared by groups of people, and that is taught by one generation to the next. Important elements of a given culture are the symbols people use to interact. The key elements of the "way of life" taught to the next generation include: (1) **knowledge** — the body of accumulated information (beliefs and "facts") that people share about how both the physical and the social worlds are constructed; the principles and rules by which they operate (e.g., the norms, mores and folkways of the social world); and about the meaning of existence (life); (2) **values** — people's shared ideas about the most abstract goals they believe are worth achieving (how to live life); and (3) forms of **symbolic expression** such as art, literature, dance, language. Essentially, by learning the basic form of symbolic expression of the culture — the language — as well as through watching others and listening to their instructions, each newcomer (child or immigrant) acquires access to the values and knowledge of the society.

Learning the Culture and the Social Order

When we arrive into our society we have to learn how it works in order to "fit in" and be seen as a "normal" member of the group. Either as small children or as adult newcomers, we don't learn how things work all at once. We discover it partly through being taught by others but, most importantly, by observing the patterns in others' everyday behavior.

Knowledge

We, like every other group of human beings, have some set of symbolic elements — a language of words and gestures — that we transfer into the minds of the group's newest members so we can answer questions like: How does the social world work? How do people work? How does the sun rise and set every day? How do all the things in life that we can't see and we can't understand work? And do we have any connection to it? All this is poured into children from the moment they are born but, somewhere between 24 and 36 months, when a fundamental understanding of language develops in the child's mind, the socialization process can begin in earnest.

Values

When we are being socialized we are usually being told about our society's values — a series of nonconscious, automatic responses to the world called deep values or "zero order" evaluative beliefs[2] — about what is right and true and proper, what we should be striving for, what things matter, and how we should act.

At the societal level, values help us distinguish ourselves from other people in other societies with different cultural histories. As we said earlier, at the individual level, values are acquired early in our development and are thus rooted in both our cognitive and emotional systems. When someone comes from a different cultural background and acquires the values of another culture, they end up with two layers of deeply held values about what is right, true and proper. This can be an ongoing struggle, especially for someone who tries to learn a new culture after the age of 10.

Norms and Mores

Values are represented in everyday behavior by a series of **norms**. Norms are rules for behavior in particular situations, or are attached to particular social positions, which are supposed to reflect the larger values. So if we think that parenthood is a good idea, then two people getting together and raising children becomes a larger value that we all take for granted. The *way* those values get enacted by the people in the positions of mother and father are called the norms. Norms are the behavioral rules that society thinks make for "good" parenting, and that reflect the larger values of what goodness and badness are in our society.

Those norms are different in different societies. Most societies think that the idea of having families and children is good. But the rules for enacting the role of parent (position-specific norms) can vary dramatically. In many societies, striking children, as a way of disciplining them, is not only accepted, it is highly recommended. In our society, and particularly in the last few decades, it has become widely condemned (although not by everyone). When there is a conflict between the agreed-upon norms and the larger values of the culture, the unconscious becomes conscious. In our society we take such conflicts to our judicial system so that the rules can be upheld or changed to fit new circumstances.

There are a number of different types of norms. Some of them are **value-centered**. Sociologists call those **mores** — general beliefs about what constitutes right and wrong and the related behavior. In our society, for example, we believe people shouldn't kill people. It doesn't mean we don't; it just means that the widely held value is that we ought not to. This is to discourage grabbing the nearest weapon and taking the life of someone who has angered you. It is on the basis of mores such as this — generally held beliefs about right and wrong, and appropriate behavior — that we build the laws of each country.

Behavior-Centered Norms

Behavior-centered norms seem to cross the whole culture, not about what is right and wrong, but about what is normal and non-normal behavior. We know when people are behaving normally or not because all of us have learned these norms early on and deeply. For example, in our society, we have a behavior-centered norm for the whole culture that says that walking down a public street talking to ourselves is strange and could possibly be seen as dangerous. However, someone walking down the street talking into a cell phone is now considered normal. Even ordinary, everyday behavior-centered norms about what is normal and non-normal behavior are adaptable.

We tend to learn these types of norms or "rules for behavior" so deeply that we take them for granted — automatically thinking that they guide everybody's talk. A good example of this is the norms for "normal" talk outlined in the box below. As you read the following, recall times in conversation when people broke these rules and you thought, "what a pain!" or "weird."

Four Behavior-Centered Rules of "Normal" Conversation

These are Grice's[3] "maxims of conversation" based on his notion of conversation being an essentially cooperative venture. The culture-wide descriptions of normal behavior in everyday talk include speaking with the appropriate level of:

1. Quality 2. Quantity 3. Relevance 4. Manner.

When we talk to people, we assume that they are following the same rules and honoring the same conventions of proper conversation as we are.

1. **Quality** of information. People are expected to tell us what they know to be true. Also, they are expected "not to say that for which [they] lack adequate evidence." This latter point relates to factual accuracy. What's very interesting is that we can break this rule by consciously choosing to lie to another but we are more likely to undermine it when we are not consciously making choices — in emotionally heated conversations or oppositely, in conversations in which we have little emotional involvement and are not really paying attention to. At these moments, we can unthinkingly make statements of "fact" for which we have little or no evidence.

2. **Quantity** of information. What that means in everyday talk is, our answers to another's question should be enough to inform them, but that's all. Saying too much or rambling on about something else suggests we don't know how to talk normally. There is an unwritten rule about what constitutes a normal amount: when I ask a simple question, I get a simple answer. And when I want a longer answer, I ask a more complicated question. And if I don't get the appropriate response, it doesn't feel right.

3. **Relevance** means that if we're talking to each other and I say, "So, what do you think about those Blue Jays?" and you say, "Well, I can see that the migratory patterns of birds are really critical in your view of the world," I'm going to think you're a bit crazy. Your response is not relevant to what I asked. I was talking about sports, making small talk. When people don't follow our comments with responses that seem appropriately logical or relevant, we become concerned. In

fact, one of the indicators of non-normalcy is the inability of the speaker to be able to follow the "logic" of a normal conversation.

4. **Manner** is another rule of conversation we have to acquire. When we're having an everyday, fun conversation with a friend, we expect a style of conversation that is reflective of that. We're just kidding around; we're not being serious. But if you say "What do you think about those Blue Jays?" and they give you that stuff about the nature of flight patterns and historical views of birding in North America, they've shifted their manner of speech as well as the relevance. It inevitably becomes more formal, more didactic. It's like a lecture and it's inappropriate to the moment. When we speak to people, we expect them to speak back in a style that is appropriate to the way we spoke. And when that doesn't happen, we begin to feel uncomfortable.

Position-Specific Norms

Another way we learn the social order is by learning the rules of behavior attached to a socially recognized position, for instance, parenting. It turns out that the person walking down the street talking to himself or herself may occupy many positions or roles in the society: citizen, mom, dad, teacher, lawyer, doctor, bank teller or soldier. Nameable positions have rules that address two things:

1) What you are obligated to do and for whom you are obligated to do it, and

2) How should you expect other people to behave toward you when you are in that particular position?

We start by figuring out how to play the role of child in our parents' eyes and then we figure out how to be a brother or sister, if siblings come along. *As we occupy each position,* we learn how to behave in ways that are representative of society's deeper notions about what is good and bad.

Situation-Specific Norms

In the formal language of sociology or anthropology, **situation-specific norms** are called **folkways.** These are rules about manners and fashion. They are the least critical of all the norms and are the most easily changed. My favorite example of a folkway occurs when we are a certain age, somewhere in our middle teenage years, when we have to be "cool." In school, the cool people are always right at the edge of the "regular" norm — the ones who look different, distance themselves from the action and still manage to get through, while the rest of us are up in the front rows, taking notes and look like everyone else. It seems important to many people that in a variety of situations, requiring a range of behaviors and appearances, that their behavior can be labeled as "cool" or "uncool." Folkways tend to be the least important of all societal norms, but following them can be essential to managing an acceptable social identity in many situations.

Although this rule learning is a critical part of the fundamental knowledge that we are socialized into, either by direct instruction or through observation and imitation, we also learn the key values, the "way of seeing" reality, and a general manner of talk while we are learning the patterns of verbal and nonverbal language in our society.

Learning Values at the Level of Everyday Talk: Framing, Style and Manner of Speech

Insights about what we learn to talk about and how we talk about it have been developed out of research that compares our culture to others. The original work was done by Hofstede[4] (1980), a Dutch management researcher who published the results of his observations on the different patterns of the talk he observed in 100,000 employees of a large multinational in 40 countries. Later researchers[5] extended Hofstede's work by focusing on nonverbal behavioral patterns across cultures.

Key Values and Framings: The Individual versus the Group

Sometimes directly, but mostly indirectly in the way we frame (i.e., see) topics of conversation, one of the key things we talk about is our values. In Hofstede's study of cross-cultural communication, we found that there were a number of dimensions that emerged in the content of people's talk, that is, what they addressed first in their conversation when they needed to explain how things happen in life. One of those dimensions was the focus on the individual versus the group.

The North American view, and generally the eastern European view, of life begins with the notion of how whatever we are talking about affects the individual, how individual actions change other individuals — what I can do for me, and what I can do for you as an individual to make everything good (or bad). Lots of other cultures believe individuals are significant, but that is not what they talk about first. What they talk about first includes categorical group words, such as *family*, *kin* and *tribe*. As Jandt[6] states:

> "Individualist cultures are loosely integrated; collectivist cultures are tightly integrated. . . . Also, in individualist cultures, there is greater emphasis on personal accomplishments, whereas in collectivist cultures, people want to know who your family is because that places you in society."

Take marriage, for example. In North America, and generally in western European cultures, the coming together of two individuals to form an emotional and social bond leads to individual choices around long-term relationships. In a group or collectivist culture, the decision around who you are going to marry has very little to do with how you happen to feel about the person at the time. In many cultures, the decision is made for you long before you meet the person or get to know them or have feelings about them.

In our culture, the feeling orientation, the individualist orientation, is what we consider to be the dominant, and therefore the only view of the world — it's the right one, the best one. In a society that holds collectivist views about marriage, the basis is an allegiance or connection between two different groups of people — two different families — that is pre-established by the rules of hierarchy and age, so the elders make the decisions.

There are always two different ways of looking at the world. Many societies do not base their mores and their laws on individual freedoms and rights, as we do. They begin by asking what is the basis for a good society, for public order? Those considerations come first and supersede the rights of the individual. As North Americans, we disagree because our ideological view begins with the individual, not the group.

Learning a Style of Talk: High- and Low-Context Cultures

Culture and communication shape the way people talk to each other beyond the particular topic of conversation or "way of seeing" a topic. Anderson's[7] (1994) research discovered that some societies focus on direct, word-centered styles of talk while others socialize their members to use fewer words and speak indirectly. He called them low- and high-context cultures.

A **low-context culture**, such as ours in North America, is one in which people consider it appropriate in many situations to speak openly about their internal thought processes and their feelings. We often say "everything" there is to say. In a **high-context culture**, there are few contexts within which people can speak openly about internal thought processes or feelings, or openly express deep emotion, and yet others are expected to understand them. In high-context cultures, people are trained much more to listen to the tone of voice, to notice the context, to watch the eyes or the face, and also to observe how carefully a speaker follows the rules for effective self-presentation. To ask others direct questions about their feelings or emotions is not appropriate and to express emotions in public is seen as possibly imposing on or disturbing the feelings of the others present. Emotional messages are communicated in the subtleties of the way people use the language and their tone of voice.

What happens if low-context people enter into a relationship with high-context people? It happens all the time in the world. In North America and low-context countries in western Europe, people say what they mean and they often don't know what they mean unless they hear it said. But half the world is high-context. So, for example, when North American business people deal with a high-context culture such as China, Korea or Japan, there is plenty of opportunity for miscommunication. In a high-context culture, it's important to pay attention to the social conventions, like getting to know each other, before doing business. Nothing is going to happen until the question, "Who am I to you in this situation, and who are you to me in this situation?" is answered. In a high-context culture, words are just words. People in a high-context culture need to hear how those words happen over time and in specific contexts in order to gain an understanding of someone as a person.

Learning a Style of Talk: High and Low Immediacy and Expressiveness

Anderson describes **immediacy** as the degree of perceived physical or psychological closeness between people, and the behavior that communicates warmth, closeness and availability for communication. In **high-immediacy** cultures, such as most countries in the Mediterranean region and eastern European countries, people express their emotions openly in order to establish connection and trust. Cultures that express themselves this way do so to determine whether someone is dependable or predictable and to discover "Who am I to you and who are you to me in this situation?" Until that happens, they can't move deeply into the topic of conversation. This kind of expressive behavior, however, makes people from **low-immediacy** cultures, such as Canada, England or northern Europe, quite uncomfortable. People from low-immediacy cultures often feel emotional expressiveness early in a relationship is unnecessary, particularly in business dealings. Since their cultural learning focuses on direct, open talk about topics of conversation with people they have just met, they already see themselves as valuing honesty and fair dealing without having to establish a relationship of trust based on displays of emotion and self-expression.

> **Marrying into a High Expressive Culture**
>
> My own experience of this stems from marrying into an Italian family. My heritage is Scots-Irish and in my family, in addition to saying hello and smiling, shaking hands is appropriate for men meeting for the first or fortieth time, and, depending on the nature of their relationship, women might give each other a hug. We are definitely on the low expressive side of the cultural continuum.
>
> In my Italian family of marriage, however, it's quite different. On first meeting them, I started with what I knew: "Hi's," handshakes and occasional hugs. I soon discovered that double-cheek kissing was the appropriate way to greet family members — close and distant, women and men — otherwise you seem standoffish. I soon got the hang of it. Now I think it's great — high expressiveness really works!

Socialization and Subcultures

These are only three of the key dimensions of cultural learning that have been revealed in the work of cross-cultural researchers, but they are critical to understanding how we learn the styles of talk in Chapters 9 through 11.

Although cultural values, both as general moral statements and as manifested through the ways we learn to talk, are shared throughout the society, the socialization of children isn't a cookie-cutter process. It would be impossible for every individual to learn our values in exactly the same way. First of all, people acquire them through the filters of their immediate family experience, which in turn is shaped by variables like family size and availability to children of one or both parents and other relatives.

Secondly, families don't just occur randomly, they are integral parts of larger communities, which vary in their social, economic, ethnic and religious characteristics. Such variations seem to drive the differences in values teaching that families located in one community provide to their children, when compared to families located in other communities. Sociologists call these community-level variations in value acceptance and socialization "subcultures."

Thirdly, we are uniquely different individuals. We bring temperamental and biological differences to the learning situation. These forces shape the way we respond to people. After all, like someone from one of the Mediterranean countries, some of us born and raised for generations in Canada are far more immediate and expressive in our communication than the "typical" Canadian. In the end, we process our society's values through our unique history of experience.

In sum, cultural learning represents a kind of contradictory complexity. Every society has a range of values it expects its members to enact in their everyday behavior and talk. At one level we are "all the same" and at every other level we're different. In other words, everyone learns about their society's values but, depending on their personal developmental experiences, will emphasize and accept some values over others in their worldview and enact some sets of norms over others in their behavior.

It's important to keep this complexity in mind as we analyze the differences between our everyday model of communication and the interpersonal communication (IP) model described in Chapter 1. Our simple, everyday assumptions about the obviousness of our ideas to others need to be tempered by the complexity of the learning process we've all been through. To make matters more complicated, this inherent diversity of learning experience also applies to our learning the languages — verbal and nonverbal — that permit us to store, recall and express our understanding of the society's knowledge, values and practices.

The Basic Tools of Talk: Words and Meaning

In Chapter 1, we said that "unlike our 'common sense' belief, words have many meanings and these will vary depending on the context [when, where and with whom] in which they are spoken." And yet we also said that people have to begin each conversation with something in common — "socially shared verbal symbols and socially defined, biologically shared nonverbal symptoms and symbols."

The essential social "sharedness" of word symbols is critical because the meaning our culture attaches to each sound or group of sounds is entirely arbitrary. Words do not have a direct relationship to the thing that they represent. They simply "refer to or stand for" something else, so we have to agree to use them in a particular way. For instance, there is nothing about the letter symbols or the sound of the word *cat* that is directly related to the "cat-ness" of cats. This three-letter collection of visual symbols simply stands for a whole family of animals that range from the feline at the foot of the bed to the feline on an African veldt.

We think of something — a mental picture develops — and then we call up a word that we have learned from others which names it for us. As long as we are using a recognized word, we can begin a conversation with an arbitrary — but shared — connection to others.

Words Have Two Levels of Meaning

Denotation

In the models of communication we described, the messages we *consciously* send to others are constructed of words, with agreed-upon meanings, strung together in an order (called syntax) that everyone recognizes. These words and their meanings are part of the **lexicon** — the verbal information base of the culture. In fact, one aspect of communication competence relates to an individual's knowledge of the lexicon — the basic dictionary meanings of words — and how well they've learned these connections.

Even though we have a list of verbal symbols and their meanings in our lexicon, we don't, or can't, learn **all** the meanings because each word may have a dozen or even a hundred meanings. Check this out for yourself: Go to any dictionary or online dictionary and look up a simple word such as *run*. How many meanings do you think might be listed? Would you be surprised to learn that Dictionary.com has 179 meanings or shades of meaning for the word *run*?

There is also a second kind of competence at work in our talk. It relates to the personal meanings we add to culturally defined words.

Connotation

Connotation refers to the personal meanings a word has for one or more members of the same community. The uniqueness of connotative meanings is the reason for a good deal of the uncertainty in our interpersonal communication. Often we are trying to convey the connotative meanings of things (what the word means to us) to each other when we speak, not the denotative meaning of our words (what they may mean to everyone else). The fact that many of the words we use have (personal) connotative meanings compels us to work harder with another person to create shared meanings in moments of face-to-face talk.

The multiplicity of denotative meanings plus the possibility of uniqueness in connotative meanings sheds light on a good deal of the uncertainty in our talk. This complicates our simplistic "I said what I meant and I said it clearly" approach to explaining communication failures. In fact, all of these sources of meaning reinforce Berlo's[8] statement: "Meanings are in people, not in words," for two reasons:

1) People can choose meanings other than the ones in your head when they are listening to you, and

2) In any *particular* conversation, in a *particular* context, a lot more is being communicated than words.

More Than Words: Nonverbal Behavior — The Other Tools of Talk

Our culture provides us with a repertoire of agreed-upon verbal symbols so that we can communicate. But that's only half the process. Now we're going to look at the other half — our nonverbal behavior. Sociolinguists argue that in the development of language, the gestural system came first. Our earliest learning as humans and pre-humans was about how to use our face and our hands and our bodies to communicate. When language developed, we simply put them both together and we learned to discriminate between gestures that contribute to, add to or subtract from communication, and the words and gestures that are irrelevant to it.

If I asked you what had more impact on you when making small talk with someone, would you say, it's the words they spoke; the way they sounded when they spoke those words; or the look on their face when they were speaking? Well, if you weren't clear about what their words meant, you would very likely depend primarily on how they looked and sounded to figure out their meaning. This is Albert Mehrabian's "truth" for applied communications: The impact of a message on the receiver, i.e., its perceived meaning, is based not on what is said but *how* it is said.

Mehrabian (1972)[9] completed a series of studies of interpersonal communication where many combinations of messages, sent via clear, blurred or blacked-out television pictures and with clear, distorted or silent audio tracks were exchanged between people (e.g., they could see the face clearly but only hear a distorted version of the words or vice versa). He summarized the results as follows: 55% of the total impact of a message on another can be attributed to facial expressions and 38% to vocal cues. Words only accounted for about 7% of the total impact of a message. People seemed to "get the message" from the 93% of the talk that was nonverbal.

In general, nonverbals operate in three ways in our face-to-face communication: (1) they affect the meanings that are conveyed verbally, (2) they significantly influence the type of relationship that forms between persons, and perhaps most importantly, (3) they express our emotions (affect displays).

Nonverbals and the Meanings of Words

We've discovered that in face-to-face communication, the gesture system — the nonverbal messages that we're communicating along with our verbal messages — allows us to figure out what the words mean. The tone of our voice, the look on our face, the movement of our hands, the tension in our muscles contribute greatly to communicating which meaning we have in our mind when we are trying to say something and, as listeners, we unconsciously depend on our own and the others' nonverbals to figure out what's going on. Nonverbals can impact verbal messages in six ways:[10]

1) ***Repeating***, as when you are giving directions to some location and you also point.

2) ***Contradicting***, as in the case of the person who is about to give a speech and says they are not nervous while, in fact, they are sweating and pacing.

3) ***Substituting*** for a verbal message. You come home from work looking beaten up and no one has to ask you how your day went. They can tell.

4) ***Complementing*** a verbal message. We blush with embarrassment while we are talking about an embarrassing situation.

5) ***Accenting*** a message. Here the nonverbal reinforces the verbal message. Pounding a table to show how angry you are while you are speaking in anger.

6) ***Regulating.*** People regulate behavior in one of two ways: (1) coordinate their verbal and non-verbal behavior when communicating a message, or (2) coordinate their verbal and nonverbal actions with those of their interacting partners. We regulate our messages in many ways, for example, by changing our posture, pausing between thoughts and shifting our eye gaze.

Nonverbals and Relationships

The second function of nonverbal messages is to define the type of relationship we are building with the person sharing our conversation. Beginning with the powerful, classic observational research on interpersonal communication by Watzlawick, Beavin and Jackson,[11] communication theorists have come to see that our nonverbal behavior provides much of the answer to the social relationship aspect of the key question in Chapter 1, "Who am I to you and who are you to me in this situation?" Nonverbal communication is the focus of axiom 3 when we assert that all IP communication has content and *relationship* dimensions.

The way we look at someone as we talk, the distance between us, whether or not we touch them, and where and how our voice rises and falls as we talk to them are just a few of the nonverbal indicators we use to tell each other about the nature of our relationship (formal–informal, close–distant, friendly–hostile, etc.) while we are talking. Although there are a variety of channels through which we nonverbally make statements about ourselves (including the appearance of the body and the face; the movement of our eyes; the sound of the voice; our use of things and understanding of the flow of time), in this chapter, we will focus on the categories that seem most central to face-to-face talk: facial gestures (the changeable looks we create as we talk) and paralanguage (the sound of our voice, including pitch, rate and vocal qualities).

Nonverbals and Emotional Communication

The third and perhaps most important function of our nonverbal gestures is the display of our emotional reactions. These reflect the third level of complexity in interpersonal communication we discussed in Chapter 1. The nature of our emotions and their effects on our intra- and interpersonal communication will be covered in more detail in Chapter 4. It's important to note that although the interpersonal communication (IP) model recognizes the importance of nonverbal messages in face-to-face talk, it emphasizes their second function — their influence on the type of relationship we are creating as we talk with another. This has meant placing nonverbal behavior primarily in the role of shaping the meanings of the words being spoken (telling the other how to "take what we say" and, indirectly, to know how we feel about them by the "way" we sound or look while talking about something else).

It is clear that nonverbals do shape the meaning of our words for others, but they also directly communicate our feelings about those others *without* words — before any words are spoken or even after the other has left our presence. Whether or not we are consciously aware of it, our nonverbals directly communicate our emotions (affect) to others and this impacts our effectiveness as communicators.

As Leathers[12] has put it: "Successful communication places a premium on the ability to identify general emotional states of individuals with whom we communicate, but also on the ability to differentiate among subtle emotional meanings that are constituents of the more general emotional states." In other words, emotion recognition, display and interpretation are becoming key competences to be studied in the research around interpersonal communication.

Face and Voice in Emotional Communication

The Face

The face is the primary site for the communication of emotional states and is the primary signal system for communicating emotions. Over the past three decades Ekman[13] and his associates have demonstrated the power of the face for communicating six basic classes of emotional meaning represented in the illustration on the facing page.

Ekman's research also revealed that these six basic categories are universal in that they are encoded and decoded at approximately the same levels of accuracy across different cultures, that is, when people from different societies feel these emotions they will involuntarily express them using the same facial expressions. When he published his basic research, contemporary scholars were not convinced by his findings. In particular,

Anthropologists argued for cultural relativism — that is, they had long believed that every behavior is shaped by local culture, including the expression of emotion. To deal with this criticism, Ekman elected to have one of his critics re-do his research to confirm his findings. He also had to come up with an alternative explanation that would assuage the concerns of those who believed in the cultural relativist model.

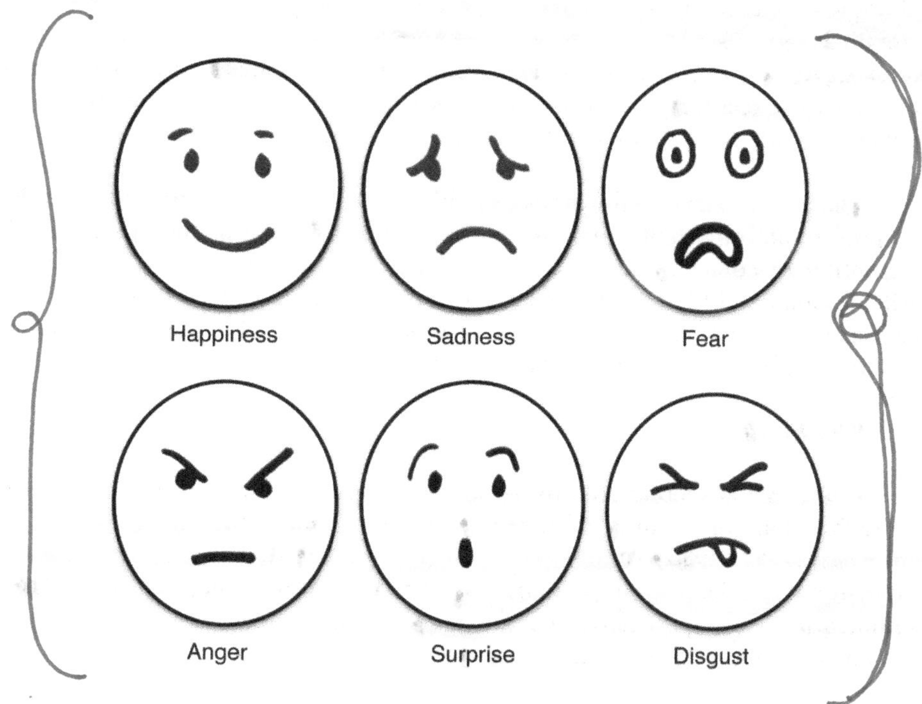

As a result, he balanced his conclusion that "expressions are universal" with a second concept — the idea of **display rules**. He argued that people do share some common emotions but they don't necessarily show them in the same way. Display rules, he argued, represent the socially learned aspect of the emotions. Each culture socializes its children using different rules about the management of emotional expression — about who can show which emotion to whom, and when they can do so.

He conducted a series of studies to demonstrate this. For instance, in one of his studies, he found that, when alone, Japanese and American students displayed the same facial expressions in response to seeing gory films of surgery and accidents. However, when a researcher sat with them while they watched the films, the Japanese masked their negative expressions more than the Americans. Japan is one of the world's high-context cultures (see page 38).

Micro-Expressions of Emotion

Over the years, Ekman and his colleagues have catalogued the movement of the many facial muscles required to express emotions and have made three other important discoveries: (1) the face can instantly communicate different combinations of these emotions at the same time; (2) behind the expressions for anger, fear, disgust and sadness there are physiological changes that generate the unique feelings for each of the expressed emotions; and finally, (3) the face communicates "micro-expressions" of emotion before a full-fledged emotion appears.[14] These emotions involve very fast movements of the facial muscles, lasting about 1/25 of a second (normal expressions last from 1/2 to 2 seconds). He argues that in conversation with another, we can't consciously see these expressions without training.

These micro-expressions not only hint at the emotion about to be displayed but they also represent an important source of emotional leakage, that is, they reveal feelings a person is attempting to conceal. Needless to say, in a post-9/11 era focused on public safety and security, Ekman and his colleagues have been teaching first responders, including police and airport security staff, how to read faces more quickly. The training is now available to everyone and can be found on line at his Web site.

The Voice

The voice is second only to the face in its power to instantly communicate emotional meaning by changing sound. Vocal cues assume a vitally important role in serving three communicative functions: (1) communicating emotions, (2) impression management and (3) conversational regulation (turn taking, etc.). The tone of the voice is also vitally important for communicating our perceived personality characteristics and, ultimately, affects the impressions we make as communicators.[15]

There is a substantial body of research demonstrating that people can both communicate significant emotions solely by vocal cues and accurately assess them in others. In addition, it has been demonstrated that vocal cues convey different emotions with readily identifiable and distinctive sound attributes. For example, sadness is expressed by downward inflections, low pitch and slow speaking rate; whereas anger is expressed by wide variations in pitch, downward inflections and a fast speaking rate. The voice rarely communicates emotion by means of a single sound attribute. Pitch alone is not sufficient to express emotion vocally, but instead it is the interaction of pitch and loudness that is critical.[16]

Having described the importance of the voice in delivering emotion messages, we also have to note that individual ability to decode emotional information via vocal cues varies substantially. So even when we are competently conveying a certain emotion through our vocal tone, we can't count on the other to decode our message in the way we sent it. Differences in communication competence always make a difference in creating and sustaining shared meaning, particularly at the level of emotional communication.

One final complication is that many people often trust nonverbal signals over verbal ones when they are presented with conflicting messages because "the nonverbal channels carry more information" and nonverbal signals are viewed to be harder to "fake." So, if others get a different emotional message than we intended, they are inclined to believe it. Generally speaking, if others think that the information being communicated in one channel lacks credibility (our words are a little hard to believe), they will likely discount it and look to other channels to determine the "real" message (our nonverbals "give us away").[17]

"All Together Now"

We are socialized into our society's language and repertoire of nonverbal behavior so we can communicate the pictures in our head to other people. In effect, we learn packages of **verbals** and **nonverbals** to help us create, sustain and manage meaning with others. We also learn to recognize changes in **context** along with the **norms** of conversation; that is, we learn **to know**:

- Where, when and with whom to say what
- In a particular **way**.

We learn when and where to say which words with the "right" tone of voice, facial expressions and positioning of our body (sometimes called our demeanor). DeVito calls these the "rules of appropriateness." To be appropriate we must learn to recognize changes in the situational and relationship contexts that we negotiate every day as we go about our lives within the larger cultural context. In an ongoing interaction, this deep learning permits us to automatically enact the correct package of words and nonverbals so that our audience will have a chance to get what we mean.

But how do we learn all these words and nonverbals with multiple meanings? Interestingly, it has to do with the way we learn while we're children. Contrary to what most parents think, children do not learn one thing at a time. They are constantly observing and internally rehearsing bundles of words and nonverbals for different situations. Cognitive scientists call them **schemas**.

Schemas are combinations of observed words, vocal tone and looks that are brought about by changes in the context — that is, the external situation. Schemas are culturally provided, pre-organized sets of expectations about people and situations that allow us to make sense of what's going on around us, much like the "line drawings" in a child's coloring book. They permit us to make instantaneous choices about what to put inside or outside the lines of our understanding of reality, and, over time, we fill in the details of each schema with our own experience, our unique emotional coloring.

Since we learn them early, they are "buried" in the mind and operate outside of our immediate awareness. Each situation calls up a deeply learned pattern of words and actions: how to begin a conversation; how to behave; what to expect.

Now you know the answer to the second of our key questions . . . those tourists! We all whisper in cathedrals because it's the schema for a particular context. The 25-foot distance between being outside and inside a holy place makes all the difference. We unthinkingly go from laughing and talking loudly to silence and whispers once we go inside, to show reverence for a holy place. We learned that pattern of behavior — that schema — long ago in our childhood. The depth of this kind of schematic learning is illustrated by a dramatic piece of research on how college-aged men handle a personal insult.

The Personal Insult Experiment[18]

In 1996, two researchers at the University of Michigan — Cohen and Nisbett[19] — did a rather simple experiment to make a complex point about the depth and lasting qualities of cultural learning.

First, they found a classroom at the end of a long, narrow hallway lined with file cabinets, in the basement of the Social Sciences building. They put about 80 college men, 18–20 years old, in the room and had them fill out a detailed questionnaire as well as give a saliva sample to the experimenters. Then, one by one, the students were let out into the hall and told to take the questionnaire to an office at the other end of the hall and hand it in to one of the staff, who would tell them what to do in the second part of the experiment.

The "real" experiment in fact took place when they walked down the hall. A man who appeared to be a researcher, but who was actually a grad student of one of the professors, brushed by them and walked quickly ahead, stopping further down the hall and opening a file drawer. This caused the hallway to be too narrow for the students to pass easily — so when they approached the "researcher" they had to squeeze by. As they did so, the "researcher" appeared angered by the intrusion. He slammed the file drawer closed, turned away and jostled the student's shoulder. Then, under his breath, he insulted the student by calling him: "Asshole!"

All this was designed to anger the students, and it did. As they approached the room at the end of the hall, their faces were observed and secretly rated for expressed anger by observers who didn't know anything else about them. When they entered the room, their hands were shaken to see if their grip was any firmer than usual — another way of testing their unconscious expression of anger. They were then asked for a second saliva sample (as part of the general experiment). Their before and after saliva samples were later tested for cortisol and testosterone — the hormones that drive arousal and aggression.

Finally, they were asked to complete a story in which a young man called "Steve" is at a party and finds his girlfriend upset because his friend Larry has made a pass at her. Shortly after learning this, he sees Larry trying to kiss her. The story asks: "If you were Steve, how would you deal with Larry?"

All the participants got angry — and showed it — but about half of them got significantly angrier than the rest. They manifested this through: (1) angrier looks, (2) more intense handshakes, (3) more violent thoughts expressed in their writing (too bad for Larry), and (4) much higher levels of stress and aggression hormones in their bloodstreams.

When leaving the experiment, they had to walk down the corridor again. This time, however, they were faced with a very tall, large, intense male, walking aggressively toward them. Every one of them stepped aside. The average step-aside distance was about 5 feet, however, the really angry students only stepped aside at about 2 feet.

When we learn more about these student participants, we discover that it doesn't matter whether they were jocks or intellectuals, physically imposing or not, or whether they had one type of personal style or another. What matters is *where* they were from, *not who they were* as individuals. It turns out that students from the southern states were significantly more enraged by the incident than students from the northern states. The outcome wasn't based in personality differences but in cultural background, and very specifically, the culture of a particular region.

Sociologists investigating crime statistics in various regions of the United States have noted a distinctive pattern in the South:

- Murder rates are higher there than in the rest the country, while property and stranger crimes such as muggings are lower.

- The homicides in the South are those in which the victim and killer know each other and know the reasons for the crime. Murder is personal — payback for an insult.

Historians assembling immigration and settlement data from the 1700s on, and anthropologists doing field work and analysis of more recent community records have argued that the South has a "culture of honor" that was imported to the United States from the highlands of Scotland. The Scotch-Irish who settled in the hilly country ranging from the southern edges of Pennsylvania to the northern edges of Georgia and Alabama were the fourth and last great wave of early Anglo-Celtic immigration, most likely because the territory looked like the land they had left.

They brought with them a culture of violent retribution for insults that led to 200 years of family feuds and murder in order to sustain family reputation. One of the more famous of these was between the Hatfield and McCoy families. Many of the participants went unpunished or were only lightly punished because of the value of "manly honor" that attached to their crimes.

These Scotch-Irish people represented the "herding cultures" of the contested, lawless lands at the border of Scotland and England. These lands were harsh, rocky country, fought over by landlords and kings for generations. The inhabitants were herdsmen because the land was too poor to farm. They formed tight, clannish family bonds, valuing loyalty to family over all else and violently defending their own and their clan's honor from perceived insults.

This makes sense because unlike other types of agricultural pursuits involving sharing land and water and thus creating more stable, cooperative communities, herding is a mobile, solitary and fluid form of occupation. Assets are easily captured and driven off. Herders are only protected by their reputation for fighting whoever challenges them or their family. A man's reputation is the core of his success and self-worth. His willingness to defend himself with violence is the key to getting others to believe and fear it.

In their monograph on the "anger" experiment, "Culture of Honor," Nisbett and Cohen stated that they needed measures of behavior before they could take seriously hypotheses about cultural differences. They said, "We examined the sequence of reactions following an insult, in an effort to determine whether southerners become more upset by affronts and are more likely to take aggressive action."

The measures they used — the looks, handshakes, willingness to face down a potential adversary, hormones, thoughts and words — all significantly supported their hypothesis. And these were not the children of Scotch-Irish herders. They were students from households making over $100,000 a year — not from the hills of Appalachia but the suburbs of Atlanta — who just happened to be brought up in the South and were attending a good school in the North.

For our purposes, this experiment is a detailed demonstration of how a deeply learned cultural schema lasts and works. With the right situational cue — a body bump and a verbal insult — our bodies know how to react and we instantly know how to feel, look, think and speak. The fact that these reactions seem to be shared by a large group of people can only be explained by cultural transmission — socialization of many generations — that goes back more than 400 years. In summarizing his review of this research, Gladwell says, "Cultural legacies . . . persist generation after generation . . . even though the conditions that spawned [them] have long since disappeared."[20]

Where We're Going Next

Let's look again at the cultural complexity underlying our simple views of communication. In Chapter 1, our everyday view of communication makes a series of assumptions about talk that we don't even notice, including our assumption that the words we speak have one or only a few obvious meanings, as we speak them. In fact, in the cultural lexicon, not to mention the dictionary, they have multiple denotative meanings whose connotations can be altered by our personal experiences.

Moreover, our nonverbal behavior can alter those meanings even as they are being spoken, and at the same time communicate feelings that we may not be conscious of. We are fully conscious about and comfortable with our abilities to communicate, even though it turns out that our perceived success in talking with others is generally structured by deeply learned patterns — schemas — that are triggered by situational cues, including other people's responses to our words and gestures. And these patterns have little to do with our conscious thought because they are deeply buried in what is called the "cognitive unconscious" part of the mind and it can't be accessed with words.

How that part of the mind works and how it supports or undermines our day-to-day talk and our relationships will be the focus of our next chapter.

End Notes

[1] Adapted from Levin, W. (1988) *Sociological ideas: Concepts and Applications* (2nd ed.). Belmont, CA: Wadsworth, p. 99.
[2] Bem, D. (1970) *Beliefs, Attitudes and Human Affairs*. Belmont, CA: Brooks/Cole Publishing.
[3] Grice, P. (1989) *Studies in the Way of Words.* Cambridge: Harvard University Press, Chap. 2.
[4] Hofstede, G. (1980) *Culture's Consequences, International Differences in Work-Related Values*, Beverly Hills, CA: Sage Publications.
[5] As cited in Jandt, F. (1998) *Intercultural Communication: An Introduction* (2nd ed.). Thousand Oaks, CA: Sage Publications.
[6] Jandt, p. 215.
[7] Anderson as cited in Jandt, p. 214.
[8] Berlo, D. (1964) *The Process of Communication: An Introduction to Theory and Practice.* New York: Holt, Rinehart and Winston.
[9] Mehrabian, A. (1972) *Nonverbal Communication.* Chicago: Aldine Atherton.
[10] Knapp, M. (1972) *Non-Verbal Communication,* New York: Holt, Rinehart and Winston, pp. 9–11.
[11] Watzlawick, P., Beavin, J., Jackson, D. (1967) *Pragmatics of Human Communication.* New York: W. W. Norton and Company.
[12] Leathers, D. (1997) *Successful Nonverbal Communication: Principles and Applications* (3rd ed.). Boston: Allyn and Bacon, p. 25.
[13] Ekman, P. (2004) *Emotions Revealed: Recognizing Faces and Feelings to Improve Communication and Emotional Life.* New York: Henry Holt and Co.
[14] Ekman, p. 15.
[15] Leathers, p. 158.
[16] Leathers, p. 163.
[17] Knapp, M., Hall, J. (1997) *Nonverbal Communication In Human Interaction* (4th ed). Fort Worth: Harcourt Brace College Publishers.
[18] This section is a summary of Gladwell, M. (2008) *Outliers: The Story of Success*. New York: Little Brown and Co., Chap. 6. References to this study and supporting research found on pp. 292–293.
[19] Nisbett, R., Cohen, D. (1996). *Culture of Honor: The Psychology of Violence in the South.* Boulder, CO: Westview Press.
[20] Gladwell, p. 175.

CHAPTER THREE

THE MIND IN COMMUNICATION: THE COGNITIVE UNCONSCIOUS

In Chapter 1 we made the case that humans are born to talk. We need to communicate with those around us to fulfill our fundamental needs to survive and to develop as whole human beings — including our deep need to know the answers to three key life questions: "What's going on here?" "What's going to happen next?" and "Who are you to me and me to you, in this situation?" To discover the answers to these questions we need to create and sustain shared meanings as we communicate, so in Chapter 2 we discussed the essential "sharedness" at the heart of talk:

1) Common perspectives — ways of seeing — regarding what's real or unreal, good or bad,

2) Shared repertoires of meanings for words and gestures, and

3) Shared schema — outlines of attributes for people and situations and for taking action toward them in particular circumstances.

We also explained how we learn this collection of shared symbols and meanings. In the process of each generation passing the society's culture on to the next through socialization, we not only learn to use the words and gestures that everyone around us thinks of as "normal," but we also learn to see our world in ways that the society thinks of as "right, true and proper" — so we can respond appropriately to most situations. Our culture — like the air — invisibly surrounds us; we breathe it in every second we're conscious. However, our earliest cultural learning is dissolved into the depths of our minds the way oxygen is into our bloodstream as we breathe. It lasts for our lifetime and operates outside of our consciousness.

Through research in the past 30 years on the roots of individual choices and actions, we have learned about the depth of cultural learning and that it is stored in a part of the mind we now call the **cognitive unconscious**. This is an aspect of the mind to which we have no direct access because the memories located here are not constructed of words and pictures but of biochemical patterns of connection between neurons. Although, this part of our mind may have no words, the information it holds gives shape to every word we say. So, in this chapter we need to review three topics:

1) The operations of the cognitive unconscious. It's the part of the mind that does most of the work of getting us through our day.

2) The three areas of decision making by the cognitive unconscious that permit us to speak and act normally.

3) The effects — both positive and negative — of these unconscious decisions on our communication relationships.

The Operations of the Cognitive Unconscious

To survive, we need to know (1) what's going on, and (2) what's going to happen next. In the womb, our body-mind knew the answers because the information was built into the biochemical exchanges that went on in the blood flow between our mother's body and ours. We developed in harmony with her. Researchers have learned that a fetus can distinguish changes in the taste of amniotic fluid, depending on what its mother had for lunch, and by 4 or 5 months, it can feel its way around the womb and react to sound and light from outside the mother's body. By the third trimester it listens and memorizes the tone of its mother's voice and comes to understand the rhythms and patterns essential to producing the language in the future.[1]

So, all was good. There we were in the womb — warm, comfortable and living a completely integrated communication relationship with our mother. Then at birth, the cord was cut and we were suddenly on our own with a collection of nonverbal gestures, trying to recreate that common union we had before we were rejected by her body.

All of our infantile grimacing, smiling, cooing and crying didn't seem like much on the surface, but beneath it important things were happening. The nonspeaking part of the body-mind — our unconscious — was continuing to answer the key questions of life for us. It was paying attention to incoming stimuli and how they affected our body, and developing a set of connections between our external efforts and our internal states so we could survive and grow.

Among other things, it was creating patterns of connection that would become the basis for our acquisition of language. This happened automatically because our developing conscious mind was occupied with differentiating between ourselves and the other "gesturing, sound-making things" around us — learning how to get their attention and connect with them. At first we did this only with facial gestures and touch, but once we learned our first words, and felt the powerful effects they had on others, we came to believe that our conscious thought and words controlled everything we do. As we will see, this powerful insight and the cultural belief built upon it, is mostly wrong.

Privileging the Conscious Mind[2]

The part of the mind that does most of the daily work that allows us to be "normal" human beings — the cognitive unconscious — was long ignored in communication theory and research mostly because our culture is based on a 2,300-year tradition of focusing on the conscious mind and its actions: thought — in particular, virtuous or moral thought — and the proper use of words — rhetoric — and the ways in which words are used to sway the thoughts of others.

Beginning with Aristotle

The philosophy of Aristotle (mid-300s BCE), focused on achieving enlightened thought and the use of rhetoric to persuade others to higher moral virtues, is still studied today. Conscious, rational choice is the cornerstone of the discipline of philosophy and of our legal system. Moreover, various models of communication based on rhetoric dominated our understanding of everyday talk in academic life until the 1950s.

Through René Descartes (1637)

Descartes, whose "Discourse on Method and Science" — on how to think in a fully rational way — endowed the conscious mind with a special status unrelated to physical laws. His summary statement, "I think therefore I am," restricted the mind to consciousness and nothing else. This idea influenced generations of thinkers to follow.

And on to Freud (1880s)

Freud does "theorize" an unconscious mind but limits it to "a storehouse of primitive, infantile thought" kept out of consciousness because it's a source of psychic pain" — the dark side of our thoughts. We defend ourselves against it but we can't reach it. It is a closed box that can only be opened with help of a psychiatrist trained in analysis. Like Descartes, Freud's thinking was very influential. The power of his ideas ensured that the unconscious would not be scientifically studied for almost 80 years.

Opening the Box: A Paradigm Shift

It wasn't until the 1960s that our view of the mind shifted from the conscious mind as a closed box to one of an open information processor. When the first computers were developed and used for research, they encouraged researchers to adopt a computational view of the mind — seeing it as an information-processing system and a symbol manipulator. They discovered that the mind computes input from the natural world to create outputs in the form of additional mental or physical states. The brain manages billions of bits of information at once, the vast majority of it entering the system below the level of conscious thought.

These discoveries led to a rise in experiments in the 1980s on the inferred outcome of brain functions. From the 1990s on, however, we no longer had to infer functions because we were able to look at the brain operations directly with the advent of imaging technologies — PET and MRI scanners.

So as our ideas about the brain progressed from the word-centered black box to an information processor, we started to answer the question: "What is a baby's mind doing while it is learning to utter its first word at around one year, two-word utterances in the following year, and full sentences between ages 3 and 5?"

From the Beginning: The Need to Connect and Learn

Once they looked, scientists discovered that before it learns its first few words, the baby's cognitive unconscious is processing a huge amount of information and communicating with touch, looks and gestures, which it learns by mimicking its "mothering other." In fact, mimicry seems to be built into baby brains at birth. As Brooks asserts:

> In 1981, Andrew Meltzoff ushered in a new era of infant psychology when he stuck his tongue out at a forty-two-minute-old infant. The baby stuck her tongue out back at him. It was as if the baby, who had never seen a tongue in her life, intuited that the strange collection of shapes in front of her was a face, that the little thing in the middle of it was a tongue, that there was a creature behind the face, that the tongue was something other than herself, and that she herself had a corresponding flap that she too could move around.[3]

There is a lot of perception, cognition and decision making hidden away in this simple act of mimicry. This experiment, replicated many times since, changed the fundamental model of infant psychology from a characterization of the newborn's mind as a blank slate to discovering how much it knows at birth and how it learns in its first year. Where we once thought that without words there could be no cognition, we have come to realize that that was a mistake.

Babies Make Choices without Words

By closely observing their reflexes in controlled situations, developmental psychologists now believe that babies are born with a set of innate, nonconscious preferences for what it is to be human. Not only can they imitate the facial movements of another within minutes of being born, but also within hours of birth (measured by their automatic eye-gaze movement) babies show that they prefer their mother's face and voice, and as noted, their first "conversation" of cries and gestures happens by automatically imitating what their mother does. Babies seem to assume that another who looks like them will feel like them and they automatically link their internal bodily sensations to the bodily movements they can see in others.[4] To learn more about themselves, they mimic people they prefer.

Within weeks, babies show a preference for human faces over geometric patterns and for familiar people rather than strangers. They soon can discriminate between happy, sad and angry faces, and within 6 months, will look longer at those who behave in ways that are trustworthy and avert their eyes from those who don't.[5] Thus, long before we can talk or develop a conscious sense of self, our unconscious mind is building patterns of emotional preferences for specific things, people and actions. In the last chapter, these patterns are called "schemas." They represent networks of neurons that fire together in the presence of an encountered thing, or person or a repeated series of actions. They permit rapid processing of data as the baby's physical self-control develops and its physical and social environments expand.

Theory of Mind: Essential for Face-to-Face Talk

The result of developing these interconnected schemas, particularly those relating to people, is called a "theory of mind" — a sense of what others must be thinking; what kind of people they might be, what might motivate them.

In her review of research on very young children, Gopnik[6] asserts:

> As babies learn what other minds are like, they also learn what their own minds are like. They learn how to have an aging Greek mind, or a Dutch 17th-century mind, or a late 20th-century West Coast mind. [One of our children, just 3 years old, suggested on a boring, rainy day that we should really go get a latte and check out some bookstores.] Communities have distinctive ways of thinking and feeling as well as dressing and eating, and children must learn these ways of being from the grownups around them.

Like all deep practice (for instance, the 10,000 hours of "right" practice that changes the brain's pathways to create highly skilled athletes or musicians[7]) our childhood cultural learning becomes deeply buried in our long-term memory but is instantly accessible to the unconscious mind's emotional "search engine" as it observes the situation in which we find ourselves. Even though these learned patterns (schemas) are essentially stereotypes of people and their behavior, our cognitive unconscious doesn't see them that way. Its job is simply to present them to our conscious mind — as an interaction is about to start — as if they were real and as if they were about the person standing right in front of us. Unless something happens to alarm the conscious mind, it simply accepts the images and words that pop up, and we start to talk. In fact, without an instantly accessible "theory of mind" we would have no place to begin — no idea of "what's going on" — and no way of being able to anticipate "what's going to happen next." A "theory of mind" is critical to our fluent engagement in interaction with others as are the words we use. And, like our theory of mind, we develop word use long before we are able to speak about it.

Words: The Other Essential for Talk

From the moment of birth, babies struggle to connect using the sound of their voices. We now know they are born with the basics of language. In their first year, their cognitive unconscious mind simply observes and stores what seem to be the discrete patterns of sounds that will become words in their language, and by the end of the year narrows the range of their babbling sounds down to the sounds of the language spoken around them. Before they can say a word, they sound like they're part of their culture.

Once they have spoken their first words their cognitive unconscious acquires new ones at a tremendous rate. Pinker[8] quotes some dramatic statistics about this process. It's estimated that by the time students graduate high school they have access to about 60,000 words. This means that from year one, when babies say their first word, the mind must learn 10 words a day. No one remembers doing this consciously because word acquisition and storage is a function of the cognitive unconscious mind. As Pinker[9] asserts, children acquire language "because they just can't help it."

The Mind and the Other 10 Million+ Bits

So scientists and philosophers have come a long way from the established belief that without words humans could not engage in mental processing. In fact, by estimating the number of neural pathways in the brain, neuroscientists argue that the mind processes 11 million bits of information per second, but the conscious mind processes only about 40 bits per second. In his book *Strangers to Ourselves*, Tim Wilson[10] poses the obvious question, "Where did the other 10 million 999 thousand 960 bits go?"

All that information enters the mind below the level of consciousness — a place without words — we now call the cognitive unconscious. The last 30 years of neurological research has made it clear that in everyday life, the conscious mind is not the dominant force we thought it was in the past. In fact, we now know that the cognitive unconscious does most of the work of daily life and the conscious mind cannot function without it.

Imagine an iceberg as the visual metaphor. Cognitive neuroscientists and social psychologists think of the cognitive unconscious as the huge submerged part of the iceberg and the conscious brain as the bit of snow and ice that shows on top. The conscious mind is no longer privileged. In our discussion of the pre-verbal learning of babies and their development of a theory of mind and a vocabulary, we have already referred to both minds, now let's review how each level of the mind works.

The Conscious Mind

The **conscious mind** works best when there is (1) enough time, (2) not too much data, and (3) the decision matters to us — i.e., we have to be motivated to do the work.

Rational, conscious thought is work. It requires real effort. In fact, during times of concentrated thought the brain burns far more blood sugar than the other organs in our body. Rational thought is controllable and flexible. It works in both the "**there and then**" and "**what if**" modes. It works on problems, what should/would happen, "if only" problems, and formulates approaches. Neuroscientists say it's seated in the frontal lobes of the cerebral cortex, right behind the forehead — the last part of the brain to develop. This is the location of the brain's speech, reflective thought and executive functions.

The conscious mind *can* work in the "here and now" if we *choose to focus* it. For instance, in daily talk, we can instantly attend to a conversation that is about to deviate from one of the norms we talked about in the previous chapter. We can consciously prevent ourselves from saying "the wrong thing." The conscious mind does keep a "distant eye" on the flow of our talk.

The conscious mind can also work in the "here and now" *if it is focused by a dramatic turn of events* or *an emergency*. But it only works well in this kind of situation when it's been repeatedly trained in routines and protocols for handling emergencies, as professional first responders are, for instance. Their long hours of repetitive training becomes stored in the cognitive unconscious and in dangerous, rapidly changing situations — too much going on and not enough time to make thoughtful decisions — their conscious minds call up their "sense of the situation" or "gut reactions" and, in turn, patterns of action buried deep in their minds. Essentially, they rely on the other mind — the cognitive unconscious — their "gut" or "intuition" — to help them make lightning fast choices in a crisis.

Mostly though, the conscious mind is effective when there is time to think, when the data is relatively simple, and there is a clear and attainable goal that matters to us: planning our day or doing our taxes. But all that thinking takes time and fluid conversation demands speed. So, in order to make time for its problem-solving work (or for daydreaming), the conscious mind hands over most of our moment-to-moment thinking to the other mind, the cognitive unconscious — the super fast, "**here and now**" thinking part of the brain.

The Cognitive Unconscious

The **cognitive unconscious** works in a completely different way than the conscious mind. It's (1) automatic, (2) fast, (3) effortless and (4) rigid.

It "sees and acts." There is no creative reflection, just pattern detection and reaction. It "decides" by association — by connecting incoming data to patterns it has already stored. It works in the "here and now" and, unlike our conscious brain, it's always paying attention. It's always on.

In his extraordinary book *Thinking Fast and Slow*, Daniel Kahneman[11] describes the operations of the two minds. For simplicity, he calls the conscious mind "System 2" and cognitive unconscious "System 1." He also calls System 1 "the association machine." He then describes a dramatic thought experiment to demonstrate how it works:

> To begin your exploration of the surprising workings of system one look at the following words:
>
> Bananas   Vomit
>
> A lot has happened to you during the last second or two. Your face twisted slightly in an expression of disgust, and you may have pushed this book imperceptibly farther away. Your heart rate increased, the hair on your arms rose a little, and your sweat glands were activated. In short you responded to the disgusting word with an attenuated version of how you would react to the actual event. All of this was completely automatic, beyond your control.

Kahneman then goes on to say that there is no particular reason for our mind to assume a sequence of connection between these two words — making a quick assumption that the bananas caused the vomit. It just does, and as readers we can't stop it. It's the power of what he calls "associative activation." The pairing of those two words sets off a chain reaction of connected elements in your brain — the ugly word *vomit*:

> . . . evokes memories, which evoke emotions, which in turn evokes facial expressions and other reactions, such as a general tensing up and an avoidance tendency. The facial expression and the avoidance motion intensify the feelings to which they are linked, and the feelings in turn reinforce compatible ideas. All this happens quickly and all at once, yielding a self reinforcing pattern of cognitive, emotional, and physical responses that is both diverse and integrated.

The coherence and automaticity of this process explains the example of deep cultural learning with which we ended the previous chapter. The "instant on" associative power of the cognitive unconscious mind triggered off in the young men from the southern United States an automatic cascade of mind-body responses to a personal insult because that pattern was anchored in generations of cultural learning in the region where they grew up.

How the Cascade of Associations Is Built

The core of the cognitive unconscious is in the midbrain, a series of organs called the **limbic system**. This part of the brain developed earlier than the frontal cortex, which is the seat of the conscious mind, and is an older part of the brain.

Every waking second as we grow, the cognitive unconscious is processing incoming data, looking for patterns in the information that flows from the rest of our bodies or from the environment — and remembering them. It remembers these patterns by adding emotional tags to them, called "somatic markers."[12] These are nano-surges of positive or negative energy which, when triggered by incoming stimuli, can create noticeable changes in the body. Since the cognitive unconscious has no word-based memories to communicate with, these *nonconscious emotional preferences* are used by the limbic system to talk to the conscious mind through the body.

Like supercomputers making speed-of-light calculations using ones and zeros, the cognitive unconscious makes a staggering number of preference decisions ("like-don't like" emotional evaluations) per second, of sensory inputs from our natural and social world. It instantly compares and contrasts them to emotionally tagged schemas it has already stored (including our community's biases and prejudices) and makes emotion-driven choices to move us.

This work is done by the amygdala — the heart of the limbic system. It is the storehouse for these deep, emotional preferences (positive or negative) which attached to patterns (schema) of neural connections representing attributes of people (e.g., overt physical differences, patterns of emotions, facial movements, vocal tones, etc.), situations and things.

The Physiology of Nonconscious Response

When something happens to us, we respond first with the **limbic system** — the emotional center of the cognitive unconscious. The process begins with the thalamus, the brain's switching center, which receives the data and does two things at the same time. It sends all of the data to the hippocampus, which registers and organizes our first perceptions of the situation and runs a quick comparison against what's stored in our short-term cognitive memory. The thalamus also sends a small amount of data to the amygdala, where the brain stores our long-term emotional memories. The amygdala compares the data to our emotional preferences — our "gut reactions" to things that have happened in the past.[13] The amygdala is the "always on" — sampling and matching — constantly dipping into the stream of incoming info and comparing "thin slices" of these huge inputs to established nonconscious preferences. It can act quickly because it receives only a simplified version of what has been perceived. As Daniel Goleman[14] asserts:

"Incoming senses let the amygdala scan every experience for trouble. This puts the amygdala in a powerful post in mental life . . . challenging every situation, every perception . . ." in terms of the essential survival questions: "Is this something to fear or hate or something that's pleasurable?"

While this is happening, the hippocampus has already moved all of the newly organized data to the brain's **neocortex**, the home of language and conscious thought — our rational brain — for more detailed processing and storage in long-term memory. Meanwhile, the amygdala having evaluated its "thin slice" of data as "good" and "bad," tells the neocortex how to react emotionally in the situation. The neocortex, which operates a little more slowly and receives much more information about the stimuli, considers this data and interacts with the hippocampus to assess the context of what is happening. It then sends back "intellectual" information to the amygdala and hippocampus, so they can stimulate "appropriate" emotional responses to a situation in the body. Describing this process makes it seem very slow, but it happens in hundredths of a second.

This is what a baby's unconscious mind is doing before birth and after it's born, while it's striving to learn to talk. It is chunking information and looking for patterns and connections to bodily states of comfort, discomfort, pleasure and pain — creating positive or negative preferences — surges of emotional energy. As we said in Chapter 2, these "chunks" of information are called schema. They act as predictors of future action for "what's going to happen next?"

The Discovery of Nonconscious Preferences

As we've said, to function as an associative machine the cognitive unconscious has to also be a "preference machine." The wordless and quick nature of its nonconscious preference learning and reaction was demonstrated in the early work of Robert Zajonc.[15] Since 1980, Zajonc has run a large number of variations of these relatively simple experiments to demonstrate the pre-cognitive learning of affective (emotional) preferences and their independent operation from our conscious thinking processes (cognition). People were shown a random series of graphics that held no meaning for them (Chinese ideograms or geometric figures). They didn't realize that while they were looking at a "blank" screen waiting for the display to begin, some of the images were already being shown at a speed that their eyes could register but their conscious minds could not. After watching the real display, participants were asked which of the pictures they liked. They consistently chose those graphics that they had previously seen in the "hidden" nonconscious presentation. Zajonc called this the **mere exposure** effect. We prefer things that are familiar.

Another variation on the experiment was based on what Zajonc called **affective priming** (emotional charging), that is, the subjects were consciously aware of a series of graphics being presented to them but were unaware that each was paired with a smiling or a frowning face that flashed so quickly their conscious mind wasn't aware of it. When people were asked which of the series of graphics they preferred, they consistently chose those that had been paired with the invisible happy face. In fact, with today's brain-scanning technology, we can now see the visual system "look" at the subliminal flashes that the conscious mind cannot see.

Philosophy Recognizes the Cognitive Unconscious, Almost

In reviewing Brook's[16] *The Social Animal*, which emphasizes the role of the cognitive unconscious in our everyday lives, highly regarded philosopher Thomas Nagel summarizes its power nicely:

> . . . vastly more of the work of the human mind is unconscious or automatic in this sense than conscious and deliberate. We do not consciously construct a visual image from sensory input or consciously choose the word order and produce the muscle movements to utter a sentence, any more than we consciously digest our food. The huge submerged bulk of the mental iceberg, with its stores of memory and acquired skills that have become automatic, like language, driving and etiquette, supplies people with the raw materials *on which they can exercise their reason and decide what to think and* what to do. (italics mine)[17]

There are two limits to his assertion about reason and choice. The first comes from Brooks himself when he states that "emotion assigns value to things and reason can only make choices on the basis of those valuations." The second is that consciously "choosing to choose" in emotionally arousing situations can be problematic for us. In these and other situations involving quick decisions and deeply learned skills, the cognitive unconscious makes choices for us before we consciously notice them. In fact, this is a natural part of the two minds working together. To be effective communicators, they *must* work together.

Three Ways the Two Minds Work Together

Let's look at the three key functions that the cognitive unconscious carries out on behalf of — and sometimes instead of — the conscious mind. It:

1) Supports rational decision making (which doesn't all happen in the conscious mind).

2) Constantly evaluates the world around us — i.e., lets us know "What's going on."

3) Initiates action in a sophisticated and efficient manner (because it knows "what's going to happen next").

Function 1: It Helps the Conscious Mind Think and Problem Solve Efficiently.

Anthony Damasio wrote a breakthrough book — *Descartes' Error: Emotion, Reason, and the Human Brain*[18] — in which he elegantly assembled historical and contemporary case studies and research on people whose neocortex (frontal lobes) had been disconnected from the midbrain by accident or surgical error.

He discovered that people with these kinds of injuries could speak extremely well and had fully functioning analytical thought processes, but their lives fell apart because they couldn't make the simplest decisions. His breakthrough insight was that the cognitive unconscious uses its emotional preference patterns to move the conscious mind through the data and the many small choices it must make to come to a fully conscious decision.

How the Emotional and Rational Brains Work Together

The integration of the emotional and the rational brains is illustrated in Damasio's work. He interviewed and did detailed observations of people who had sustained damage to the neural link between the prefrontal lobe of their neocortex and the amygdala of their limbic system. They showed no loss of cognitive functions — they retained their IQ and language skills — but began having trouble with simple and mundane tasks like getting up in the morning or preparing for work. They could think about and discuss those everyday events in detail, they just couldn't do them. He also noticed that they couldn't feel anything. Nothing seemed to touch them emotionally.

Damasio argued that they were prone to making terrible choices in their lives because they had lost access to their emotional learning. At every point in our decision making — even about the simplest things, there are choice points. We have to show a preference or choose to go one way or another. Feelings, he asserts, are absolutely necessary at these points for rational decisions because they point us in the proper direction. Our cognition may organize information and review possibilities but our emotional reactions — often unspoken gut feelings and emotional memories — "move us" to choose.

The cognitive unconscious stores our words, but can't use them to communicate with the conscious mind. It has to stimulate the body to get the conscious mind's attention. The somatic markers we referred to earlier — gut feelings, a sense of knowing — appear in the body at every "choice point" in a focused, rational decision-making process and give the conscious mind a sense of which way to go. Since Plato and Aristotle we have believed that the conscious mind did all the work of deciding. Now we know that without the support of the cognitive unconscious, we can't make decisions at all.

Function 2: It's "Always On" — Assessing People and Situations to Answer the Question, "What's Going On?"

The cognitive unconscious constantly evaluates the world around us. It's evaluating the context for threats and opportunities. As we said earlier, the amygdala is constantly processing "thin slices" of incoming data — comparing it to what we already know and assessing it in terms of "good-bad" or "reward-threat." It generates those "gut feeling" somatic markers Damasio talked about.

How does this happen in face-to-face talk? In 2008, Alex Pentland[19] and his colleagues at MIT published an overview of their research that shows us, by using a very small device, about the size of a credit card, and worn like an ID badge — called a sociometer — to continuously measure various nonverbal aspects of people's interactions, described below. This is the same information that's being processed by our senses and through the limbic system of the brain and the amygdala.

Pentland calls them "honest signals" — they happen quickly (in milliseconds); they're hard to fake; and they tell the mind something important about whether an emerging relationship will continue or end momentarily. As an observer, it would be a very difficult task to consciously perceive the subtle variations in behavior that mark immediate states of interest in a relationship. As someone participating in the conversation, it's impossible to do. So the nonconscious mind does it. It communicates its findings to your conscious mind through the various somatic responses we've discussed earlier. Pentland's sociometer data shows us what our cognitive unconscious notices in the person we are talking with for the first time:

- **Activity levels** — small movements in the body; changes in posture such as leaning toward or away; changes in tone of voice (not words); talking starts and stops.

- **Mimicry** — when people's movements and speech patterns automatically begin to imitate another's to indicate the beginning of empathy and trust.

There's been a lot of research in the past decade on pathways in the brain called **mirror neurons**. These are distributed throughout the brain and they trigger micro imitations of other's behaviors in our bodies at the muscular level. It's how we learn to feel how others feel. Our brain and body subtly imitate what we see in others so we can feel it in ourselves. Many scientists argue that we may have discovered the neural foundation of empathy. It is also argued that mirror neurons are the mechanism for the nonconscious rehearsal aspect of childhood learning.

- **Interest and attention** — if two people are talking and each of them is anticipating when the other will pause, and jumping in exactly at that point, they're paying a great deal of attention to each other.

- **Influence** — is shown by the "extent to which one person causes another to match their speech patterns." You may have noticed this in yourself if you've ever spoken to someone with a regional accent different from yours. You tend to imitate the sound of their voice or accent as you talk.

Speed Dating Research

Pentland and his colleagues seem to have found the perfect venue for testing out his device. In a speed dating situation, people come together for a short time with the intention of creating a connection with someone. In this case, each man and woman wore sociometers and spent 5 minutes chatting with 10 members of the opposite sex before moving to the next person. At the end of every encounter, each of them secretly wrote down whether or not they wanted to exchange numbers and handed in a form to an organizer. If they *both* said yes, organizers passed on numbers at the end of the night.

The common assumption was that men would give their numbers to almost anyone whereas women would be far more selective. This turns out to be wrong.

- Men only gave their numbers to women *who they somehow knew* were also going to say yes. Since the women's responses were kept secret until the end of the night, how could the men know after only 5 minutes of talk?

- A pattern of paralanguage and movement predicted to whom the men would give their numbers in 71% of the cases.

These men and women made their conscious choices with the help of their unconscious minds. No doubt, each was "sizing up" the other based on micro-expressions of emotion in the first milliseconds of contact (see Chapter 2), while Pentland's data measured the next steps in the process — what he calls the women's "exploring displays." When the women had high activity levels (interest and excitement) and openness to influence, it showed in a strong variation in vocal emphasis and rhythm, as they unconsciously matched their speech flow to the man's. This pattern accurately predicted the woman's decision about whether or not to trade phone numbers. Their conscious decisions may have been kept secret until the end of the evening, but the women's unconscious signalling had already delivered their decisions to the men's unconscious minds loud and clear. The cognitive unconscious knows "what's going on" and influences our conscious decisions.

The "Look of Competence" Research

Without fancy electronics and complex mathematical algorithms to process the data, the "always on" function of the cognitive unconscious was demonstrated by social neuroscientist Alexander Todorov.[20] He demonstrated the "instantaneity" of the "sizing up" process by showing his experimental participants pictures of two people, side by side, for **one second**. All he asked them to do was hit a key that told him which of the two faces they thought looked more competent. He showed them three sets of pictures but didn't tell them that the third set of pictures were candidates for U.S. Senate races in the 2006 election.

When his subjects hit the competence button, they picked 72% of the winners of those U.S. Senate races. This was a much higher positive outcome than that of the political theorists who had been analyzing and discussing all the data for months before. In fact, Todorov even replicated that approach by having some of his participants analyze their decisions before they made them. He told them to deliberate, to make a good decision. Their accuracy rate collapsed when compared to those participants who did it on "gut feel" and first impressions.

The outcome was so astounding to political researchers that his experiment was replicated in a half dozen other democratic countries, in both national and local elections, within the next two years. His data were confirmed every time. Todorov has also replicated his own work in more recent experiments by showing the faces for only 1/10 of a second. He achieved the same results.

In a review of research on this effect, he argues that the amygdala processes cues based on the shape of the face as a whole, and on the relationship between different elements of the face (e.g., subtle differences in eye, eyebrow and mouth shape and jawline). He found that in the competence studies, "winners" seemed to combine two facial dimensions that evoke feelings of strength and trustworthiness in the raters — a strong chin with a small, confident-looking smile. The amygdala may overgeneralize from these very small bits of data to make choices for us along the dimensions of competence and trustworthiness.

This research provides an even more obvious example of how our cognitive unconscious can make sense of what's going on before our conscious mind does, and then help our conscious mind to decide.

Function 3: Initiating Action in a Sophisticated and Efficient Manner.

The associative activation process of the cognitive unconscious operates 80,000 times faster than the conscious mind in terms of making decisions. It energizes the body for action more quickly than the conscious mind can think. How do we know this?

In the early 1980s, neuroscientist Benjamin Libet[21] did a series of studies on an increase in measurable brain activity that precedes bodily action called the "readiness potential." He wired up volunteers with scalp and wrist electrodes and asked them to perform a very simple task:

- Stare at a clock,
- Flick their right wrist whenever they felt like it and
- Report exactly the time when they were first aware of their intention to make the movement.

Their announced intentions always came before the action. That made sense. The surprise was that changes in the brain's readiness potential *preceded* the conscious intention to move by up to a half second. Since our the brain's synapses connect at about the speed of light, a half second difference means that the body-mind was prepared to move the wrist a long time before the subject had the conscious thought to do it. When he published in 1983, Libet triggered an intense debate in neuroscience and related fields about the nature of our ability to chose — our free will. It continues today.

Libet's early lab experiments ignited years of research to discover how the cognitive unconscious operates. We now take its speed for granted and that helps us to explain how the conscious mind works in rapidly changing, real-life situations.

Reading the Context at Bat

Jonah Leher[22] describes how a professional baseball player hits a major league pitch. He argues that a typical pitch travels from the pitcher's hand to home plate in about 0.35 seconds — the average interval between human heartbeats. The batter's muscles require 0.25 seconds to initiate a swing leaving him only 0.10 seconds, or 10 milliseconds, to make up his mind about whether or not to do it. Leher says that even this estimate is too generous, since it takes a few milliseconds for the information to travel from the batter's retina to his visual cortex, so he likely has only 5 milliseconds to decide. But this can't happen, because it takes 20 milliseconds for the frontal lobes of the brain to respond to any sensory stimulus. So, he asks, how does the batter do it?

His cognitive unconscious mind does it by collecting information on the pitch long before it leaves the pitcher's hand. It's watching the windup and the "anticipatory clues" that the pitcher is giving off as he moves through it. As Leher states:

> A torqued wrist suggests a fastball, while an elbow fixed at a right angle means that a fastball is coming, straight over the plate. Two fingers on the seam indicate a slider, and a ball gripped with the knuckles is a sure sign that a wavering knuckleball is on its way.

Batters aren't consciously aware of all this information but are able to act on it. A particular combination of cues triggers schema in the cognitive unconscious that narrow the list of possibilities and, at the right moment, the urge to swing appears in the batter's conscious mind. Batter's can't say why they swing at certain pitches except perhaps, that "it felt right." This feeling happens because in their thousands of hours of batting practice and play they were doing far more than improving the body mechanics of their swing, they were educating the "eye" of their unconscious mind and building up their schema of what "good" and "bad" pitches look like *before they are even thrown.*

Threat and Action

The cognitive unconscious can move the body without talk or conscious thought and, if necessary, it can find indirect ways of communicating with the conscious mind to get through three kinds of situations: (1) no threat, (2) moderate threat, and (3) high threat situations.

Let me give you a quick example of each of these.

No threat — It works with your conscious mind.

In my neighborhood, at a four-way stop on a quiet day on the street, I am waiting for the car coming in the opposite direction to make a left turn after stopping. When it does, I can clearly see that the driver is gesturing intensely with both hands while on a hands-free phone . . . so who's turning the car? Her knees and her cognitive unconscious — situational cues indicate safety: no traffic, stop-sign turn — and allowed her to give control of the car to her cognitive unconscious's deeply learned driving habits while her conscious mind is fully focused on the phone call.

Moderate threat — The cognitive unconscious lets you know indirectly what's going on.

At the University of Iowa, researchers[23] devised a gambling game with two decks of cards, one red and one blue. When a subject turns over a card, he or she gets a payoff and makes money. The red decks, however, are dangerous. They give big payoffs at first but then generate big losses. The blue decks are safer. They generate steady but smaller payoffs and smaller losses.

After turning over 50 cards, participants seemed to get a hunch about the red deck problem, but couldn't explain why when asked by the researcher. After 80 cards, they were able to explain it. Explicit or conscious learning had occurred.

However, the researchers also measured their "galvanic skin response" (increasing sweat on the skin) to stress. It rose dramatically by the *10th* card — the body-mind, the cognitive unconscious knew the danger in the red deck when it saw it. Without speech, it can't "tell" the conscious mind what to do, so instead it creates hesitations. Without realizing it, players gradually began to pick fewer red cards from the 10th card on, even though by 50 cards, they still couldn't say what was going on.

High threat — The cognitive unconscious takes over for direct action.

Consider the moment we step off the sidewalk and in our left peripheral vision a dark mass suddenly appears. Before our conscious mind can say, "That looks like a car," our cognitive unconscious has already flooded the body with hormones that trigger automatic muscle contractions, halting our forward motion, shifting our center of gravity and balance, and putting us back on the sidewalk just as somebody speeds by without hitting us.

How did we do that? The self that we're conscious of and which thinks out loud in our head didn't do anything. The automatic, unspoken, self-protective responses of the cognitive unconscious saved our life.

The Effects of the Cognitive Unconscious on Our Talk

Let's consider how this "always on," emotion-based, wordless decision-maker — our cognitive unconscious — can have both the positive and negative impacts on our communication relationships.

Positive Effects

We would not be able to talk effectively without:

1) The speed and automaticity of the cognitive unconscious, which calls up our deep cultural learning of the language and the order of words, i.e., syntax, for a recognizable sentences. (Recalling Nagel's earlier comment, we don't consciously create a visual image from sensory input or choose the word order and produce the muscle movements to utter a sentence.)

2) The instant recall of conversational schemas — what to do first, how to pause, then respond appropriately — that allow us to perform fluently and "normally" for the other.

3) The instantly invoked, stereotypical schema of people and their patterns of talk, including their nonverbal emotional displays, and of situation or context we're in — the "where and when" of our talk.

4) Our theory of mind — our unconscious ability to anticipate what's going to happen next built on an instant interpretation of the meaning of the other's words and nonverbal displays, in this particular situation.

Our cognitive unconscious helps us to do this very quickly and with great certainty. Without it we'd sound like tourists struggling to order dinner in someone else's language, hesitant and awkward. But, as we said, the cognitive unconscious isn't perfect and, given its speed, when it goes wrong, it can go very wrong.

Negative Effects

The part of the mind that presents us our ideas, and smoothly reads situations so we can speak with confidence, can suddenly turn against us if the external situation changes rapidly from positive to negative. Unlike "first responder" professionals, we are not deeply trained to handle difficult situations before they happen.

In every conversation we are putting a bit of ourselves on the line. Remember the IP communication model. Talk is more than words, it's a "transaction in selves," and the words we utter and decisions we come to — with some conscious effort — are extensions of ourselves. But if someone actively disagrees with us and particularly if that disagreement comes as a surprise, or is done in a way that seems to diminish our sense of self, the cognitive unconscious reads their response as a threat.

Remember, the cognitive unconscious is **rigid**. It can't tell the difference between a psychological threat to your self-esteem and a physical threat to your body. And, as we said, it's **fast**. It's already "on" before your conscious mind knows it. Like Pentland's speed daters and Leher's professional hitters, it has already read the situation. It's paying attention to the changing feelings displayed in the face and body behavior of our "opponent" before the words even appear. It's running a "compare and contrast" analysis of emotional expression to anticipate what's going to happen next. And, before our conscious mind can react, it's running its body-centered, threat-response schema:

- Speeding up the heart; increasing sweat on the palms; raising the hairs on the forearm; tightening the neck or throat muscles.

- Anything to let us know "IT'S COMING" — get ready to fight or flee.

Before the other can attack us, we are ready to defend ourselves. Our conscious mind surges ahead on the energy of this somatic communication. We begin to talk to ourselves as if the thoughts appearing in our mind are about what's going on in front of us. They're not. They're automatic word reactions to the other's actions. These have been overlearned at a much earlier period in our lives and most likely in very different circumstances. Our conscious mind has instantly entered its reactive defence mode — a "there and then" mode of thinking — as we say to ourselves:

- "What a jerk!" (A powerful judgment of the other's *possible* character, based on our emotional reactions to their *previous* behavior)
- "What an idiot!" (More judgment — our perceptions of their *past* choices) or
- "He can't talk to me like that" (too late, he already has).

These appear to us as "here and now" reactions but none of them is really about the behavior that has actually just happened in the moment. They are habitual responses — learned long ago — arising from our body's being "primed to defend" by our cognitive unconscious mind. We will describe these reactions in more detail in Chapter 10 under the topic "heavy C.O.N.T.R.O.L. talk." Our thoughts are emotion-driven and if we allow our emotions to override our conscious mind in the moment, and erupt into action, we suffer a collapse of emotional competence — "an emotional hijack." We will discuss this in detail in the next chapter.

In its efforts to warn us and prepare us for attack, our cognitive unconscious automatically sets us up for more problems, because the other's unconscious mind is already reading our face and body, anticipating our reactions, creating a downward spiral of automatic responses — the third layer of communication complexity in action (see Chapter 1).

So, before we say the first, worst thing that can come out of our mouths, we need to stop or at least slow our emotional reactions, and call upon our slower, effortful, controllable conscious mind to focus on what has actually just happened in the here and now. To become more effective communicators, we need to become conscious of what is happening in our bodies and use the power of our conscious mind to delay or deflect the automatic responses of the cognitive unconscious.

Where We're Going Next

Managing our first reactions to difficult or threatening situations is so important that we are going to describe the process in detail in Chapter 8. But before we explain how we can call our conscious mind into the present to manage our unconscious reactions, we need to know more about how it operates. So, in the next three chapters, we are going to describe the conscious mind's three basic processes: (1) feeling, (2) perception and (3) cognition. We'll show how they work in our conscious mind, while demonstrating how they depend on the energy and schematic learning of the cognitive unconscious. Most importantly, for each process we analyze, we'll provide clear, practical advice for effectively communicating how we feel, see and think about ourselves and those around us, while managing our nonconscious reactions.

END NOTES

---

[1] Brooks, D. (2011) *The Social Animal*. New York: Random House.
[2] This section is based on Wilson, T. (2002) *Strangers to Ourselves: Discovering the Adaptive Unconscious*. Cambridge, MA: Belknap Press of Harvard Universsity Press, Chap. 1.
[3] Brooks, p. 34.
[4] Unless otherwise noted research findings are summarized from Gopnik, A., Meltzoff, A., Kuhl, P. (1999) *Scientist in the Crib*. New York: Wm. Morrow and Company.
[5] Poulin-Dubois, D. et al. (2011) "Infants prefer to imitate a reliable person," *Infant Behavior and Development* 34 (2), pp. 303–309.
[6] Gopnik, et. al., p. 24.
[7] Gladwell, M. (2008) *Outliers: The Story of Success*. New York: Little Brown and Co.
[8] Pinker, S. (1994) *The Language Instinct*. New York: HarperPerennial.
[9] Pinker, p. 32.
[10] Wilson, T. (2002) *Strangers to Ourselves: Discovering the Adaptive Unconscious*. Cambridge, MA: Belknap Press of Harvard University Press.
[11] Kahneman, D. (2011) *Thinking Fast and Slow*. New York: Penguin Group, pp. 50–51.
[12] Damasio, A. (1995) *Descartes' Error: Emotion, Reason, and the Human Brain*. Toronto: HarperCollins.
[13] Based on key concepts in LeDoux, J. E. (1996) *The Emotional Brain: The Mysterious Underpinnings of Emotional Life*. New York: Simon and Schuster; Dharma Singh Kalsa. (1997) *Brain Longevity*. New York: Warner Books; Gottman, J. (1999) *The Marriage Clinic*. New York: W. W. Norton and Company; and Goleman, D. (1998) *Working With Emotional Intelligence*. New York: Bantam Books.
[14] Goleman, D. (1995) *Emotional Intelligence*. New York: Bantam Books.
[15] As cited in Forgas, J. P. (ed.). (2000) *Feeling and Thinking: The Role of Affect in Social Cognition*. New York: Cambridge University Press.
[16] Brooks, op. cit.
[17] Nagel, T. (2011) "David Brooks's Theory of Human Nature," *New York Times*, March 11.
[18] Damasio, op. cit.
[19] Pentland, A. (2008) *Honest Signals*, Cambridge, MA: MIT Press.
[20] Todorov, A., et. al. (2005) "Inference of Competence from Faces Predict Election Outcomes" *Science*, 308, pp. 1623–1626.
[21] Libet, B., et al. (1983) "Time of Conscious Intention to Act in Relation to Onset of Cerebral Activity (Readiness-Potential): The Unconscious Initiation of a Freely Voluntary Act," *Brain*, 106, pp. 623–642.
[22] Leher, J. (2010) *How We Decide*. New York: Mariner Books.
[23] Bechara, A. et al. (1997) "Deciding Advantageously Before Knowing the Advantageous Strategy," *Science*, 275, pp. 1293–1295.

CHAPTER FOUR

THE CONSCIOUS MIND AND EMOTION

When someone tells us something, we struggle to understand their meaning using three fundamental, interconnected processes:

1) **Emotion** — how we give our perceptions and thoughts energy and allow them to affect our behavior

2) **Perception** — how we see things, and

3) **Cognition** — how we name them, or label them, and think about them.

We will review these processes in the next three chapters.

Emotions in Communication

Emotions are made up of three elements:

1) The biochemical reactions that our brain creates in response to changes in our external and internal environments

2) The nonverbal reactions of our body to those biochemical shifts, as well as,

3) Our cognitive interpretations of these bodily reactions.

As we move from uncertainty to certainty as information flows through our perception and cognition processes, we notice some bodily changes: our edgy, fidgeting body movements, and tension in our shoulders and neck changes, to a moment of stillness in the body, dropping of the shoulders, unclenching of fingers, relaxing of the stomach muscles. These muscles are responding automatically to biochemical changes deeper in the mind-body — in Chapter 3 we called them "somatic markers." Once we become aware of these physical reactions, we begin to name them and call them our *feelings*.

As a society we talk about feelings a lot — isn't it the first question a reporter asks of someone who's just experienced something dramatic? But, at the individual level, awareness of and ability to talk about feelings varies significantly. Moreover, few people are conscious of the interaction between their feeling and thinking processes and the effect they have on the way we communicate with each other. In this chapter, we will describe how developing an awareness of our feelings, *naming* them, and *describing them accurately* to ourselves, and to others, is central to our becoming more effective communicators.

First, Some History . . .

In our studies of human thought and talk, we find that emotions and cognition have been separated for millennia:

- Feelings can be dangerous.

  "Rule your feelings, lest your feelings rule you."
  Publius Syrus (first century BCE)

- Feelings are not as important as thought.

  "I think therefore I am."
  Rene Descartes (1630s)

- Feelings interfere with thought.

  "Emotions cause a complete loss of cerebral control [and contain] no trace of conscious purpose."
  P. T. Young (1936), author of a widely read psychology text

- But by 1960 we see a dramatic shift in the conventional wisdom about emotions:

  "The emotions are of quite extraordinary importance in the total economy of living organisms and do not deserve being put into opposition with 'intelligence.' The emotions are, it seems, themselves a high order of intelligence."
  O. H. Mowrer (1960), professor of psychology, University of Illinois

The Functions of Emotion

By the 1980s, researchers saw emotion as a part of our fundamental evolutionary adaptation to nature. Emotion permits humans to process complicated situational information very rapidly in order to survive. Contemporary emotion theory builds on this basic idea. As Elliot and colleagues argue:

> Emotion identifies what is significant for well-being and prepares the person to take adaptive action. Emotion also coordinates experience, provides it with direction, and gives it a unifying wholeness. In other words, emotion tells people what is important, and knowing what is important tells them what to do and who they are.[1]

We discussed the physiological aspect of **emotions** in Chapter 3. These represent the biochemical energy we use to pay attention to stimuli, retrieve information from memory, sort out our perceptions, and decide things. We might think of it as the fuel of the cognitive unconscious. In this chapter we will examine the body's nonverbal reactions to changes in emotional energy, and how they emerge from the wordless levels of our mind into our conscious internal chatter, to be interpreted and named as feelings. These latter steps shape how we talk with others.

Becoming Aware of Our Feelings: How We Notice and Name Them

Our culture provides us with a "common sense" model of feeling awareness.

1) Something happens outside of us,
2) We experience it, and then,
3) We respond physiologically with an emotion — we feel it.

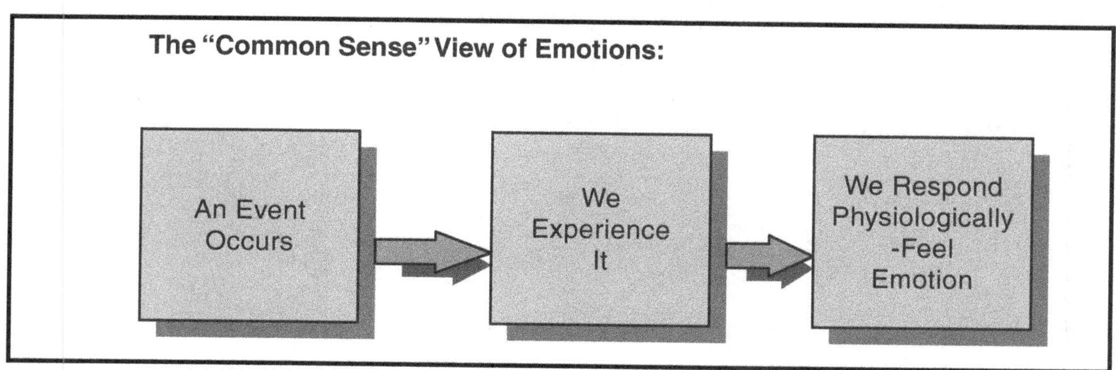

This common sense model was overturned by psychologists Schachter and Singer in 1962.[2] Their hypothesis, called the Affective Appraisal model, was that something happens outside of us and our body reacts first. Then our conscious mind matches our internal emotion to the situation by calling up and naming a feeling. This was a point of contention at the time.

Affective Appraisal Model of Emotions

Schachter and Singer's Affective Appraisal model of the brain's functioning was supported by an important experiment he ran on how we name our emotions.[3] They hypothesized that for anyone to feel an emotion they had to be in a general state of physical arousal and that different emotions arise out of the same general state of bodily excitement. He also argued that the way individuals described their feelings would depend on how they interpreted what was going on around them — the situation or the context of their reactions. He had students do the experiment in pairs — one was the naïve subject who received a small amount of synthetic adrenaline in a glass of water — the other was the experimenter's helper — who drank only water. As the symptoms of arousal (speeded up heartbeat, some sweating, faster breathing, etc.) began to appear in the naïve subjects, the experimental helpers were told to pretend they shared the symptoms and to act one of two ways — as if this were an enjoyable and exciting experience or as if it were uncomfortable and frightening.

Needless to say, most of the subjects responded to what was happening internally by listening to how the helper was defining the situation and imitating how the helper was behaving. Changes in the helper's behavior shifted the context and the meaning of the students' reactions. Their amygdala was sending quick evaluations of the chemical stimuli to the neocortex and enacting a series of bodily changes that reflected general physical arousal ("Do something!"), while the neocortex waited for more information, responding with a definition of this internal state which depended on how it perceived and named the external situation, as shaped by the helper ("We're doing something; we're laughing and having fun," or "We're doing something; we're acting scared"). This is the opposite of the "common sense" model of emotional reaction we talked about earlier.

Schachter and Singer's Model of Emotions

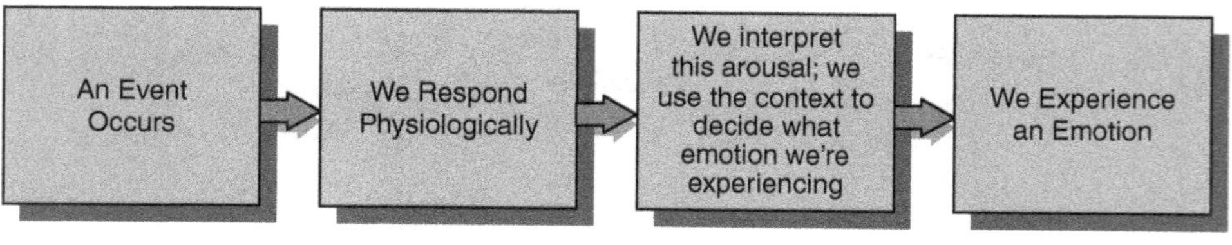

This effect has been demonstrated in many subsequent experiments — mostly in the laboratory — but also in real-life moments. Usually the experimenter puts a naïve subject to the test. In the following case the subjects chose "the test" themselves.

The Swinging Bridge Experiment[4]

The researchers' hypothesis was that strong emotions are re-labeled as sexual attraction when two conditions are met: (1) an acceptable object is present (in this case, a good-looking female), and (2) the emotion-producing circumstances do not require the full attention of the individual. In other words, the conscious mind will use cues in the external environment to explain automatically triggered bodily sensations. Remember, our brain is always trying to figure out what's going on — matching internal states to something it notices in the situation. In this experiment the brain misattributes the physiological arousal caused by the fear of a swinging bridge to feelings of sexual attraction toward a young woman who happens to appear in the situation.

Lust on a Swinging Bridge

Eighty-five males between 18 and 35 were interviewed just after they'd walked across one of two bridges over the Capilano River in North Vancouver, British Columbia, Canada. The researchers called the Capilano Suspension Bridge the "experimental bridge." It's a 5-foot-wide, 450-foot-long bridge constructed of wooden boards attached to wire cables that run from one side to the other of the Capilano Canyon. It has "a tendency to tilt, sway and wobble" and has "low handrails of wire cable, creating the impression that one is about to fall over the side." It's a very long drop to the ground. On the other hand, "[t]he 'control' bridge is a solid wood bridge further upriver. This bridge is wider and more stable than the experimental bridge. It's constructed of heavy cedar, and only 10 feet above a small, shallow rivulet. It has high handrails, and does not tilt or sway."

Like all good researchers, the experimenters tested the fear-inducing qualities of each bridge. All those interviewed rated the "experimental" bridge as very scary, whereas those on the control bridge rated it not scary. Needless to say, everyone interviewed coming off the swinging bridge was in some state of physical arousal (Diffuse Physiological Arousal or DPA) when the "experiment" occurred.

The experiment consisted of the subject simply being stopped and interviewed by an attractive young woman at one end of the bridge. The "interviewer" explained that she was doing a project for her psychology class on the effects of exposure to scenic attractions on creative expression. She then gave the subject a two-page questionnaire. The first page contained six items, including age, education, prior visits to the bridge, etc. The second page contained the "creative" part: The subjects were instructed to write a brief, dramatic story based on a picture of a young woman covering her face with one hand and reaching out with the other. The stories were later scored for manifest sexual content.

A story with any mention of sexual intercourse received 5 points; but if the most "sexual" reference was "girl friend," it received a score of 2; "kiss" counted as 3 points, and "lover" 4.

On completion of the questionnaire, the interviewer offered to explain the experiment in more detail when she had more time. She then tore the corner off a sheet of paper, wrote down her name and phone number, and invited each subject to call, if he wanted to talk further.

The experimental subjects were told that the interviewer's name was Gloria, while control subjects were given the name Donna, so that they could easily be classified when they called. On the assumption that curiosity about the experiment should be equal between control and experimental groups, it was felt that a difference in calling rates might reflect differential attraction to the interviewer.

The subjects on the swinging bridge expressed significantly more sexual content in their "creative" story than people on the solid bridge — in fact, double the amount. Also, more of them took the interviewer's phone number. As well, 50% tried to call her back while only 12% of the control subjects called.

The young men from the swinging bridge were in the midst of a full-body reaction (DPA), and their *conscious* brain found a "logical" answer for it: they were "hot" for the young woman — not afraid of the bridge. Their unconscious mind used the "self-serving" bias to explain the situation. They showed this by the *non-conscious* use of sexual imagery about a neutral picture and in their conscious interest in the woman. The fact is that our brain needs to match our arousal to a feeling-thought quickly, and it's not all that careful. The cognitive unconscious matches up the changes in biochemistry to a stimulus that looks "about right" — and presents it to the conscious mind. This means we can consciously attribute our arousal to the wrong thing.

What Does This Mean for Effective Communication?

One possibility is that it might be wise for us to consider the circumstances under which we have a conversation. If one or both of the people are trying to talk to one another in the midst of a tense or frightening situation, they might attach some surprising emotions to the conversation. If, for example, your supervisor has just had news of a serious medical diagnosis, and you approach him or her to talk about a raise or time off, you may be unhappily surprised by what he or she makes of your request later on.

To summarize, there are always *three levels* of reaction to a changing situation:

1) Emotions begin as an instant biochemical response to changes, i.e., an instant positive or negative evaluation, which produces

2) Rapid bodily reactions to those biochemical shifts (Diffuse Physiological Arousal — changes of breathing, sweat, muscle tension — the "somatic markers of our cognitive unconscious), which causes

3) Our conscious cognitive brain (the left frontal lobe) to match up our internal state with the external context — to interpret these reactions (even though they may have little or nothing to do with one another) and then to name them as our feelings.

Feelings and Mood

Feelings are our way of noticing emotions that *interrupt* cognitive processes and behaviors and that *require attention.* After the immediate intensity of the feeling has subsided, it usually lingers on in the form of a mood. We may have moved on to "feeling" something else but the biochemistry from the first reaction isn't done with our body.

Mood and Opinions

In survey research, nicknamed the Sunny Day study, researchers found that people contacted on a sunny day were more positive about their current state of happiness and life in general than people contacted on a rainy day. They also found that people given a small, virtually worthless gift were in a better mood and gave higher ratings to items such as household appliances, when later interviewed, than others in the vicinity who were stopped and asked the same questions at the same time, but who received nothing.

Bad moods, on the other hand, have the opposite effect. They make life in general and other people look more dangerous. It seems that our brain has the same problem as it does with *misattributing arousal* (see swinging bridge experiment above). If we haven't figured out why we're in a particular mood, we sometimes allow that mood/feeling to inform our opinion of things in general.

Feelings and mood matter mostly when we're *not paying attention*, because *when we do notice* them, mood doesn't affect our opinions. In the above-mentioned mood and weather (i.e., Sunny Day) study, when students were casually asked at the beginning of the conversation — "How's the weather there?" (i.e., the weather was brought into their consciousness) — they didn't let it confuse their thoughts about their state of being ("It's a lousy day but I'm having a pretty good life."). In other words, once they were made consciously aware that their mood was likely due to the weather, they dismissed the weather as irrelevant to the questions being asked. Thus, we don't have to be under the automatic control of our moods; we just need to awaken to the fact that we are "in a mood," and come up with a reason why (which often has nothing to do with the present moment). When we do this, the factors that determined the mood no longer shape our next thoughts or decisions.

Emotions and Problem Solving

Our emotions are pervasive. They permeate much of our thinking and most of the decisions we make, as well as our perceptions of the world, even though we would like to think that these processes are entirely based on rational thought.

In his **Affective Infusion Model** of decision making, Forgas[5] argues that emotions infuse rational decision making and noticeably color the outcomes under two sets of conditions where we have to "construct" reality:

1) Where the decision is complicated and requires accurate judgment in a situation that is ambiguous, and where new information needs to be assimilated before a decision can be made

2) Where the decision is simple; it doesn't matter much to you; the information is typical; there is little pressure to be accurate and you have other things going on in your head (heuristic thought)

Where the decision is complicated, needs to be accurate, but must be made in an ambiguous situation full of new information, we tend to "go with our gut." Where the decision is simple and doesn't matter, we're distracted, and we're working with information we've processed before, we tend to ask ourselves "How do I feel about it?" When we don't have to think about things we automatically let our current feeling-state shape our decision making (sunny day reactions).

In both of these situations, decision-makers are more likely to deduce their final judgments from the way they feel than from the relevant facts and choices. In fact, Forgas's experimental data showed that people in the second situation don't respond to situational stimuli at all but only to whatever feeling reactions they call up.

Emotions and Judgment

Immediate and intense feelings are like moods — they can influence the judgments we make without our being aware of it — as demonstrated in this experiment. Among the student volunteers for the experiment was an actor (a confederate of the experimenter) paid to appear as just another volunteer, but who behaved in ways that encouraged the other subjects to like her or dislike her.

- In the first scenario of the experiment, the actor comes in late wearing a t-shirt from the university; apologizes nicely for her lateness; puts away her headphones; then opens a bag of cookies and shares it with the group.

- In the second scenario, the actor shows up late wearing the rival university's sweater; acts with hostility toward the experimenter when she comments on her lateness; puts on earphones and blasts her music loud enough for everyone to hear; and proceeds to eat her cookies by herself.

Volunteers in both groups (good actor and bad actor scenarios) were told they were to be either a player or observer of a simple computerized tennis game. The actor was purposely selected as a player in both scenarios. The point of the experiment was that all the *real* volunteers were observers. They were to watch the tennis game within an individual cubicle and act as a linesman. They were told that while they had **no control** over judging or calling the game, they were still to make the calls according to what they saw, because they were providing excellent data to the experimenter on the clarity of the game.

The volunteers also knew they had no influence on the game so there was no purpose to be served by falsely reporting the balls falling inside or outside the boundary line. Nevertheless, their feelings biased their reports. When the ball fell just inside the line, the volunteers who had been treated uncivilly by the actor called it "out." When the actor's computerized opponent hit a ball that was just out, they called it "in." Those who felt warmly toward the actor did just the opposite. They made calls to enhance her game. This was all done without their realizing it. In their minds, and as they later reported to the experimenter, "They called 'em like they saw 'em."

The subjects had no personal agenda. They didn't know anybody in the experiment before they showed up. Yet even though they knew they had no control over the game, their feelings toward the actor powerfully influenced what they saw.

An Observation on Talent and "Niceness"

My TV-watching guilty pleasures include two reality shows, competitions about things I like and know something about: singing and ballroom dancing. I have found that in the early rounds, no matter how talented individuals are, I know that they *won't move ahead* in the competition and have a chance to win if they aren't also pleasant, personable *and* a bit humble in the face of criticism. That's because the audience votes — and, at least on these shows, warm feelings in the viewers can take a competitor a long way toward winning.

Feelings Influence Our "Causal Attribution" of Others' Behaviors

Generally speaking, when individuals try to explain others' behaviors, they make what psychologists call the "fundamental attribution error." That is, they believe that people act as they do because of the type of people they *are*, not because of the situation they are in. This reflexive use of beliefs about another's character is a mental shortcut (a heuristic) the conscious mind uses to avoid having to analyze complicated situations. But, how we feel about the other makes a difference in our automatic analysis. In *happy* relationships, this "attribution error" is less likely to occur. John Gottman,[6] whose relationship research we will explore in a later chapter, found that in happy long-term relationships, if one person does something negative, the other tends to evaluate the negativity as *fleeting and situational* (e.g., he or she suspects that the individual is just in a bad mood or having a stressful day). In *unhappy* relationships, the same behavior is interpreted as *stable and internal* to the person.

Almost all of the processes we've discussed are automatic, low-effort ways of noticing and naming our feelings and the outcomes of these processes can affect our connection to others and our communication with them in important ways. In terms of our communication competence (see Chapter 1), to be better communicators we need to be more competent about our feelings. We need to become more conscious of when they appear in our mind and more precise in how we name them. This competence is called "emotional intelligence."

Competent Communicators Are Emotionally Intelligent

The concept of emotional intelligence was introduced to the public in 1995 by Daniel Goleman in his book *Emotional Intelligence*.[7] In it, he reviews the implications of this concept based on the research of a number of scientists, including Reuven Bar On, who invented the widely used shorthand designator EQ for emotional intelligence, and who defined emotional intelligence as, "Our ability to recognize, understand and use emotions to cope with ourselves, others and the environment." For our purposes, "recognize, understand and use" means knowing and naming our feelings, and "cope" means being able to regulate our feelings and effectively communicate them. We will discuss this communication competence in more detail and provide guidelines for communicating our feelings effectively in the last section of this chapter.

Naming the Emotions

Words describing the general states of *anger*, *fear*, *sadness* and *happiness* are commonly used to describe our emotional experiences. In Chapter 2, we reviewed the work of Paul Ekman on the role of the face in expressing these emotions. Ekman considers these four, plus *surprise* and *disgust*, as "universals" — that is, they are expressed the same way on the faces of people across a wide variety of cultures. Robert Plutchik, in his research, has identified these emotions, along with acceptance and anticipation, as the primary emotions.

His data showed that acceptance was seen to be the opposite of disgust, and anticipation the opposite of surprise.

He argues that other emotions, such as love, contempt and disappointment are a mixture of the primary emotions. He calls them the *secondary emotions*. Both levels are shown in the graphics below.[8]

Interestingly, the emotions in this "circumplex" can be organized like a color wheel to demonstrate their similarity and, in combination, to produce new emotions. Plutchik puts similar emotions close together and opposites 180 degrees apart, like complementary colors. Other emotions are mixtures of the primary emotions, just as some colors are primary and others are made by mixing the primary colors.

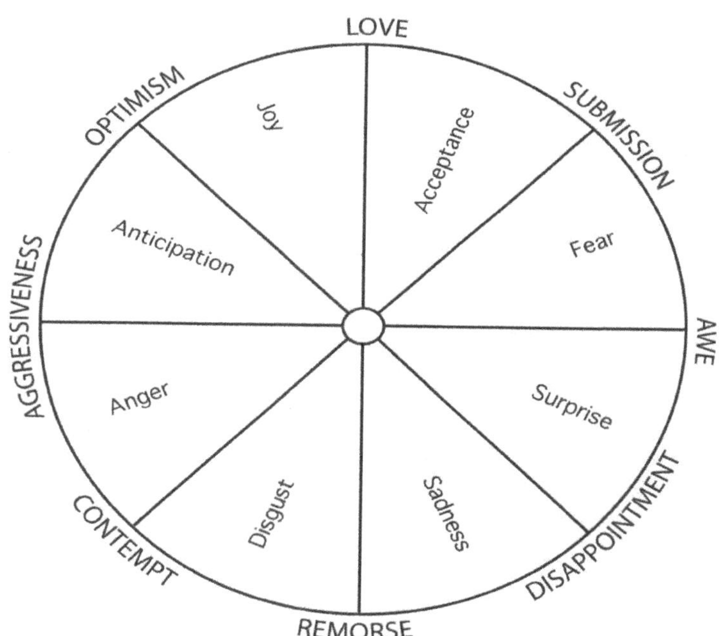

In addition, Plutchik's model of emotions also includes a third dimension, which describes the intensity or strength of feeling around each type of primary and secondary emotion. Notice in the diagram below that the inner ring of Plutchik's first model above is now the second ring from the center in his second model (on the next page). Along each emotional dimension of this second model, the center represents a highly intense level of the key emotion and the outer ring describes a low level of intensity. Starting with the emotion of fear (on the right side of the graphic), one can see that fear can begin as a general sense of apprehension (low-level uncertainty, worry, sense of concern) or, depending on the situation, can develop into terror (in the center of the circle). Likewise, pensiveness can become sadness, which over time, or depending on circumstances, can turn to grief or despair.

Although debate continues on how to classify emotions, there seems to be agreement on the six basic "families" of emotions — fear, anger, enjoyment, sadness, surprise, disgust — found in Ekman's cross-cultural work on the wordless expression of emotions by the face, and in Plutchik's detailed research on the words we use (adding acceptance and anticipation to Ekman's list) to name and describe emotions in our culture.

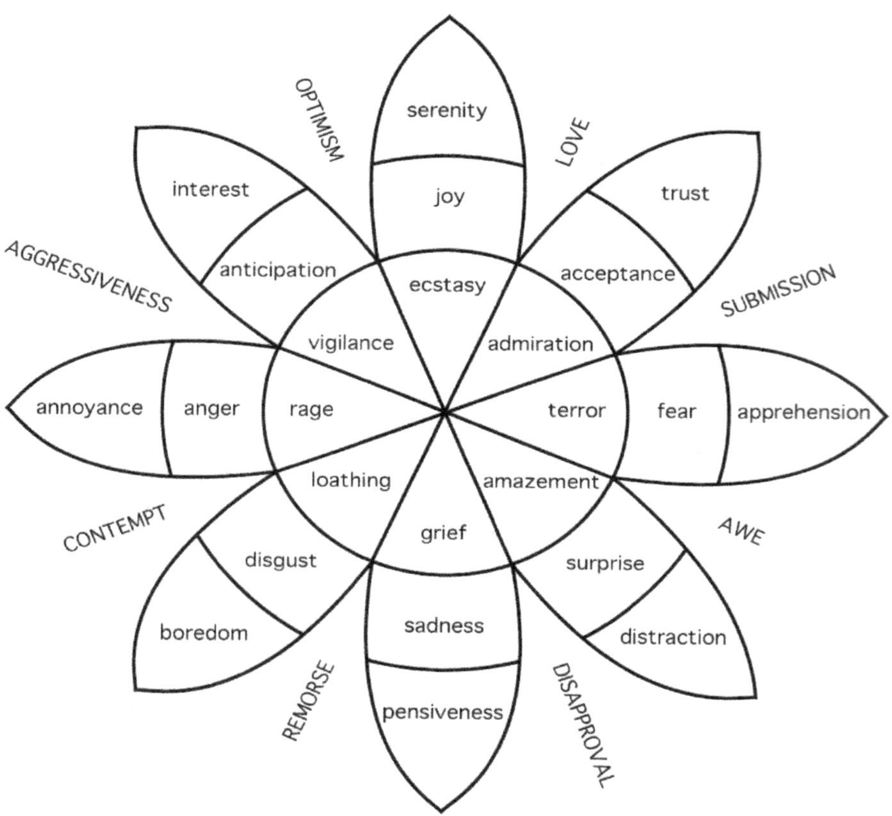

Plutchik's research demonstrated that people have a high level of agreement on these combinations — they seem to represent something *real* to us. His model gives us a direct and simple way of noticing and naming our feelings and this can lead us to more "*emotionally competent talk.*"

Emotions and Thought in Everyday Talk

Unless we are facing brand-new situations or are consciously challenged to do so by others, *we don't think before we talk, we feel before we talk.* While our expressed thoughts and opinions appear to be about the "objective" topic of conversation — the incoming data — they are really about our personal constructs, stereotypes and the moment-to-moment emotional reactions the incoming data stirs up in our mind.

In some situations, to be effective communicators, we must choose to be "rational" — we have to consciously slow the process of our mental talk and decision making and focus on the reality that's in front of us. In this type of situation, Forgas[9] argues, we become rational decision-makers in the traditional sense. We must use "substantive" decision making, which forces us to consciously select and learn new information and compare it to what we already know. Otherwise, he argues, we are "effort-minimizers," using the simplest and quickest methods to decide — our emotion-laced schemas, containing heuristic cues to trigger automatic thought. As Daniel Goleman argues, "In the dance of feeling and thought, the emotional faculty guides our moment-to-moment decisions, working hand-in-hand with the rational mind, enabling — *or disabling* — thought itself. Likewise the thinking brain plays an executive role in our emotions, except in those moments when emotions surge out of control and the emotional brain runs rampant."

Noticing Our Emotions

We have looked at the automatic, nonconscious shaping of our perception and cognition processes by automatic and nonconscious emotional processing — mostly apparent in changes in our body chemistry and in symptomatic nonverbal displays (blushing, sweating, eye movement). When we finally notice such changes, we name them as feelings. In other words, when the intensity of the internal response is large enough to interrupt our current flow of thought and potentially affect our behavior, we begin to consciously perceive our emotions and name them as part of our internal and external communication processes.

Noticing Feelings That Can Deeply Affect Our Talk[10]

- **Sadness:** feelings can range from slight gloominess to overwhelming grief at loss of cherished loved one or object, or past; represented by turned-down mouth, slumped posture, crying, difficulty with eye contact, irregular breathing in trying to control self.
- **Fear:** immediate feelings of threat of harm, either physical or psychological; rapid breathing; hair rising on arms, back of neck; face momentarily frozen (blank) and losing color as blood rushes to the large muscles of the body; tensing of muscles, tightened gut; or generally anxious moods, anticipate difficulties, constant vigilance and worry.

- **Anger:** feelings of exasperation, indignation or hostility; often stimulated by the perception that someone is getting in the way of our achieving a valued goal; represented by physiological changes like increased heart rate; blood pressure increases; galvanic skin responses (sweat); shallower and quicker breathing, reddening of the face.
- **Contempt** is only felt about people or their actions and contains feelings of condescension — "looking down" on someone. May also be felt as "fed up" disgust by the complainer in long-term relationships plagued by repeated complaint and avoidance. Shown in "rolling the eyes" — looking up when the other speaks — and lips slightly turned down at corners, because it contains undertones of disgust, i.e., feelings of repulsion triggered by strangeness, disease, misfortune, and morally repugnant behavior.

Most often, if we notice our emotions we can deal with them, but there are at least two moments when we can't: (1) when they emerge suddenly and take over, and (2) when they hang around as moods after we think we've let them go.

The Sudden Takeover: When Rational-Emotional Harmony Collapses

The two minds operate in an integrated fashion most of the time but there are times when emotions can dominate. The amygdala, which is constantly comparing incoming data against our deepest emotional memories, can instantly shift the thought-emotion brain balance to pure, uncontrolled emotional response when it perceives an immediate threat. As described in Chapter 3, this can happen because, as neuroscientist Joseph LeDoux[11] discovered, there is only one neural link between the thalamus-switching center of the brain and the amygdala, as compared to a longer pathway of several links between the thalamus and the neocortex.

If the amygdala senses a threat in the incoming data it can take over our brain and body in a 25th of a second and push us into action by starting the biochemistry of "flight or fight" (fear/anger) response. Before the neocortex can think about it, we are in action. For example, jumping out of the way of an oncoming car is the perfect example of our "flight" response. It's literally a thoughtless stimulation of the body to action — the kind of response that ensures our evolutionary survival. The problem (also noted in the previous chapter) is that, depending on the individual's history of emotional memories, the amygdala can treat a dirty look or a verbal criticism like an oncoming car, and induce an **amygdala hijack** (also called "emotional flooding"). It might involve losing our temper and verbally or physically abusing a loved one just because he or she "pushes our buttons" by saying or doing something we don't like.

Hijacks undermine our emotional intelligence and communication competence in the moment and potentially undermine any efforts we might make to apologize or make amends in the future if they recur. To avoid this situation, we not only need to be aware of our feelings but know how to manage them and talk about them in ways that enhance our relationships not undermine them.

Talking about Feelings: Effective Emotional Expression

We may not be able to choose our emotions — they begin below the level of consciousness — but when we notice them, we can choose how to name them as feelings and how to express them. To be successful communicators, we need to use and improve our skills in these areas. These skills represent elements of our **emotional intelligence** (EI). There are four ways we can increase our EI[12]:

1) Become more aware of our emotions as bodily reactions

2) Be more aware of others' emotional states

3) Regulate the way we talk to ourselves about our own and others' feelings, and

4) Manage the expression of our feelings in ways that positively shape the emotional context of our communication with others (shift ego states and "voices").

How we name and express feelings can make all the difference to how people hear and accept what we have to say. We use Plutchik's model to provide ourselves a basic vocabulary, but we can't do that effectively if we don't know what's going on inside of us.

Emotional Self-Awareness

The first key to emotionally intelligent expression of feeling is **awareness** of our feelings. There is now a considerable amount of data that suggests that people who can read their own emotions and recognize their potential impact on perception and thinking are seen as more dependable and trustworthy by others. Emotionally self-aware people seem to know their strengths and limitations and are more likely to be able to talk about their feelings appropriately rather than simply act them out.

Awareness of Others' Emotions: Empathy

The second aspect of emotional intelligence is our awareness of emotions in others — often called **empathy**. When we can sense how others are feeling, it can open the door to seeing the situation from where they are and responding accordingly. This means being able to describe others' feelings with some accuracy in a nonthreatening way and taking them into account in our thinking and decision making. Again, this permits a kind of connection with others that can be achieved in no other way. Individuals who practice empathy are seen as much more influential in their communication because they can accurately appraise how others feel and influence them to be more receptive to and supportive of the individual's thoughts and decisions. Empathy is the fundamental skill that lies behind the kind of interpersonal influence used by successful coaches, counselors, therapists and teachers.[13]

Emotional Self-Regulation

The third aspect of emotional intelligence focuses on our emotional **self-regulation** — our *inner* talk around emotions. How we perceive and name our emotions makes a difference in how we experience their intensity and duration, which in turn affects how we communicate them. Research and practice in cognitive psychology has clarified that it is our perceptions and beliefs about situations that shape our feelings, that is, how we interpret our emotional reactions. If a good friend suddenly turns on us, accuses us of evil behavior and calls us terrible names, we might feel intense shock, hurt and anger. If these same accusations are hurled at us by a stranger on the street, who we noticed was talking to himself before lashing out at us, our feelings are more likely to be surprise, pity, perhaps fear. Our interpretation of the situation makes all the difference in terms of what we feel.

Since we are dealing with the surfacing of deeper emotional reactions, which are altering our biochemistry even as we notice them, we need to deal with our emotional arousal before it overtakes us completely (the hijack) and while we can still reframe our thoughts and feelings. To regulate our thoughts and feelings, we first need to alter the biochemistry of our body. This means we need to calm ourselves — pause before we speak; slow and deepen our breathing; and, as a result, slow our heart rate.

Emotional self-regulation allows us to speak in a self-managed way. Self-managed expression means we can speak *with* emotion or *about* our emotions without being overwhelmed by them or lost in them. To illustrate the concept of self-regulation, let's consider the following list of recommendations, summarized from a number of different communication texts on how to communicate effectively about our feelings.

Guidelines for the Effective Expression of Emotions

- Accurate description
  —Tell the other exactly what you are feeling.
- Identify reasons for your feelings
  —Tell them why you are feeling the way you are.
- Anchor in the present
  —Stay focused on the feelings you are having in this moment.

- Avoid "allness" statements
  —Avoid using "always" and "never" in your descriptions.
- Own your feelings
  —Start your sentences with "I" ("I'm feeling . . .) not "You" as in ("You make me . . .").
- Say what you want the other to do

These are clear, straightforward recommendations and they *do* work, but notice the degree of emotional self-regulation that is required to make them work. When our feelings are aroused, we need to shift from *emotionally reacting* to *thinking about* our emotional reactions (calling on the brain's frontal lobes to reframe the first responses of its limbic system) before we respond externally to another.

To describe our feelings in detail, we have to think about them and then give the other person reasons for them. Moreover, staying anchored in the present when we are emotionally aroused means that we have to consciously back down from our emotionally driven judgments to the description of "the data" — what's going on now — and our ownership of our feelings ("I am feeling . . . now"). By doing this, we are less likely to talk in sweeping generalities ("Allness" statements) using inflammatory words, and more likely to be able to tell the other what we actually want to happen. In the end, all of this will allow us to speak to others so they will actually listen to us. We need to become self-managed communicators.

How to do all of this will be covered in detail in Chapter 8 where we will provide more detailed information on how to regulate our emotional responses so we can speak as self-managed communicators in difficult situations.

Automatic Emotional Expression: The Third Level of Talk

Within the traditional analytical frame of the interpersonal (IP) model of communication (Chapter 1), theorists have argued that our exchanges have both a content and relationship level (axiom 3). Our definition of **communication** asserts that people use both verbal and nonverbal messages to communicate and, in fact, those nonverbal messages substantially affect what the IP model calls the "relational" level of interpersonal talk. They do this in two ways: (1) they can alter the meaning of the words we are saying (change the pitch of your voice on one word in a sentence and it can shift from being a description of the other's actions to a criticism), and more directly, (2) they act as "affect displays" (remember the research of Paul Ekman and his colleagues on the role of the face in expressing emotions). They demonstrate how we feel about ourselves, and others, while we are talking to them. These two elements are so important that research shows that anywhere from 65% to 93% of the **impact of our talk**[14] on others is derived not from what we are saying but from *how* we are saying it, that is, what our face, voice and body are doing while we are talking.

Despite the IP model's clarity about the "relationship" level of talk, and on how nonverbals shape the meaning of our talk for our relationships (for example, do we speak to someone in a *tone of voice* denoting a relationship of equality or superiority?), there does not yet seem to be any recognition that emotional signals might operate in a predictable way independently of our talk, although several decades of recent research indicate that they do.

We have learned that many of our nonverbal gestures are automatic responses to others. They are the unthinking expression of our feelings about the other and ourselves that occur *before* we utter our first words in a conversation — as soon as we see them. Todorov's research suggests that we "size up" people within a tenth of a second of seeing them. And as we begin to interact, Ekman's research suggests that we unconsciously recognize and interpret micro-expressions of emotion that happen in the first 1/25th of a second. As a result, unconscious and unspoken emotional communication shapes our relationship with another so early in a first encounter that the topic and the words we speak hardly seem to matter.

Pentland's data makes it clear that after only a couple of minutes of ritual exchanges of greetings and small talk at a speed dating event — the emotional exchanges — both parties "know" what's going to happen next, i.e., they have gut feelings about who they are going to give their phone numbers to. In effect, emotional communication, happening at the level of the cognitive unconscious between two people in face-to-face conversation seems to be a third level of communication which infuses the content and relationship levels of talk.

In Table 1 in Chapter 1, the concept of **feedforward** is defined as a kind of talk — words that are spoken to set the other up for what is coming next. Our emotional displays seem to be a nonverbal kind of feedforward. Also as noted in Chapter 1, it is this automatic emotional messaging that makes the concept of "self-feedback loops" so vital to understanding why people respond the way they do in any conversation. Self-feedback loops are emotion-based and become particularly important to understanding conversations that involve some level of disagreement.

Since emotions seem to directly shape our perceptions of others and influence our thoughts and the way we express them, it is important for us to become more aware of how emotional reactions and our thoughts about those reactions — our feelings — emerge in us and in others while we are talking. It is also important that we learn — where and when it's appropriate — to put them on the table — discuss them openly.

Emotions, "Real Meaning" and Communication

The early, quick and automatic attachment of emotional memories to incoming stimuli by the emotional brain adds a new level of uniqueness to the idea of meaning. We've already accepted the axiom that the meanings of words are in the minds of people, not in the words themselves. When that axiom was stated in 1960, it argued that people cognitively constructed meanings out of their cultural learning (socialization) and personal experiences. There was always the potential for uncertainty in talk because we are socialized differently and lead unique lives.

Research on the operations of the brain since the 1980s shows that the possibilities for personal differences in the construction of meaning (how they "get" your message as well as how they create their own) go far deeper than differences acquired in learning the vocabulary of our language. They reach down into our early learning of wordless, emotional memories.

In other words, cognition can't work without emotion. Moreover, emotional learning is a mixture of the learning that comes out of not only the conscious internal dialogue between the left frontal lobe of the neocortex and the amygdala, but also a much deeper wordless collection of somatic responses to life around us. It might even be argued that since the deeper responses come first and so quickly, and color what happens in our rational mind, to us the *real* meanings of the words we use to describe our lives *are* their emotional meanings.

We now have to consider the possibility that the struggle for understanding comes out of both individual differences in conscious learning and life experience, and also out of unconscious learning and emotional experience that happen at an earlier stage of life and at a deeper level of socialization. This deeper learning involves reactions that are out of our conscious control ("I don't know what it is; I just don't like him"). The research on emotions and thinking suggests that in many areas we simply "feel" something is right or wrong and then build our reasons for having this view, after the fact.

If we take it to heart, this insight may compel us to pay attention to our first schematic emotional reactions and judgments, suspend them for a moment and seek more information from others when we are confronted with reactions we don't understand. Instead of labeling them in our head, we could admit that we aren't sure of what's going on and ask a question. This insight and extra effort is particularly important when we hear, see or produce reactions that take us by surprise.

All this may make logical sense, and emotional self-management sounds like the "right thing" to do — so why don't we do it? After all, we always have our "conversational face" (Chapter 1) on display in any conversation and words and gestures are never emotionally neutral. We don't do it because emotional self-management isn't easy so, as we said above, we are going to give an entire chapter over to the subject.

Where We're Going Next

But before we get to the point of calling on our conscious mind to manage our unconscious reactions in difficult situations, we need to learn more about its other functions. In the next chapter, we'll take a closer look at the perception and cognition functions of our conscious mind.

End Notes

[1] Elliot, R., Watson, J., Goldman, R., Greenberg, L. (2004) *Learning Emotion-Focused Therapy.* Washington, DC: American Psychological Association.

[2] Schachter, S., Singer, J. (1962) "Cognitive, Social and Physiological Determinants of Emotional State," *Psychological Review*, 69, pp. 379–399.

[3] As cited in DeVito, J. (1992) *The Interpersonal Communication Book* (6th ed.) New York: HarperCollins.

[4] Dutton, D., Aron, A. (1974) "Some Evidence for Heightened Sexual Attraction Under Conditions of High Anxiety," *Journal of Personality and Social Psychology,* 30 (4), 510–517.

[5] Forgas, J. P. (1995) "Mood and Judgment: The Affect Infusion Model (AIM)," *Psychological Bulletin,* 117 (1), 39–66.

[6] Gottman, J. (1995) *Why Marriages Succeed or Fail: And How You Can Make Yours Last*. New York: Simon and Schuster.

[7] Goleman, D. (1995) *Emotional Intelligence*. New York: Bantam Books.

[8] From Plutchik, R. (1994) *The Psychology and Biology of Emotion*. New York: HarperCollins College Publishers; and Plutchik, R. (2003) *Emotions and Life: Perspectives from Psychology, Biology and Evolution.* Washington, DC: American Psychological Association.

[9] Forgas, J. P. (ed.). (2000) *Feeling and Thinking: The Role of Affect in Social Cognition.* New York: Cambridge University Press.

[10] Ekman, P. (2007) *Emotions Revealed: Recognizing Faces and Feelings to Improve Communication.* New York: Henry Holt and Co.

[11] LeDoux, J. E. (1996) *The Emotional Brain: The Mysterious Underpinnings of Emotional Life.* New York: Simon and Schuster.

[12] These characteristics of EI are derived from Salovey, P., Mayer, J. (1990) "Emotional Intelligence," *Imagination, Cognition and Personality*, 9, 185–211; and Goleman, D. (1998) *Working with Emotional Intelligence*. New York: Bantam.

[13] Goleman.

[14] DeVito.

CHAPTER FIVE

THE MIND IN COMMUNICATION: PERCEPTION

In this chapter we talk about the operations of the mind, the context between our ears into which the culture is poured during the socialization process. It's important to understand how our minds process the information that flows through us every second in order to understand a fundamental aspect of interpersonal communication — our drive toward creating quick, automatic certainty in our responses to what is essentially an uncertain world.

In Chapter 1, our search for moment-to-moment certainty and predictability in our talk was described, and in Chapter 2 we noted that this is provided in a general way during socialization by learning a common language and a repertoire of meanings assigned to non-verbal behavior. In Chapter 3 we also asserted that we learn life in a more specific, moment-to-moment way as we grow — in clusters of specific words and actions we called schema — through the operations of our cognitive unconscious. We described its constant observation and evaluation of the world around us and its attachment of positive or negative tags of emotional energy to these deeply learned patterns of behavior to aid in their automatic production as verbal and nonverbal patterns for each situation in which we find ourselves.

In Chapter 4, we brought the emotional forces behind all of our automatic behavior into the conscious mind by showing how our body-mind's biochemical responses to change (emotions) emerge into our consciousness as feelings. We argued that becoming aware of our feelings, being able to *name* them and *describe them more accurately* to ourselves, *and to others*, is central to our becoming more effective communicators.

In the following section of this chapter we discover that the cognitive unconscious is also intimately connected to the second conscious mental process that is critical to interpersonal communication — how we perceive ourselves, others and the situations we are in. The relationships between the "two minds" is critical in shaping how we see the world around us.

Perception: Structures for Seeing the World[1]

What is perception? The simplest definition is: a process of observing and selecting stimuli, organizing them into recognizable patterns, and giving them meaning. So, when something does get our conscious attention, the conscious mind uses a three-step process.

1) It selects what to see,

2) It organizes that data into patterns, and

3) It interprets the pattern, giving it meaning and describing it.

The world is full of chunks of information that are trying to get our attention. To create shared meaning with someone, we use words and nonverbals to communicate the way we see the world in our mind. We organize our perceptions into recognizable structures that we and they can then interpret, using our perceptual powers to create patterns, and our cognition — our thinking powers — to name, evaluate, and then transmit those patterns.

The Necessity of Selection

Our mind can't possibly manage all the information that is pouring in through all the senses: sight, sound, smell, touch, taste. Since these sensory systems deliver millions of bits of information to our mind every second, our conscious mind must ignore most of it and select the bits that have the most meaning for us. We do that by using pre-packaged forms of reality to deal with the data flood. These early-learned forms or cultural categories are like the cookie cutters that are used to make specially shaped cookies out of unbaked dough — stars or crescents or gingerbread men. If the dough represents reality — the shapeless flow of data our sensory systems process every second — then our schemas represent the "cookie cutters" of our minds.

Schemas: Organizing Cultural Learning and Personal Experience

Our minds don't simply create patterns from nothing. In fact, without our culture providing us some pre-existing structures around which to build our own patterns, we couldn't even begin the process of perception; our conscious minds would be overwhelmed from the start. However, as we have noted previously, the cognitive unconscious mind has been building and storing patterns of reality since birth — our schema — including our negative and positive emotional preferences for them — so it can gently prod the conscious mind through the selection and organization processes. In slightly different words Brooks[2] says, "Emotion assigns value to things and reason can only make choices on the basis of those valuations." The foundation of the ways we consciously see the world are the emotion-tagged patterns created by and stored in the cognitive unconscious part of the mind.

These schemas affect our access to reality: what we notice, think about and remember. Researchers have found that when people are confronted with information that is inconsistent with a particular schema, they will usually fail to notice it, or ignore it, or if they do see it, quickly forget it. It seems as if we would rather be certain than accurate in our perceptions of the world around us.

Prototypes

Our minds use *two types of schemas* — cultural prototypes and personal constructs. A **prototype** represents our cultural learning. It is the socially organized knowledge that reflects the "typical" examples of a category of relationships, objects or situations. For instance, we each have a collection of:

- **Person-relational** prototypes based both on role or character names, such as teacher, parent, computer geek or jock, and on our potential connections to people who might be playing such roles, like "great teacher," "good friend," or "untrustworthy jerk," and,

- **Situational** prototypes like "meeting his/her parents for the first time" or "first day on the job." These types of prototypes are often called scripts because we learn the sequence of behaviors that are supposed to be performed in the situation.

We may not know any computer geeks or jerks but these prototypes hover in the background of our mental processing and organize a set of expectations we can call up to guide our behavior. In addition, situational prototypes provide us with scripts that are guides to action in typical situations so we know what to expect or do next.

Prototype categories exist in the society's knowledge base and are learned through direct instruction and by the observation and imitation of others' behaviors. Thus, the detail they contain and their accessibility to aid perception varies by individual. Moreover, as we grow and learn, we add more personal experience and new levels of personal certainty to the "prototypical" models. We develop them into **personal constructs.** Personal constructs allow us to make more detailed judgments about individuals, relationships and situations, but they also increase the uniqueness of our reactions to the world. In fact, when others don't agree with us, we are surprised that they don't construct their realities in exactly the same way we do. The very act of increasing the certainty of our personal views has the potential to increase the level of uncertainty in our conversations.

Perception: Processes for Seeing

We know that the basic process of perception is **selection**. We have to choose which data to notice from the flood of it hammering our sensory receptors every second we're conscious. Our schemas permit us to do this by simply leaving out — filtering — what doesn't seem to fit with what we already expect to see. We look at and pay attention to what is meaningful for us: the familiar, the intense and the new.

Intensity and Novelty

In addition to noticing things we are familiar with — things we have seen before (whether we are conscious of it or not) — we tend to pay attention to those things that are more intense — louder, for instance — which is why when we get angry and frustrated with people, we almost always raise our voice. We also notice things that we haven't noticed before, things that are new.

We notice the novel and the intense — at least for a moment — because of the mind's efficiency in moving information from short-term memory into long-term storage. The process is called **habituation**. In Chapter 3, we described the habituation process that occurs when we learn to walk. After a period of conscious trial-and-error learning and repeated rehearsal (holding on to the furniture, letting go, lurching forward and falling down, again and again), we begin to "forget" what we're learning, that is, we get to the point where we don't have to actively call up patterned perceptions into our consciousness in order to use them. We just "know" what to do. This knowledge simply appears in our minds because of what social psychologists call "chronic association" — when the appropriate cue appears in the environment the schema is instantly called up.

Once we have selected key bits of information, we use two relatively simple rules — called "heuristics"[3] (mental shortcuts) — for organizing them within the outlines of our schema: the rules of proximity and resemblance.

Rule of Proximity

One of the devices we use to organize reality to make pictures in our head is the rule of **proximity**; that is, our brain assumes that things that are closer together in space and time are more alike and therefore belong together. For example, two people who are walking along arm in arm create a different picture in our mind than two people who are walking three or four feet apart. If we see three people walking in a parallel line, even if they are total strangers, we think they are connected.

We also use the rule of proximity along the dimension of time. When things happen close together in time — one right after the other, for instance — we assume that they are somehow connected and, most often, that the first event "caused" the second.

Rule of Resemblance

We also use the rule of **resemblance**. Things that look like each other go together. When things have similar attributes, whether it's color, shape, height or weight, our mind automatically begins to group these things into a common schema. In the extreme, this can lead to stereotypical perceptions of people and situations and create some real communication problems for us.

The rules of proximity and resemblance go together to help the mind seek closure — the automatic completion of an established schema or the creation of a personal construct — to shape the reality we are dealing with into a satisfying, recognizable pattern — to interpret or give it meaning. Our mind is built for speed and certainty. We seem to dislike the slow work of making decisions as well as the uncertainty that such work might create, so we develop personal constructs (whether they are "realistic" or accurate views of reality or not) so we can quickly name and evaluate things and move on. Ultimately, our perception of things contributes to the way we communicate about them.

The Perception Process: Seeing Ourselves in the Context of the World Around Us

The selective attention process chooses what to look at based on intensity and novelty and then organizes what it has selected into patterns. If something is too novel, we tend to ignore it. This is also what we do when the world doesn't respond to us, or our behavior, in ways that we find consistent with our perceptions of ourselves. If we can't change the incoming data, we ignore or distort it — it's an automatic response. Let's review both of these processes.

Ignoring Reality to Be Consistent

Simmons and Levin[4] ran a simple experiment at Cornell University. They made a short movie that started with a long shot of an actor walking through an empty classroom. He stops and begins to sit, and as he does, there is an edit to a close-up of a different actor completing the action. Only 12 out of 40 students watching the movie noticed. Their minds simply "missed" it.

"Mistakes" like this happen in movies all the time; they're called "continuity errors." Filmmakers watch for them during the making of the movie but it's like trying to edit your own writing: your mind simply constructs each scene the way you expect it to flow, and an error, such as a door opening the wrong way, a black eye or a mustache missing from an actor's face, is missed.

We can see this from the studies of "eyewitness" accounts of frightening events. They provide the least reliable form of evidence. For instance, in a potentially dangerous situation where people witness someone else using a gun, they rarely remember details about the person's appearance or the situation, because their minds are focused on the most threatening element of the situation — the gun. We "miss" stuff all the time.

To summarize, low mental effort and the drive to be consistent are the most important forces behind all of these processes of selecting, organizing and interpreting patterns of data. When we perceive the world around us, consistency is vital. To feel good, right and calm, the elements of our perceptual schema must be consistent with each other (i.e., hang together) not just in the moment, but also over time. Much of this mental work is done automatically but when a changing external situation demands it, we seem to be willing to put in the extra, conscious effort to achieve consistency between our perceptions of self, our own behavior, and feedback from the world around us.

Distorting Reality to be Consistent and Pain Free

We all want to be right, certain and calm to avoid the psychic pain of perceptual inconsistency, which social psychologist Leon Festinger[5] identified as **cognitive dissonance** over 50 years ago. Cognitive dissonance is a state of tension and discomfort that occurs whenever a person holds two cognitions (perceptions of self and behavior) that are psychologically inconsistent.

We strive to make sense out of contradictory ideas and to lead lives that are, at least in our own minds, consistent and meaningful. For example, we know that smoking could kill us, yet we continue to smoke two packs a day. This kind of dissonance produces mental discomfort, ranging from minor pangs of guilt to deep anguish, and we can't rest easy until we find a way to reduce it.

Using the smoking example, the most direct way for smokers to reduce dissonance is to quit smoking. But if they have tried to quit and failed, they must now reduce dissonance by convincing themselves that it's okay, and they do this by changing the way they see smoking. They may tell themselves:

- Smoking isn't really so harmful; they had relatives who smoked until they died in their 90s, or

- Smoking is worth the risk because it helps them relax or prevents them from gaining weight (and after all, that's a health risk, too), and so on.

In fact, the drive for consistency — also called consonance — between our perceptions of ourselves and our behavior is so important we will go out of our way to claim supportive evidence for our perceptions as well researched, and arguments for it as well taken and important, while dismissing contradictory arguments as stupid, poorly researched and based on rare occurrences.

This effect is so pervasive that social psychologists call it the **confirmation bias** We see what we need to see to be internally consistent. So, for example, if you believe you are a capable, kindly and attentive spouse and your mate criticizes you for being incompetent, cruel and dismissive, you might ignore or distort the message in some way. Either you attribute the message to the fact that your mate may have had a bad day at work, or you decide that they are imagining things or playing some weird joke on you. (As we mentioned in the previous chapter, this positive attribution is more likely to happen in emotionally positive relationships.)

This process is also supported by the unconscious operations of the mind. In one study, a group of people had their brain scanned using magnetic resonance imaging (MRI) while receiving critical information about their favorite presidential candidates. The scans indicated that the reasoning areas of the brain — the frontal lobes — virtually shut down when this dissonant information was being delivered, and when consonance was restored (by telling them the first information was fabricated), the emotion circuits of the brain happily lit up again.

The fact is that it's hard to change a mind. That is, unless you can get someone to do something they wouldn't ordinarily do . . . then a change can happen. For example, if they ordinarily wouldn't harm another person and they do, their perception of the other becomes much more negative. They blame the victim: they must have deserved it. On the other hand, if someone does a favor for another person that they wouldn't ordinarily do, then their perception of the other person changes positively — they must have deserved it because they are such a good person.

Think of these arguments as the "I'm not the kind of person who would do that without a good reason" arguments. I find that "good reason" by changing my perception of the action or the target of the action.

Distorting Reality to be Consistent and Pain Free: The First Research

As a doctoral student in 1955, Leon Festinger infiltrated a small religious cult whose charismatic leader had predicted the imminent end of the world and the arrival of a spaceship to take the faithful to a new planet. In this field study, Festinger made firsthand observations of group members' behavior on the night the spaceship was supposed to arrive. He successfully predicted that the most committed members of the cult — those who had already given away their worldly goods — would become more committed to their beliefs and their leader rather than less, when the world didn't end.

The subjects in the room awaiting the arrival of the spaceship began to worry when the ship didn't show up at the appointed hour but they were transformed into believers when, four hours later, their leader — a Mrs. Keech — suddenly had a vision and announced that their faith had saved a doomed world and prevented the landing.

Within minutes they were calling local radio stations and newspapers to report the good news, and within hours they were on the streets buttonholing people to join the group. In essence, they were enacting the statement: "We are not the kind of people who would give away all of our worldly goods, so we must have had a good reason . . . we saved the world."

Interestingly, people who stayed in their own homes to wait and worry soon lost faith in their leader. Mrs. Keech's own husband — a nonbeliever — had gone to bed at his regular hour and had a sound sleep that night.

This field study led to lab experiments — the first of thousands of "I am not the kind of person who . . ." studies. In one early experiment, Festinger had subjects come in to do a really boring task for an hour and at the end, he had them rate how interesting the work was. They uniformly thought it was awful. But as part of the debrief, he told each subject that half the participants in the experiment had been told that this was a really exciting task and half were not told this, and that they were part of the "not told" group. He also told them that this was really an experiment about the impact of positive expectations on performance.

Festinger then feigned embarrassment — "I have a conflicting appointment. My colleague hasn't shown up and can't talk to the next subject. I need every one I can get to complete my data set — so as the subjects arrive, would you please tell them the experiment is really interesting?" (In other words, lie for me.) He then gave half the subjects $1 to do this and the other half $20.

When questioned a week later, the $20 liars who had told the arriving subjects that the experiment was interesting, hadn't changed their original perception of the task because they were given a big enough sum to lie (this was the 1950s) and the experimenter had asked them to do it. In other words, they still considered the work boring.

The $1 liars, however, when asked to rate the experimental work, had unknowingly changed their impressions of the task. Their responses showed they thought it was fun after all. Essentially, "I am not the kind of person who would tell a lie for a measly buck . . . so I didn't lie." Therefore, it must have been fun.

And, by the way, we are so sure we need to be right that not only do we reconstruct our memories of what has recently happened but, by extension, our lives as a whole. We need to be a coherent narrative that supports our current sense of self. As Daniel Gilbert said in his book *Stumbling on Happiness*[6]: Bogie was wrong in the movie *Casablanca* when he told Ingrid Bergman she would regret it, "maybe not today, maybe not tomorrow, but soon, and for the rest of your life," if she stayed with him in Morocco instead of leaving with her Nazi-fighting husband. Quite the contrary: She would have found reasons to justify her choice and lived happily ever after.

Four Axioms of Perception

As with the IP communication model, we can summarize the internal and external dynamics of the process of perception with four axioms.
In our conscious responses to incoming data from our environment:

1. We are highly selective in the data we consciously perceive.

    - We use selective attention to perceive only a small amount of what is happening within us and without us.

2. Our selective attention reinforces our drive toward consciously maintaining consistency — a coherent balance — between our perceptions of ourself, our own behavior and the information from the environment.

    - When we think that we, and the world, perceive our actions the way we perceive them, we feel a sense of inner calm, certainty.

3. When we consciously perceive data that contradicts or challenges the consistency of our perceptions of ourselves and our behavior, we feel some level of psychic discomfort even pain (feelings of uncertainty, fear or even a sense of threat).

    - To reduce or eliminate this pain our automatic response is to ignore the data, or if necessary, deny or distort it to return to a state of psychic balance and comfort.

    - An unintended outcome of the denial or distortion process can be an unconscious change in our perceptions.

4. People can consciously choose to change their perceptions of themselves and their behaviors — to learn something new — if they also choose to become actively involved in the process.

    - This often requires the help of another person who provides therapeutic support and a positive climate for personal change. We have to be willing to go outside our comfort zone and do the hard, often painful work. It takes a long time and a lot of courage, and people often quit when the going gets too tough.

So far we've been dealing with the perceptions of one's self and behavior, but what about how we see other people?

Perceiving People: Tools for Creating Internally Consistent Pictures

Thing versus Person Perception

Most of our understanding of the processes of perception — proximity, resemblance, closure — has emerged from studying how people see things. Culture provides us with established schemas for this process: schemas for shape, size and depth (such as circle, square, triangle, cube) so we can instantly create pictures of reality and have more certainty in our lives. We see how easily this works in the physical world. Most objects — chairs and rocks — don't directly interact with us the way humans do. They exist in a very slowly changing reality, so we can see them once and think we have seen them forever. But "person" perception is different. Human beings are complicated and in process all the time; that is, they move, they grow, they think, they change. People, unlike things, are an odd mixture of their personal physiological inheritance, their upbringing, their individual community settings and their larger community experiences. They are complicated systems of physiology and psychology and each one of them is unique. Moreover, they engage us — our hearts, minds, emotions and thoughts — so, theoretically, we should "learn" them one person at a time because they are not like tables and chairs and rocks.

Unfortunately, that's not the way our brain works. We treat complex people the way we treat unchanging, uncomplicated things. We see them in terms of simple schema — as still photographs rather than as movies being written, directed and edited right in front of us. Like triangles or chairs, the essence of the other person is seen through our person/relational prototypes or stereotypes, out of which we build a personal construct as we get to know more about them. We also expect consistency across time. Once I see you, and I think I know you, I think I know you across future time in the same way.

First Impressions

We have a series of person prototypes we use to create and maintain the mental pictures we have of others. The first time we meet somebody, one of our schemata will kick in and that first impression — the **primacy effect** — happens very quickly and deeply (Todorov's research). We get a picture in the first few seconds of seeing them, and it gets reinforced in the first couple of minutes we interact with them (Pentland's research). We do this kind of first-impression work all the time and it is based upon the rule of resemblance — do they look like and "feel" like a certain type of person? We select little bits and pieces of information and plug them into our schema. Most often we use some combination of elements along two dimensions — emotional openness and physical attractiveness — to create a coherent, whole picture — in a very short period of time.

Malcolm Gladwell[7] calls this "thin slicing." This is a key operation of the "always on" cognitive unconscious. It allows us to make very quick judgments using very "thin slices" of all the information that is available to us when we perceive others. Gladwell argues that our cognitive unconscious is invoked "whenever we meet someone for the first time, whenever we interview someone for a job, whenever we react to a new idea, whenever we're faced with making a decision quickly and under stress."[8] He reviews research data which demonstrates that (1) people create an almost instantaneous first impression (primacy) of others, and (2) they are often very accurate.

One of the experiments he reviews is summarized in the "research box" below.

Student First Impressions of Professors

Psychologist Nalini Ambady[9] gave students three 10-second videotapes of professors with the sound turned off. The students easily rated the teachers' effectiveness. When the tapes were reduced to 5 seconds, the students' ratings were the same and remained that way when the students were shown only 2 seconds of videotape. When these "snap judgments" were compared to the evaluations of the same professors made by their students after a full semester of classes, they were essentially the same. Gladwell asserts that the similarity of ratings made after a few seconds versus those made after 12 or 13 weeks indicates the power of the cognitive unconscious.

Emotional Openness: Warm versus Cold

One of the key dimensions we use in creating first impressions is approachability, i.e., where the person seems to be on the warm–cold dimension. The importance of this dimension was discovered in a classic experiment conducted by Kelley.[10] To one group of students he read a list of personal traits: "intelligent, skillful, industrious, warm, determined, practical, cautious." Another group was read an identical list, except that "cold" was substituted for "warm." All the participants then wrote a brief paragraph describing the type of person to whom the traits applied. When the responses were examined, the descriptions obtained from the two groups were found to be strikingly different. The "warm" trait generated impressions of a person who was more popular, wise, humorous and imaginative. Moreover, the students who rated him like this were also more likely to ask questions and engage him in discussion. Kelley called traits such as "warm" and "cold" central traits because they seemed to be implicitly correlated with the existence of a wide range of other traits — as indicated in more of Ambady's[11] research.

Coolness, Dominance and Medical Competence

In another study on first impressions, Professor Ambady let people hear 2-second clips of recordings of discussions between doctors and their patients. The participants in the study could hear "the sound" of doctors' voices — their words were intentionally distorted but the tone, pitch, rhythm were clear. They were then asked to rate the doctors' voices on dimensions like warmth, dominance, hostility and anxiousness. On the basis of the participants' ratings she could easily predict which of the doctors in the sample had been sued and which hadn't. The voices of the doctors who had been sued sounded dominant and cool while the doctors who had never been sued sounded less dominant, warmer and more concerned.

Physical Attractiveness

A second key dimension that shapes our first picture of someone is physical attractiveness. We now have data that indicates that both the content of this prototype and its importance in shaping our perceptions of others vary by culture. Studies have found that physical attractiveness is associated with social competence (popular, likeable, friendly), capability, and, to a lesser extent, intellectual competence (though more for men than women), positiveness, as well as dominant behavior in men and submissive behavior in women. When we look for physical attraction we look at the face for men, and the face and body for women (and not just any body type, but a very distinct body type).

Not surprisingly, perhaps, people who grow up in cultures that think the group is more important than the individual spend far less time talking about individual surface characteristics like physical attractiveness, whereas in highly individualistic cultures like ours, physical appearance shapes a big part of the pictures we form of ourselves and others. Moreover, we add characteristics to our initial impressions. For instance, we don't just build a picture of a particular man as simply good-looking and approachable, we build a picture that says he is good-looking, popular, sociable and dominant. And all this "thin slicing" happens within a few seconds of seeing him, before he's even opened his mouth.

Implicit Personality Theory

When we think of someone as good-looking, and automatically associate that characteristic with others, such as "smart, sociable and dominant," we are instantly creating a coherent whole — a perception process that social psychologists call **Implicit Personality Theory**. (It is also called the "Halo Effect.") Person perception research has demonstrated that we need the pieces and parts of our schema to hang together in a consistent fashion and work well together. The recognition of the need to create these patterns emerges out of many experiments in which people not only consistently clustered personality traits into particular patterns but were also able to predict that others would create similar groupings. There seems to be a broad agreement that certain personality traits go together, so completing a statement like "Fred is handsome, smart and . . . clumsy / capable" is easy for us. We consistently choose capable over clumsy because it "fits," even though we don't have all the parts. The implicit personality theory schemas we all carry around in our head permit quick, comforting certainty. They can also prevent us from seeing how people "really are."

Person and Relational Prototypes: Role Names and Expectations

Teacher and student or doctor and patient: do we know anything about the people who happen to be playing these roles? We think we do. In a superficial way, these role names help us understand people's behavior, and over time, we see enough performances of these roles to infer things about the types of people who play them. In our mind, these very general cultural categories evolve into relational schema as we learn the behavior patterns or scripts that are built into these schema and our emotional reactions to them. We develop personal constructs for what a "good doctor" or a "bad teacher" is and we apply them automatically to the next doctor or teacher we meet. This process also occurs when the "roles" we confront aren't necessarily recognized in the wider society — what is a cool dude or a hot chick? There may be no absolute definition for these performance roles, but within our part of the community, we observe, discuss and develop relational schema for them in our head, and we treat these pictures, these little schematic diagrams, as if they were real.

Stereotypes

Closely related to prototypes are **stereotypes**. Stereotypes go beyond simply categorizing people or situations. They are focused on predicting behavior. Stereotypes are sets of expectations that have hardened into beliefs about how individuals think and act because of their membership in a particular group. Stereotypes tend to include extreme generalities about shared characteristics or behaviors framed as "allness" statements — "they all act like that" or "this is the way they are."

Stereotypes are a major part of cultural knowledge and they certainly make our world more organized and predictable, but they may or may not be accurate and are most often unfair to individuals. They help us perceive individuals as "things" rather than as unique beings. Finally, stereotypes share a common characteristic with other types of schema in that they often persist in the culture long after any evidence that may have supported their invention has been discredited. Racial and gender stereotypes continue to exist happily alongside the mountain of both social-historical and scientific evidence that we have accumulated in the past century that discredits their explanatory value.

Stereotypes enable us to make shortcut decisions about individuals based on their group membership. The trouble with stereotypes is that they tell us what people *may* share, but not what they actually *do* share. Members of the same categorical group may or may not share the same thoughts, beliefs or behavior patterns. But if we assume they do because of our stereotypical perceptions, then in fact we've blocked off any other possibilities of learning about them as individuals. But it works for us because we'd rather be certain than accurate in the way we see the world.

Television, Stereotypes and Humor

We use stereotypes all the time to make jokes. All stereotypical humor is built around a series of schema where we think we have whole pictures of people just because they fit a category. Television comedy is built on stereotypical characterization. It has to be. Television doesn't have the time to build character. It uses stereotypical behavior acted out by people who represent schematic versions of human beings rather than real people. It reinforces some of our worst stereotypes: all men or all women are a certain kind of way, all black people or all people from Asian backgrounds are a certain kind of way. As children we watched television or hours and were socialized into cultural stereotypes long before we could consciously think about people as individuals.

Stereotyping works well at giving us the illusion of dealing with a consistent and dependable reality because our mind uses two quick fixes to deal with any information that might contradict our stereotypes. First, when we stereotype an individual as belonging to a particular group so we can predict their behavior, we simply ignore or forget instances where we dealt with someone whose behavior fell outside our stereotype of members of that particular group. We automatically think of the stereotype first to keep up the illusion of stability in our mental world. Second, where we are compelled by the context or by repeated contact with that person to consciously recognize the limitations of our stereotype in explaining their behavior, we invoke the "exception-to-the-rule" version of the stereotype ("You're not like the rest of them"). In this way, we can hang onto our stereotype and still recognize the individual's differences.

Stereotyping and "The Door" Experiment

Professors Simmons and Levin[12] of Cornell University had "strangers" (who were actually their confederates) on campus ask pedestrians for directions. As the two people talked, they were rudely interrupted by two men who passed between them, carrying a door. The interruption lasted a second, during which time one of the men carrying the door traded places with the "stranger" asking for directions. When the interruption was over, the pedestrian was confronted with a different person who continued the conversation as if nothing had happened.

The question was, would the innocent pedestrian notice? The answer is that less than half — about 47% — reported noticing the change. It turns out that those who noticed the change had something in common with the "stranger" they had been talking to. Generally, they were about the same age and dressed like them.

There is a lot of data showing that when we meet people who are like us, we momentarily pay more attention to them than when we meet people who are different. So the next question became, "Would this shift of attention extend to whether or not we actually 'see' others who are not like us?"

To answer this, the professors did the experiment again, except this time the "stranger" was dressed as a construction worker — hard hat, boots — and only approached people his own age. He encountered 12 people and asked for directions. The door passed between them and the switch was made, but this time fewer people — only 33% — noticed. The higher miss rate was based on the fact that the students didn't really see the person. As they said afterward, they only saw a "construction worker" — no details like face and eyes — just the boots and hard hat.

Stereotypes are tied to role names, differences in skin color, hair color, perceived differences in national background, dress, and many other noticeable differences we encounter every day. We manage incoming information by "thin slicing" for speed and certainty. And by the way, when the professors explained the experiment to a class of 50 and asked how many thought they would catch the trick — all 50 of them said they would. They believed they were "not the kind of people who could be tricked." And why not; we all think we are "better than average."

Perceiving People: Tools for Creating Consistency through Time

We seem to be compelled not only to *perceive* individuals as unrealistically simple and internally consistent collections of attributes but also to *maintain* our view of them over time. Since we have invented these pictures, they are extensions of ourselves. We built them the first time to assure ourselves that we knew what was going on with the other as well as in the relationship between them and us. Any changes in our perceptions of them and our relationship to them would require changes in our perceptions of ourselves. This has the potential for discomfort and, in the case of unanticipated, negative changes, the possibility of real pain — something we are driven to avoid.

External Consistency Model

The balance between our perceptions of ourselves, our own behavior, and of other people and the world around us is the basis of the **External Consistency Model** of perception (Perception Axiom 2). We need to see both ourselves, and the world around us, in this way:

- I expect the persons I like to like me,
- I expect them to like the things that I like, and
- I expect them to dislike the things (or people) that I dislike.

Isn't that why we have friends? Our friends help us to maintain a carefully constructed balance of perceptions about who we are and who everyone else is by supporting us in our efforts to influence others to our way of seeing things, defending us when others criticize us, and just simply enjoying the world from a perspective that is close to ours.

This consistency drive can create some interesting problems when we are first getting to know someone new. As we are learning about them and fitting them into our schemas for friend or lover, we may have our first perceptions of them challenged — sometimes deeply challenged. It's the "I like you, you like me, I like X, and I now find out you hate X" problem. The feelings of surprise and discomfort are the "cognitive dissonance" we referred to above. Our reality is jarred by their reality. Sometimes we even change our expectations of the other to rebalance our perceptions: "Oh well, it doesn't really matter that he hates cats." Or we may decide to end the process of connecting: "Sorry, I can't meet you again. I don't like smokers."

One of the ways we maintain stable perceptions of people we like over time is to limit our future information about them to the "good" stuff, or at least the stuff that already fits our perception of them. We've all heard the saying, "If you haven't got anything nice to say, don't say anything at all!" This turns out to be a basic cultural rule. We can maintain a consistent view of them and of ourselves, because we are not going to rush to tell them the bad stuff. In fact, we will ignore or explain away any negatives about them for as long as we can. This approach allows us to keep intact whatever pictures of them we have in our head.

Self-Fulfilling Prophecy

Another powerful and subtle way we do this is through the process of the **self-fulfilling prophecy**. Because of our schematic view of another, we think we can predict their behavior; then we act toward them as if our prediction were true. If we believe they will act cool and distant when they meet us, we act cool and distant to protect ourselves from possible hurt or embarrassment. Not surprisingly, in response to our style, they act the same way — cool and distant. Of course, we don't see their actions as a response to us; we attribute it to their character or personality and say, "See, I knew it. He's an arrogant jerk."

Attribution Process

The "arrogant jerk" outcome of our self-fulfilling prophecy example represents our continual efforts, as amateur psychologists, to explain the motives for other people's behavior — called the **attribution process**. Our perceptual schema, however, don't allow us to be very accurate in our predictions, since we tend to have a **self-serving bias** in our attribution of motives to our own and others' behaviors. When we see negative behavior in ourselves, we tend to explain it in terms of the circumstances that caused it, using "It wasn't my fault" or the "devil made me do it" types of explanation. But when we see negative behavior in somebody else, we make the **fundamental attribution error** — we make the automatic judgment that it's about the way they are as a person. Our interest in the situation suddenly disappears. In addition to providing instant answers to our questions about "what's going on" and "who are you in this situation," the self-serving bias prevents us from learning things about ourselves, while maintaining the consistent view we hold of others.

Another aspect of attribution has to do with our need to use only a few characteristics to create quick pictures of others. Called **overattribution** — another way of saying "thin slicing" — this process not only names and evaluates someone but also predicts the motives for their actions. In other words, we use one or two obvious characteristics to explain everything there is to know about the person. Considered objectively, overattribution is simpleminded and silly but it's also unambiguous, clear and certain and that's important for the way our mind operates. So we say something like, "They were born rich and never had to work for anything, and that's why they are the way they are." Again, we never look at circumstances that might drive their behavior.

Perception and Effective Communication

When we are trying to understand another person and their behavior, we shouldn't jump to conclusions, because we are reacting to our schema, not them. Our schema of them is a highly simplified model into which we pour limited amounts of information as a way of reminding ourselves that we know them. Most importantly, it encourages us to jump to "one-clue conclusions." There might be several reasons why a person does something. When we're looking for motives, it's a bad idea to mind-read — for example, telling someone, "You don't care!" We don't know whether they care or not, because we haven't asked them. All we're doing is risking the fundamental attribution error. When we need to know somebody's motivations, it's better to say, "This is how I see you behaving in this situation. Can you tell me what's going on?" Communication falls apart when we assume we already have all the answers and say nothing.

To summarize this section, here are some guidelines about how we can consciously manage our perception processes to be better communicators.

Improving the Quality of Your Interpersonal Perceptions

Don't jump to conclusions about what you see

- Wait, watch and then ask what's going on. Remember, you're dealing with your "schema" not with their reality.

Avoid one-clue conclusions

- Respond with a "hypothesis" not a conclusion. Then seek more information.

Avoid "mind-reading" for motives

- No matter how much you see, you are still guessing. Ask about their intentions; don't just attribute motives to them.

Describe your perceptions

- Ask for confirmation of what you see or hear.

Where We're Going Next

We have a pretty good idea now of how our conscious mind perceives things — selects and organizes things. In the next chapter, we'll take a look at how our conscious mind names and thinks about things. This last step in the perception process is **interpretation** — giving our pictures meaning. We do this by consciously naming and evaluating what we see.

END NOTES

[1] The perception section of this chapter integrates key concepts from Trenholm, S., Jensen, A. (1996) *Interpersonal Communication Book* (3rd ed.). Belmont, CA: Wadsworth Publishing; DeVito, J. (1992) *The Interpersonal Communication Book* (6th ed.). New York: HarperCollins; and Hinton, P. (1993) *The Psychology of Interpersonal Perception*. London: Routledge, Chap. 6.

[2] Brooks, D. (2011) *The Social Animal*. New York: Random House.

[3] More specifically these are "representative heuristics" according to Aronson, E., Wilson, T., Akert, R. (2006) *Social Psychology*, (6th ed.). Upper Saddle River, NJ: Pearson Education, p. 75.

[4] As cited in Hallinan, J. (2009) *Why We Make Mistakes*. New York: Broadway Books, p. 17.

[5] Festinger, L. (1957) *A Theory of Cognitive Dissonance*. Stanford, CA: Stanford University Press.

[6] Gilbert, D., (2007) *Stumbling on Happiness.* Toronto: Random House Canada, pp.196–197.

[7] Gladwell, M. (2005) *Blink: The Power of Thinking Without Thinking,* New York: Little, Brown and Co.

[8] Gladwell, p. 12.

[9] Ambady, N. as cited in Gladwell.

[10] Kelly, H. H. (1950) "The Warm-Cold Variable in First Impressions of Persons," *Journal of Personality,* 18, 431–439.

[11] Ambady, N. et al. (2002) "Surgeons Tone of Voice: A Clue to Malpractice History," *Surgery,* (1), 5–9.

[12] Simmons, D., Levin, D. (1998) "Failure to Detect Changes to People During Real-World Interaction," *Psychonomic Bulletin and Review,* 11 (3), 414–435.

CHAPTER SIX

THE MIND IN COMMUNICATION: COGNITION

Cognition: Thinking about Our Perceptions[1]

If, as our definition of communication suggests, we act together to create and sustain meanings, then the words we use to name our perceptions are critical to the way we speak about them. We send each other socially shared verbal symbols that only stand for the pictures in our head — we can't send the pictures themselves. So if we want to stimulate similar pictures in the mind of another, the words we use make a difference. Understanding our thinking processes — our cognition — helps us understand how and why we attach certain words to those little pictures in our head.

The cognition process involves two aspects of thought:

1) How we name and think about the patterns we create.

2) How we deal with differences between our expectations and reality in day-to-day life.

As we learned in Chapter 3, our conscious mind can and does work its way through the process of rational problem solving and decision making, but it's a relatively slow, energy-demanding process (think of what goes into preparing a presentation for work or doing your taxes each year). Everyday talk, however, demands a quicker form of cognition — we instantly size up a new situation, figure out who the person is, what's going on and, perhaps most importantly, guess what's going to happen next using the schema from our early learning and life experience. If we didn't, our mind would slow down to the point that we would appear to be "lost in thought" every time we tried to speak. In fact, we now know that we effortlessly create first impressions of people and things around us and we interact, using low effort, automatic forms of thought (schemas), calling words and thoughts into our conscious mind instantly. In *Thinking Fast and Slow*, Kahneman[2] clarifies this process.

The Distractable Controller

In his detailed analysis of research on the relationship between the conscious mind and the cognitive unconscious, Kahneman[3] makes clear that in everyday thought the list of "heuristics" — shortcuts — provided by the cognitive unconscious to the conscious mind is extensive and that judgmental thinking is natural and generally unnoticed by the conscious mind. As he says,

> In the picture that emerges from recent research, the intuitive . . . [cognitive unconscious] is more influential than your [conscious] experience tells you, and it is the secret author of many of the choices and judgments you make.

Our conscious mind *can* perform fine discriminations between events in a situation, and make complex decisions. As Kahneman states, it can do things like focus on the voice of a particular person in a noisy room; monitor the appropriateness of your behavior in a social situation; check the validity of a complex argument and do your taxes. However, when we complete these complex tasks, we must exert continuous effort to *pay attention.*

Despite our current beliefs about the value of multitasking, the conscious mind can't really focus on two things at once unless both tasks are very easy (driving and texting don't mix). It is easily distracted, as we discovered in the now famous, "invisible gorilla" research. Chabris and Simons[4] demonstrated the limits of conscious attention in a simple and dramatic experiment. They asked participants to watch two teams in the same space, one in white shirts and one in black shirts, passing basketballs. They were told to ignore the team in the black shirts and to count the number of passes made by the white-shirted team.

Halfway through the video a woman appears on the screen, wearing a gorilla suit and thumping her chest before moving on. She's on screen for 9 seconds and of the thousands of viewers of this video, only half actually saw her. The request to pay attention and to count the number times the white team passed basketballs, was enough to blind them to an obvious event.

And Lazy Too

Kahneman reviews research demonstrating that "the defining feature" of the conscious mind is the real bodily effort it requires to operate and that one of its main characteristics is "laziness." We seem to have evolved as decision-makers who invest as little energy as possible in our moment-to-moment thought. We are "energy misers" when it comes to thinking. As a result, our "conscious judgments" and the words to describe them are either guided by or directly provided by the cognitive unconscious. It uses its huge database of past preferences to create a coherent set instant associations, in the moment. It is driven to make them fit together into judgments that don't have be "true" in the objective sense. They simply have to "make sense" to us — be plausible.

Combining a light speed, coherence-seeking cognitive unconscious with a lazy conscious controller means that it will accept the intuitive judgments and beliefs of the unconscious mind without checking the "real world" data. As Kahneman[5] summarizes, the cognitive unconscious never stops:

> Its input never ceases. Jumping to conclusions on the basis of limited evidence is so important to an understanding of intuitive thinking, and comes up so often . . . that I will use a cumbersome abbreviation for it: WYSIATI, which stands for what you see is all there is. [The cognitive unconscious] is radically insensitive to both the quality and the quantity of the information that gives rise to impressions and intuitions.

WYSIATI at Work

The "What You See Is All There Is" operating system of the cognitive unconscious permits us to be quick thinkers — perfect for everyday talk. It makes it easy to find order in the moment by using a set of heuristics — shortcuts — to build coherent stories that reward us a momentary sense of "mental ease."

Accessibility or Ease of Availability Rule

> We base our judgments on the ease with which we can bring something to mind — what's most familiar. WYSIATI's hidden logic is that the easier something is to recall, the "truer" it must be.

Assertiveness and Ease of Recall[6]

An experimenter asked participants to recall and write down six times they were assertive in their lives. Since it is not difficult to recall six events, at the end of the exercise, people rated themselves as pretty assertive.

Other participants were asked to recall 12 times they were assertive — a much more difficult recall task. When they were finished, they rated themselves as far less assertive. The thinking was that they must not be so assertive because these events were difficult to recall. They judged themselves, not the task.

Overconfidence Rule

If a judgment comes quickly and seems to plausibly explain the situation, we become very confident in it truthfulness. If we feel it's true, we'll defend it. Remember, the cognitive unconscious is not concerned with either the quantity or quality of the data in the actual situation.

The Representativeness Rule: How Similar Is A to B?

This involves classifying something — a person or situation — using a typical case in our past. This is an instant "compare and contrast." In the flow of action around us, the cognitive unconscious pays attention to certain elements (representing things it already knows) and instantly goes into WYSIATI mode. These elements become the focus of our thinking as it makes a quick match with the past. Close enough is good enough and this judgment is instantly presented to the conscious mind. This gives us the ability to talk without actually seeing what's really happening in front us ("He looks like one of them, therefore he could be a threat"). As we said, the intuitive decision of the cognitive unconscious is based on coherent plausibility rather than accuracy.

Framing Rule: Taking Things at Face Value

We accept things we hear first — both words and numbers as true. They anchor our next thoughts and act as a starting point for subsequent decision making. What comes first shapes what comes next. The classic example is the doctor describing the possible effects of a surgery to a patient. If he says that the odds of survival after surgery are 90%, a patient is far more reassured than if he made the logically equivalent statement that chance of dying after surgery is 10%. The cognitive unconscious's first emotional reaction is "all there is."

Contextual Cues

We can also see how WYSIATI complicates communication when it comes to using contextual cues. Recall from Chapter 3 Lehrer's example of a big league batter hitting a professional pitcher. The decision to swing is made before it occurs in consciousness because the cognitive unconscious is reading the pitcher's body movement before the ball leaves his hand. The cognitive unconscious is always paying attention to "what's going on" well before it presents low-effort decisions to the conscious mind. As a result, contextual cues play a far bigger role in our conscious decision making than we recognize.

Contextual cues trigger nonconscious framing. They can change the way we consciously think about our reality in the moment without us noticing. For instance, we take our beloved to a movie whose plot is about one member of a loving couple cheating on the other. On the way home we may have an argument about something minor and unrelated to the movie. Why? Because our fears about infidelity have been triggered by what we saw in the movie. (Remember unnoticed moods affecting opinions in Chapter 4.)

Specific and momentary changes in our environment affect our thinking all the time. This is why retail stores, particularly those selling food or drink, alter the aromas that waft through the store or the background music being played. These cues trigger positive "chronic associations" in the nonconscious mind that affect our conscious decision making. In fact retail chains regularly collect data on this effect.[7]

Answering the Easier Question

Along with providing answers based on intuitive judgment to questions that arise in interaction, our unconscious mind does something else that can sometimes be a real problem in interpersonal communication. It substitutes easier questions for harder ones when it needs to. When the conscious mind is given a difficult question like, "What is really going on in this situation?" it must shift its attention away from the moment and search its memory for an answer. We have to stop talking. To avoid this, the cognitive unconscious instantly substitutes an easier, heuristic question, "How do I feel about what's going on in this situation?" It answers this question instantly, the lazy conscious doesn't notice the switch, and we keep the conversation moving.

We are rarely "stumped" by the questions that arise in our daily talk because we have a wealth of intuitive judgments and opinions about everything in our lives.[8] This is simply a low-level version of the cognitive unconscious doing what it has evolved to do — provide basic, emotion-based assessments of every situation — so we'll know what's going on (threat or opportunity) and know what to do next.

The Affect Heuristic

We have been discussing the more-or-less subtle effects of the unconscious mind's ability to affect our moment-to-moment thinking about what's going around us. Its effects become much more obvious when our emotions are aroused, when our beliefs and attitudes are on the line. Then the unconscious mind's use of heuristic thinking to protect us from what's going on and predict what's going to happen next, takes over. Conclusions and strong judgments take over from any possible rational argument and a search for the information. The conscious mind's tools of memory search, comparison and choice are overwhelmed and, instead of exercising appropriate self-criticism, the conscious mind accepts the intuitive judgments and beliefs of the cognitive unconscious as if they were real. Only then does it go to work and search its memory for data to support the judgment.

In effect, the conscious mind acts like a kindly kindergarten teacher in most conversations — as if the mind were a child at play. It monitors our talk and accepts our production of intuitive judgments — in lieu of descriptions of the reality in front of us — and only occasionally intervenes with a firm but gentle "no" when it looks like we're about to say something inappropriate. However, when our emotions are aroused and we do utter a powerful judgment, it instantly changes role to "hired gun lawyer." It comes to the defense of ourself by searching its memory for data to justify the judgment. It helps us be right. It also stops discriminating between facts and judgment and begins to think in general, black-and-white labels, rather than descriptive specifics. If the goal of interpersonal communication is building shared meaning, then the conscious mind, under emotional pressure, doesn't help. It makes an already complicated process worse, and "shared reality" doesn't stand a chance.

Everyday Talk Is Complicated by Thinking in Labels

When we attach words to images in our head, we tend to use simple terms. We can describe our thought-images in a few words. The positive aspect of this is that simple labels help the conscious mind call up complicated memories if it chooses to search for them. The downside is that this cognitive simplicity reinforces the nature of the low-effort thinking and schematic pictures of others held in the cognitive unconscious. If the conscious mind doesn't pay attention, these are what appear when it asks the question, "Who is this person?"

To function easily, schemas already leave out a good deal of "reality." For instance, we may use only one or two words to describe our personal constructs of people — "great worker" or "arrogant jerk" — but those don't call up as much information as we might need to describe them adequately either to ourselves or others. Research has shown that people who are able to call up more descriptive words when discussing their perceptions of others are also more accurate in their predictions of others' behavior than people who use simple, polarized descriptors like "weak" or "strong," "good" or "bad." Such simplified labeling of others makes our conscious mind more likely to treat them as if they were the label itself rather than the complex human being they are. This is called an **intensional orientation**.[9] This compounds the error of seeing them in only one way over time — **static evaluation**.

Making Things More Complicated: Using Abstract Judgment Words

The simple labels that connect us to our schemas of other people are most often abstract judgment words. They may be a natural part of our thinking process, but they really are problematic when they enter our talk. The reason is that in speech we often treat abstract labels as if they were factual descriptors of the features or characteristics of things or people. They're not and we often don't notice.

For instance, when asked about our colleague George, we could say that George is about 5′ 9″, 160 lbs. He's a grad student from another country, working here as an intern. Simple, verifiable and unlikely to trigger anything in the other's unconscious mind. Or we could move to a high-level abstraction for something more powerful and positive: George is a really great guy. Less verifiable, a value judgment, but more likely to tap into other experiences, or someone's feelings about what makes a "really great guy" and what doesn't.

The more abstract we become in our talk, the more information we leave out, and the more we depend on others' intuitive judgments (emotion-based beliefs about how the world should be) to create our meaning.

As we move from describing George in detail to exclaiming that George is a great guy (or a real jerk), we go from words that are concretely descriptive of his characteristics — things that other people can observe and agree on — to words that are abstract and evaluative and contain very little information about George. These words are not very good for creating shared meanings about him because they are really about us — our feelings, our judgments about George. And what's missing is what other people need to know — which is *why* we feel that way.

To understand why we made the judgment we did, we would need to focus our conscious mind. When we actually ask ourselves why we said something judgmental, we're trying to untangle the automatic emotional judgments of our cognitive unconscious from our conscious thinking and exercising a feature of the conscious mind — enlightened self-criticism. In fact, we can say that effective communication begins with asking ourselves "Why."

If, by explaining how we came to think that George is a great guy, people are going to understand us better, why don't we do it?

- First of all, it's harder work. It would slow down our talk and force us to think about our thinking. As we said earlier, we prefer low-effort approaches to thought in most of our daily talk. Moreover, judgmental abstractions can imply more than we say and that frees us from doing the work (and taking the risks) of saying what we think.

- Second, we get other people's attention with these kinds of assertions. We can quickly engage their emotions at several levels — positive or negative, hope or hate — without having to provide much in the way of information.

- Third, we *like* using abstract and judgmental language. It makes us feel competent. We sound clear, definite, sure of ourselves when we talk like this. Powerful judgments about others also connect us to our own emotions in the same way they connect others to our feelings.

Unfortunately, when we talk like this, things not only go quickly but, when our emotions get involved, they can go very wrong, very quickly. Poor word choices, spoken in inappropriate contexts, can get us into trouble because we can't know for sure (until they tell us) how others will "get" our judgments. Words can hurt. People respond to the emotional energy attached to *their* meanings for *our* words. Words carry those somatic markers of positive or negative energy we talked about in Chapter 3 and they often mark in conscious memory chronic associations with situations that were either threatening or joyful as we, and they, grew up.

Distinguishing Facts from Inferences

We are now aware how our cognitive unconscious "creates" information. Its perception process is built for speed and certainty rather than accuracy and it works from schemas that operate as quick and dirty representations of reality. In order to "make sense" of situations in the moment, it notices only the data that fit into those schema. Its intuitive judgments leave out lots of information that we may later discover would have been useful.

If we discover we're missing useful information when someone asks us a question, we "make sense" of the situation by creating plausible, not necessarily truthful, answers. The cognitive unconscious is not only an association and preference machine, but is also a plausibility machine.

This might not be a problem if we called up our conscious mind to help discriminate between what we know from direct perception and what our unconscious mind has inferred or assumed to be "real," using heuristic shortcuts. Most often, we don't — there's no time for that. Thus, in our inner dialogues and in our talk with others, we automatically mix together three, quite different, levels of thinking.

- **Report data (factual statements)**

  Things we can report that we've seen and heard and are verifiable by someone else. This level is closest to the literal meaning of the words "I know."

- **Inferences**

  Ideas that we have invented out of that data, statements about something that we don't know made on the basis of something we do know. We add information automatically. This is what we mean by the words "I know" most of the time.

- **Evaluations** or **judgments**

  Statements about whether or not we like something, and about how it fits with our beliefs and values. We add the expression of approval or disapproval to an assumption we made (whether or not that assumption is based on something we have seen or heard). This level of "I know" can be the most oppressive form of language — particularly when we share gossip or rumors about others.

We often do this without thinking about it. In fact, automatic assumptions and judgments are a mostly unnoticed part of our everyday small talk. Unnoticed, that is, until we're challenged by someone and we find ourselves in one of those 3 D moments we talked about earlier — unexpected differences and disagreements — that can take us by surprise and make us feel ineffective as speakers.

To be better communicators we need to recognize the quality of the information we are sharing. We need to know the differences between statements of fact and inference. We can move instantly from what is observable to that which we allow to be added to our thinking *as if it were real.* "I think you're terrific" and "I really like you" are two interesting statements, but they are not based on fact, they're based on inference; that is, if you have characteristics x, y and z, and I really like that, then I really like you. The final inference is, "You're my kind of people." That's the ultimate evaluation or judgment: acceptance or rejection. When we think or speak, these levels of knowledge are woven together as if they were all factual.

Differences Between Factual Statements and Inferential Statements[10]	
Factual Statements	**Inferential Statements**
• Can be made only after observation	• May be made anytime
• Are limited to what has been observed	• Can go beyond what has been observed
• Can only be made by observer	• May be made by anyone
• Can only be made about past or present if easily verified by a third party	• May be about any time without verification

The Inference Ladder

This model shows how our mind "naturally" works in the face of ambiguity or direct challenge by someone else.

This ladder metaphor illustrating how the mind moves upward from many facts to a few judgments — from description to abstraction — is adapted from one published in 1994 by Peter Senge[11] and his colleagues. It is a valuable teaching tool because it combines into one easily remembered image all of the processes of the mind we are reviewing in this part of the book, including:

- How our mind automatically uses deeply learned schemas to select data from the millions of incoming bits of information about "concrete" reality and organize them into recognizable patterns, and then
- Instantly, adds information from our previous learning — makes inferences — so we can give them meaning, and then
- Immediately evaluates them — draws conclusions or makes judgments about them.

THE INFERENCE LADDER

I talk and act on the basis of my judgments
I ACT!

I draw conclusions on the basis of my inferences
I JUDGE

I make inferences; add meaning; achieve closure
I INFER

I select from data and organize using schemas
I PERCEIVE

Concrete reality
DATA

The following is an example of how the ladder of inference works when dealing with ambiguity.

The Boss Criticizes Jane

Jane has been late in delivering several important reports to her boss, but we don't know this. We simply overhear the boss say, "Jane, your performance is not up to standard!" We begin to construct some meaning out of the boss chewing out Jane. Then we add some inferences, or assumptions, such as, "The boss is 'picking on' Jane." This assumption begins to feed into our belief system, and becomes a conclusion we draw based on the inferences, beliefs and feelings we may hold about how men manage women. Our conclusion is that the boss is picking on Jane because she is a woman. In the micro-moment between inference building and conclusion creation, we are being moved by deeply held emotional memories of past situations in our own life. We label the boss a typical male chauvinist who shouldn't be supervising women. We tell Jane, "You should go down to human relations and complain because your boss is a pig."

All this can happen in seconds. We say the wrong thing because we don't know everything there is to know about the situation. We have constructed it in our head because that's the way the mind operates. And we didn't construct it in terms of Jane's reality, which is that she regularly shows up late with the reports; we constructed it in terms of our reality. And then we tell Jane our reality as if it's her reality.

Our reactions to incidents like this can be based on very little information. We just don't notice. Our cognitive unconscious instantly assesses the situation, ignores the real question, "What really happened here?" and answers the easier question "How do I feel about what happened here?" It makes an intuitive judgment and communicates it as if it were an objective truth.

When we are in disagreement with another and our emotions are aroused, the process simply speeds up. In such difficult situations, the conscious mind gets recruited to provide supporting "data" for our beliefs. Then we speak/act as if:

- Our beliefs are *the* truth.
- This truth *is* obvious (or should be to anyone listening).
- Our beliefs are based on *real* data.
- The data *we select* are real data.

To these four axioms, I add one more. It is based on my observation of what people actually do in difficult situations. Like the seventh axiom in the IP model it is a pragmatic axiom that explains how people change the way they communicate at the point in a disagreement when they feel the other is being unnecessarily resistant in accepting their truths and data. At that point the sender simply stops asking any questions and will go out of their way to prevent the other from adding more information. The offended sender acts as if:

- "I have all the data I need, and your thoughts don't matter."

The Ladder in Action When We Are Confronted

The first two steps of the ladder — perception and inference — are always automatic, but the third step is instantly included when we are challenged. The conscious mind's ability to discern differences and describe reality is instantly replaced by the cognitive unconscious mind's use of shortcuts — the representative heuristic, for example — to create intuitive judgments about our reality. As this happens our thoughts are reframed. We stop using concrete and specific words and begin to use emotionally powerful and abstract descriptors. We ignore information about the current reality and use simple labels to capture and reproduce responses we've learned long ago. As our emotions become more intense, our thinking and words become more abstract. As the arrows in the diagram below indicate, each step up the ladder represents a higher level of emotional intensity — either expressed directly by the speaker or intended to be evoked in the other by the words being used and the way they are being expressed.

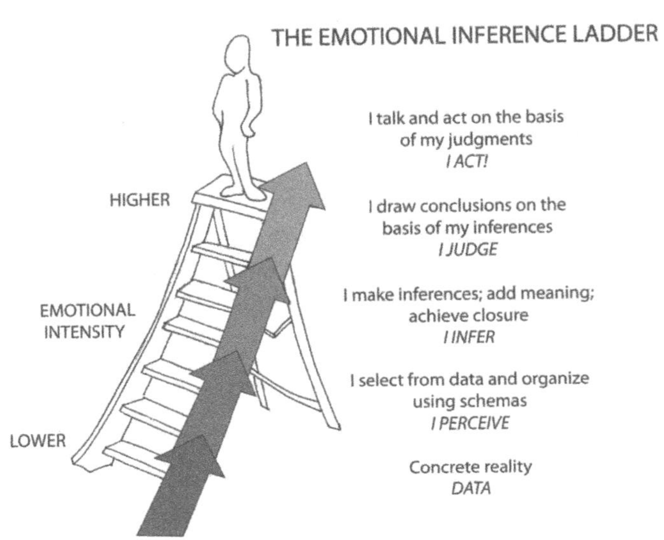

When we disagree with another person about "what's real," we are in a competition to be right (driven by axiom 7), to sustain or protect our face in the situation. Consider what's happening in this excerpt from the first half of an article by couples' therapist Jeffery Rubin[12]:

Hang Up the Gloves

I heard them yelling in the waiting room. By the time I emerged from my office to greet them several minutes later, the well-dressed couple in their early 40s were silently fuming. I introduced myself and ushered them inside. The wife, Cathy, sat on the sofa; the husband, Robert, chose a nearby chair. They glared at each other.

Without even waiting for me to ask why they'd come to see a therapist, Cathy exploded at Robert. "You're always working. You don't spend enough time at home. I feel like a work widow." First Robert seethed, then he lit into Cathy. "Nothing is ever good enough for you," he said angrily. "I'm always working because you're always spending so much money."

She came right back at him. "At least I'm at home with the family, not married to my job. I might as well be single. In fact, I am."

"Yeah, but I'm not a critical bitch who's bankrupting the family."

It was time for me to intervene. "Throw me your wallets," I said.

They looked at each other, then at me. "Hand them over." They complied, intrigued enough to call a cease-fire. I took the wallets and put them on the ottoman at my feet. "Do you enjoy throwing your money away?" I asked. They stared at me blankly.

"No," they both said.

"If you follow one principle — which I'll try my best to help you with — you'll save yourselves a lot of time, money, and tears," I said. "It's this: Be more interested in understanding your spouse than in winning. Otherwise, this process will take longer than it needs to, and you'll waste a lot of money trying to win, trying to be right. And you'll both lose. Guaranteed."

Now I had their attention.

In their competition to be "right," Robert and Cathy continually speak from the judgment level of the inference ladder. "You're always working" and "Nothing is ever good enough for you" is typical. The inference ladder clarifies the mind's response to information, particularly in situations of disagreement. It moves quickly and naturally from selected limited information to whole pictures, compelling us to speak as if our conclusions — and the emotions that drive them — are facts. And what are these "facts"? They are our feelings or emotional reactions.

As conscious communicators we need to be aware that when we talk, we're talking only about our own internal reality, not the objective facts of the reality in which we happen to be immersed. These processes are at work anytime we talk with another person; *they are simply more obvious when we are in a disagreement with them*. We need to wake up to this.

Errors in Cognition and Talk[13]

If we don't get conscious about our thinking processes, we often think and speak in error, and particularly in difficult situations, we make some common mistakes:

- ***The Uncalculated Risk***

We take the uncalculated risk when we don't know where we are on the inference ladder when we speak. We do this when we talk as if we have real information, quoting data and facts, but we are actually stating our own conclusions, judgments and beliefs. We also run the risk, once our views are questioned, of staying up the ladder and defending our conclusions, moving toward more polarized thinking, static evaluation and "allness" talk. Why? Because every label we attach to our version of reality and every conclusion we draw comes with a surge of emotional energy.

- ***Allness Talk***

When we are emotionally intense, we often speak as if what we are saying is all there is to say about a subject. We use extreme words like *always* and *never*. For instance, "You never help." "You were always a jerk." We act like we know all there is to know about someone or something. Of course, logically that couldn't be true. The reality we live in constantly changes, but the meaning of these types of words doesn't.

- ***Polarization***

When we think abstractly and quickly, we think in opposites — "all or nothing," "black and white." This encourages "Allness" talk.

- ***Indiscriminate Thought***

This is where we assume all the people in a category have identical characteristics. This is the basis for stereotyping in our speech and for what we have earlier called the intensional orientation — viewing people only in terms of the labels we give them. This leads to:

- ***Static Evaluation***

Having given someone a particular label, we don't change our descriptor when they change.

Some Guidelines to More Effective Thinking in Conversation

Every error in thinking (and talking) — particularly the error of letting our emotions drive our thinking up the inference ladder — can be avoided or mitigated through several conscious choices. When discussions get heated, we need to wake up and remember that what our mind does in the first two or three steps of the inference ladder is done by the cognitive unconscious. It evokes a schema — provides information to us — but only *from within* us. It's not about external reality but only about our schematic view of reality. We need to use information we can share with the other.

Getting Conscious: Talking Ourselves Down the Ladder

To become more effective communicators, we can consciously talk ourselves (and the other person) back down the inference ladder. We can reconstruct our mutual reality by making our own thinking processes — and the other's — a part of the data that's being exchanged to deal with or resolve the issue before us. Rather than simply "talking in conclusions" and assuming we have all the facts, we need to add new facts to the flow — the facts about how we seemed to reach our conclusions; how we saw the issue in the first place; what data we selected; what assumptions we must have made on the way to making up our minds. In addition, we need to ask the other questions that encourage them to put these same aspects of their thinking onto the table. In Chapter 8 we will call this kind of talk *metacommunication* — talk about our talk. Only when we do this will we find out whether we are actually discussing the same thing. Many times we're not, and that's why the discussion is so difficult in the first place. The following list provides more detail on this process.

Talking Ourselves Back Down the Inference Ladder

1. Slow down our reactions — get conscious and think before we speak.
2. Make our perceptions and thoughts more conscious to ourselves, and others, by describing what we think we saw and heard in the situation. In a struggle over "the truth" of a situation:
    a. "Look, these are the facts as I see them. . . ."
    b. "This is the way it looks to me."
3. Describe to others (and ourselves) the assumptions and inferences we must have made that led to the judgments and conclusions we just uttered.
    a. "I assumed that. . . ."
    b. "I came to this conclusion because. . . ."
4. Avoid speaking in sweeping generalities (indiscriminate, polarizing, "allness" statements), and as if our words were the "capital T, Truth."
5. Ask others for their reactions to the same information to find out if we are talking about the same things.
    a. "I see things this way, but how does it look to you?"
    b. "Are we talking about the same thing, here?"
6. Ask them to describe the thinking behind their words — how they reached their conclusions — and take the time to really listen to what they have to say.
    a. "What caused you to say that?"
    b. "Are we looking at different things here?"

In Conclusion

It's important to understand how our mind manages the enormous amount of information our senses receive every second we are alive. Using concepts from the IP model, the encoding-decoding processes of our mind seem to operate to keep the work the mind has to do to understand the world around it down to minimum. The key operating principles of our perception and cognition in everyday talk are focused on creating quick, automatic certainty in our responses to what is essentially an uncertain world.

What happens is that in most situations our cognitive unconscious automatically runs up the inference ladder. As millions of bits of data pour in, we unthinkingly use schemas (organizing rules and pre-learned categories) to leave out most of the information coming into our mind and instantly organize what's left into patterns our mind recognizes. Within the next eyeblink, we positively or negatively label (evaluate or judge) our inventions and then use this as a basis for action and talk in the "real world." This works to make much of our talk smooth and effortless. This judging process works even faster when we suddenly find ourselves in a 3 D situation where our emotions are aroused and not only our words but also our self is suddenly on the line.

Where We're Going Next

In the past three chapters we have reviewed the key processes of the conscious mind separately to clarify their operations but, of course, they don't work separately in our lives. In reality, they operate in a fully integrated way through a unique collection of perceptions, beliefs and feelings called the self. In the next chapter we are going to review how we develop our unique sense of self.

End Notes

[1] The cognition section of this chapter integrates key concepts from Fisher, D. (1981) *Communication in Organizations*. St. Paul, MN: West Publishing Company; and DeVito, J. (1992) *The Interpersonal Communication Book* (6th ed.). New York: HarperCollins.

[2] Kahneman, D. (2011) *Thinking Fast and Slow.* New York: Penguin Group.

[3] Kahneman, p. 13.

[4] Chabris, C., Simons, D. (2011) *The Invisible Gorilla: How Our Intuitions Deceive Us.* New York: Three Rivers Press.

[5] Kahneman, p. 86.

[6] Aronson, E., Wilson, T. et al. (2010). *Social Psychology* (4th Canadian ed.). Upper Saddle River, NJ: Pearson Education, p. 76.

---

[7] Halliman, J. (2009) *Why We Make Mistakes: How We Look Without Seeing, Forget Things in Seconds, and Are All Pretty Sure We Are Way Above Average.* New York: Broadway Books.
[8] Kahneman, p. 97.
[9] See DeVito, J. *Messages: Building Interpersonal Communication Skills* (5th ed.). Boston: Allyn and Bacon, 2002.
[10] DeVito, J. (2004) *The Interpersonal Communication Book.* Boston: Pearson Education, p. 161.
[11] Senge, P. et al. (1994) *The Fifth Discipline Fieldbook: Strategies and Tools for Building a Learning Organization.* New York: Bantam Doubleday Dell Publishing Group.
[12] Excerpted from Rubin, J. "Hang Up the Gloves," *O Magazine*, August, 2004.
[13] The concepts in this section on errors in thinking and talking have been taken from Fisher, *Communication in Organizations*; and DeVito (2004) *The Interpersonal Communication Book.*

CHAPTER SEVEN

THE SELF IN COMMUNICATION

Aspects of the Self: Personality, the Self-Concept and Self-Esteem

In the previous chapters we talked about the mind's emotional, perceptual and cognitive processes. We need to know how these processes operate in a general way in order to understand how all of us make sense of our inner and outer worlds. To understand how each individual notices different things in the same situation, or thinks about the same things differently and reacts uniquely, requires that we also understand the "operating system" that energizes these mental functions. We need to recognize that intimate collection of perceptions, cognitions and emotions we develop called the "self."

Everything that is in our life and everything that comes into our life is processed through this unique system. Until we have some understanding about how the self works, we won't understand how we each react to life uniquely — differently than other "selves" out there — using the same three mental processes. Ultimately, we need to understand the nature of our selves so we can anticipate our reactions to others and learn how to manage them to become more effective as communicators in a variety of situations. The self can be understood from three different perspectives: (1) the foundational personality, (2) the developed and slowly changing self-concept, and (3) the worth that each of us places on our self-concept — our self-esteem.

Personality

As the foundation of our sense of self, **personality** is broadly defined as an enduring set of characteristics — needs, perceptions and emotional reactions — which each of us can call "me." These characteristics emerge out of a combination of our biochemical inheritance from our parents and the families they represent. This inheritance defines our individual temperament — our unique pattern of energy, responsiveness to external stimuli, emotional reactivity. Our temperament shapes a good deal of how we connect to and communicate with other people and is something we can analyze in order to learn how we understand and talk to the world we encounter.

When we are born, our brain already comes with a series of biochemical predilections that shape the degree and quality of our engagement with the world around us. One look at newborns in a hospital nursery shows the differences almost immediately. Some will be placidly sleeping after having the most extraordinary and traumatic experience they are ever going to have in their whole life. Others will be crying or squirming, while still others are lying perfectly still with their eyes wide open, taking it all in. Our unique biological inheritance, and the effects that the immediate environment has on that biochemistry, contribute over time to our deepest sense of who we are. We've been aware of this for over a century, but our theories of how this all works to shape our individual patterns of behavior have undergone some notable changes over the years.

Freud's Unconscious and the Cognitive Unconscious

In many respects current theories of personality began with Freud's late 19th century ideas of personality, including his breakthrough concept of the **unconscious mind**. While his concepts remain current in some parts of the therapeutic community today (and have rooted themselves firmly in the vocabulary of popular culture), the newest model of our deep self is gaining considerable scientific interest and is built around the idea of the cognitive unconscious. Wilson[1] compares them as follows, beginning with a summary of Freud's concept of the personality as a product of the struggle between the conscious mind and the uncontrolled drives of the unconscious:

> [T]he defining feature of personality is how people deal with their repressed drives, such as sexual and aggressive impulses. The battles, compromises and truces among the id, ego and superego define who we are."

On the other hand, he argues, the cognitive unconscious is a set of deeply programmed, uniquely individual thinking and feeling processes, not accessible from the conscious mind (i.e., "talk therapy" won't change them), that shape how people construe situations. And he notes that the cognitive unconscious "has distinctive ways of interpreting the social environment and stable motives that guide people's behavior." In addition, he states that these dispositions (inclinations to see things in particular ways) are measurable — unlike Freud's concepts — using indirect means; are determined in part by genetics and by early childhood experience; and are not easily changed. Wilson also argues that the cognitive unconscious is outside the direct access of the conscious mind and can be measured using indirect means.

An Intermediate View of Personality

Like his early mentor, Freud, Carl Jung conceived of personality as a balance of forces within each developing child between the demands for immediate satisfaction of unconscious needs (Freud's concept of the Id) and the limitations on behavior represented in the Superego (the demands of the larger culture mediated through the parents). This balance is maintained by the Ego — the conscious "manager" of our personality. Unlike Freud, however, Jung put more emphasis on both unconscious and conscious "cognitive and affective" operations of the Ego; that is, on what we *can* manage, what we *can* know, what we can do about it. While Freud focused on the unconscious and on how all our uncontrolled drives and needs get in the way of our becoming well-adjusted people (leaving us to struggle with guilt and anxiety), Jung put more emphasis on human learning and effectiveness rather than our neurotic darkness.

He argued that the relationship between the unconscious and the conscious is a positive one and that the unconscious is a reservoir of those aspects of ourselves, and the larger society of which we are part, that we can call upon to become effective *once we are aware of them*. Although he framed the operations of the Ego in ways that reflect our current idea of the cognitive unconscious, unlike today's theorists, Jung thought humans could become conscious of the surface levels of the unconscious if they were asked questions that were very indirect in their phrasing, and whose connections to the deeper processes of the mind they couldn't guess ahead of time.

In the end, we may not be able to articulate the deepest part of the self in detail, but by using psychological inventories based on Jung's work, like the Myers-Briggs Type Indicator, we can bypass the filters of our self-perception and, at some level, understand how the personality operates and affects our behavior.

Myers-Briggs Type Indicator

The **Myers-Briggs Type Indicator** (MBTI) is a personality preference inventory that helps individuals distinguish how their personality may be the same as or different from somebody else's. The theoretical model that supports the MBTI suggests that when we are born, we inherit a biochemical reservoir of energy from both of our parents that, at first, we have no control over. This energy flows out of us, and we "call out" to others through our behavior while those around us respond to these "calls." The developing conscious sense of self — the Ego — in turn, reacts to their reactions, and so it goes.

For example, a child with an inherited temperament based on high energy and activity levels, will likely be responded to differently by parents who are soft-spoken and deliberate in their reactions than those who are energetic and spontaneous in their responses to the world. From Jung's point of view, what emerges through the differences in these two versions of the **call-and-response effect** is not mental health in one case and neurosis in the other, but uniqueness in both cases. Each child, although beginning with the same general kind of physical inheritance, will develop as a unique assemblage of biochemical and experiential differences — preferences — in the way their mind functions.

The difference between measuring uniqueness versus measuring one's degree of mental health is important to remember. The MBTI focuses on clarifying the combination of nonconscious cognitive and affective processes an individual can have but, unlike every other form of psychological inventory, *does not* evaluate an individual in terms of his or her mental health just because their inventory choices represent a particular combination or *type*. All combinations are functional and healthy, just different.

The MBTI focuses on personality differences by describing the psychological functions of the Ego. These functions represent the ways our mind processes information both from within us and from the world around us. In fact, Jung's emphasis on the personality as an information-processing system seems perfect for a communication-theory approach to personality. Jung, and later Myers and Briggs, argued that our mental functions could be analyzed along four dimensions:

1) **Extroversion (E)–Introversion (I)**: the source and direction of an individual's search for information and energy expression
2) **Sensing (S)–Intuition (N)**: how an individual perceives information
3) **Thinking (T)–Feeling (F)**: how an individual processes that information
4) **Judging (J)–Perceiving (P)**: how an individual uses the information they have processed to deal with the world around them.

When these four dimensions are combined, sixteen personality types are generated, each of them representing unique but effective ways of engaging the world.

Self-Concept

The next facet of our sense of self is our **self-concept**. Our self-concept is constructed as we learn the language of our society. Some time between the second and third years of our life, we learn to name things, including our feelings and reactions to those aspects of our behavior that seem to make us distinct, and separate us from others in the world. This becomes our self-concept. It is a set of self-referring beliefs and attitudes, statements that begin with the words "I am." The self is, in fact, the story we tell ourselves about our self.

In analyzing this aspect of how we know who we are, Wilson[2] argues that since people don't have direct, word-based access to many of the traits, dispositions and temperaments that make up the personality, they

> are forced to construct theories about their own personalities from other sources, such as what they learn from their parents, their culture, and yes, ideas about who they prefer to be. These constructions may be driven less by repression and the desire to avoid anxiety than by the simple need to construct a coherent narrative about ourselves, in the absence of any direct access to our non-conscious personalities . . .

> [however] people often construct narratives that correspond poorly to their non-conscious dispositions and abilities.

Although criticizing Freud's model of personality in this statement, Wilson admits what Freud calls "the defense mechanisms" and what I will call "defensive talk" back into his assertions about the importance of the cognitive unconscious in our daily interaction. Our sense of self may just be a story built up out of our ongoing conversations with the world, but we act if we desperately need a coherent and plausible story about who we are, just to feel sane. As we gain more experience, the narrative of our self will change gradually and we will de-emphasize some past "me," with its associated behaviors, and slowly integrate new experiences into our sense of self. If, on the other hand, life directly challenges our story, we automatically fight to retain the coherence of our narrative — we defend our selves.

Our Self-Concept as "I and Me"[3]

At the beginning of the 20th century, George Herbert Mead developed a model of the self, constructed out of two perspectives — the "I" and the "Me" — which represent something more than inherited traits and early developmental experiences. His model of the self focuses on an internal dialogue between two perspectives that develop out of the changing communication relationship between our self and the rest of the world as we grow. In Mead's model of the self, the "I" represents the spontaneous and creative side of our personality; it responds to inner needs and is more concerned about getting what it wants as opposed to responding to the needs of others or to social norms. This is akin to Freud's Id, except the process is not unconscious. The "I" is consciously self-centered, demanding; it doesn't care much about the rest of the world and it cries to get what it wants.

Mead's Three Stages of Self-Development

Mead argued that the spontaneous need fulfillment of the "I" is managed through the other side of the self — the "Me." His argument was that within the first two years of life, we begin to import the rules of the world into our mind. This **first (imitative) stage** of the "Me" emerges as the child imitates others' behaviors and is rewarded and punished for its efforts, but truly develops when the child acquires language — at around 3 years of age. After this point, the **second (play) stage** emerges. The child can remember and mentally re-enact its own and another's behavior. When the "I" wants something, the child can run the movie in their head of what might happen before acting it out. Mead calls this "taking the role of the other." By practicing this internal skill in the playing of simple children's games with few guiding rules, the child can put itself in another's shoes (the significant other), watch its possible reactions in its head before behaving, and, as a result, manage the spontaneous "I."

Mead then argued that, within a few years, children enter the **third (game) stage** of self-development when they learn to play more complicated, rule-driven games. At this level of play, the child learns that general social rules (the "generalized other" — that is, beyond those of family members and friends) must be taken into account when managing their behavior. Essentially, the child's "Me" becomes a repository of social role learning — the social self. As pointed out in the chapter on culture, the norms attached to social positions help us learn the larger value demands of our society.

Throughout our life, there is a constant tension between the spontaneous demands ("I want what I want when I want it") of the "I," and constraints of the social self — the "Me" ("Do what's appropriate or right, not just what you want"). It's this tension that we face when we ask ourselves, when remembering something we did: "Why did I do that?" The "I" and "Me" are the two different perspectives on (or sides of) the self that we appear to be every day in our inner dialogue.

Keeping Our Story Straight

It is clear that our self-concept is established through sustained communication relationships with other people. And as we said earlier, while we hang on to a core of stable beliefs about the way we "really" are at one level, we are slowly changing the way we see ourselves at another. To manage this paradoxical complexity, and to maintain a coherent narrative of our selves over time, we regularly deceive ourselves about, or simply refuse to notice, the changes as they accumulate.

Some levels of the self-concept change more easily than others. Clearly the "Me" – built on the social roles we play and the identities they provide us – changes throughout our life. And while these changes are fairly quickly integrated into our sense of self, our deeper personality needs for affection, control and connection with others seem more constant and unchangeable.

Social (Cultural) Identities

As part of our self-concept, we have **social identities** that are given to us by others, based on the family we are born into (ethnicity, language and religious community), where we come from (neighborhood, class background), as well as those created by us in terms of the folkways we choose to enact (the style of clothing we wear, music we listen to, people we hang out with). We also live in a media-rich environment. The media, written, oral and audio/visual — particularly television, fills our life with identity messages about how we ought to be, or at least how people who look like us or act like us ought to be. Also, whether we choose them or they are imposed on us, some identities may not fit well with our internally generated story of self. This can lead to considerable psychic conflict.

Situated Identities

At the same time that we are playing various roles (and enacting social identities), we're also presenting different aspects of ourselves to the people we are "playing" with. We manage the public facet of our inner selves — our **situated identity**. For example, when we get that first job interview, we play the role of the ideal employee-to-be. We think of what it is that this employer is looking for, and we enact it — we take off the nose ring and torn jeans; we speak and act differently. We base our choices on a stable sense of self — "I am a good person, hardworking, dependable, trustworthy and kind; I am also a wild party animal on Friday nights; I go to church on Sunday; and I'm very polite" — but we only show the aspects of our self that are required in a given situation. We manage our self-presentation in the moment. This is our "situated identity."

Conversational Identities: Face[4]

Within every moment of managing our "situated identity" in face-to-face conversation, we are presenting a conversational "**face**." In face-to-face conversation, our nonverbal and verbal acts *are* the way people see us. We express ourselves through those acts toward others in the situation. We also react emotionally to our own performances. We can't be free from our words because whatever direction they take us (our conversational "line"), it represents us — our identity in that conversational moment — our conversational "face."

Self-Monitoring

Because we can name our "selves," we can see ourselves as objects and monitor ourselves. As part of this self-monitoring process, we can also, as stated above, "take the role of the other" in our everyday conversations — and adjust our behavior accordingly. We are constantly trying to figure out what the consequences of our actions might be, and monitoring the outcomes of what we do. As in every other facet of life, however, some people seem to be more attentive or effective self-monitors than others.

Self-Esteem

The third element of the self — **self-esteem** — refers to how we evaluate ourselves. We mentioned the key questions that underlie our sense of self-esteem in Chapter 1. They are part of an insightful and practical model of self-esteem authored by Stephen Glenn, clinical psychologist, who focused his career on the positive development of young people. He argued that our self-esteem is based on how we hold three vital beliefs[5]:

- "My life is significant: there are places outside of my self where I am of value."
- "I am a capable person: I can learn and do things when I need to."
- "I am influential: although I can't always control what happens to me, I can always determine how I let life affect me. There is much I can do to shape my life."

He also argues, "That's not how we're born: we're born powerless, with no sense of who we are, and totally at the mercy of the others in our world who take care of us. And the sooner we emerge out of that, the more of our potential we can realize."

Of course, there is nothing neutral about our self-monitoring process. As we watch ourselves and watch other people watching us, we judge ourselves against these beliefs about ourselves and our conclusions are energized by our emotions. Our sense of self-esteem at a particular time could be seen as a sum of the "emotional ratings" we give ourselves in response to Glenn's three key questions:

1) Do I matter?
2) Am I competent?
3) Can I influence my life?

The importance of getting positive answers to these three questions was demonstrated in the results of an experiment by Langer and Rodin.[6] Benefits were given to two floors of a nursing home for the aged, including live plants in their rooms and a movie screening once a week. On one of the floors, the nurses chose the plants, watered them and decided which night the movie would be. On the other, the patients were allowed to choose their own plants and were responsible for watering them. They were also responsible for deciding which night they would screen a movie.

Having choices made a huge difference. Where residents had increased control, they were happier, more active and alert. These changes were still visible 18 months later, but more dramatically, these folks were measurably healthier and had *half as many deaths* as those whose environmental improvements were controlled by the nurses. Being treated as if they mattered; were competent enough to manage the changes and, as a result, had influence over their situations, actually extended their lives. Positive answers to these questions *do* make a difference in people's lives.

These three questions are the key components of the larger life question that, we argued in Chapter 1, underlies every conversation: "Who am I to you (and you to me)?" We are always trying to find out how we are going to be treated by the other, because the potential for being treated badly — as if we don't matter (others ignore us or our words); we aren't capable (others are condescending or contemptuous of us), or we have no influence (it's their way or the highway) — can drive us to protect and defend ourselves in everyday talk. We live in a world of reflective appraisal (the "looking glass" self). How other people see us affects how we see ourselves. We are always comparing ourselves to others, both real (those we know directly) and virtual (those presented to us as ideals through the media). When we are directly interacting with another, we can't help but infer their evaluations of us from their behavior toward us.

Perception, Cognition and the Self

In terms of how we see, think and feel about ourselves, our mind works for us in the same way it does when responding to the external world. It is highly selective. Seeking to create a stable, but gradually changing, narrative of self over time, we strive to create consistent connections between our sense of our self and our perceptions of the world around us.

Perception: Self-Fulfilling Prophecy

Our self-perception operates exactly the way our other-perception does. We focus on consistency and stability. For example, we use **self-fulfilling prophecy** to tell ourselves we can or can't do some things and we act accordingly. If we see ourselves as slightly depressed and highly dependent, then we behave in those ways and life passes us by and reinforces our belief. When we suddenly get it right or we achieve something we didn't expect we would achieve, we say, "I was just lucky. I just happened to be in the right place at the right time, and it will probably never happen again."

Perception: Perceptual Accentuation

We also use **perceptual accentuation** — we look at those things in us that we want to see and that we expect to see and we remember them, while we ignore or deny the things that we don't expect to see, that don't fit with a consistent and stable self-image. It's our cognitive unconscious acting like our "hired gun lawyer."

Perception: Attribution Bias

We use the **attribution bias** to ensure that we keep everything in place. If something happens that fits with our self-concept, we take credit for it. If something happens that doesn't fit we say, "I had to do it. In the situation, I had no other choice."

Cognition: Labeling

We **label** ourselves; we name key elements of ourselves in the same way we name the elements in our cognitions of other people. We identify other people as "good friend," "terrific person," "really love her," or "really hate her." We name "our selves" in exactly the same way.

Labeling and "Allness"

We use the same language when we are talking about ourselves as we might use for other people, particularly when we are either very excited or very angry. We often speak in **allness** terms about ourselves: "I never do this." "I always do that!"

Cognition: Static Evaluation

As with our perceptions of others, when it comes to who we *really* are, we see ourselves as a coherent whole — often as a static picture. Realistically, as we gain new experiences, our self-concept should change, but we often don't notice changes, so we can continue to tell ourselves: "This is the way I am." Such inner talk may make us feel sane and stable, but it can set us up for some surprises and problems when we interact with others.

The Self as Communication Filter

The self is the anchor for all our judgments. It's the place we go to when we decide what's real, right or wrong, clever or just plain dumb. We measure all these things through the construction in our head called "my self." It contains all our anchoring attitudes. We never approach the world neutrally. We never see the world as it is; we see the world as we are.

Having a stable sense of self is so important to having a stable sense of outer reality that we cannot easily recognize (or accept) reality if our perceptions, thoughts and feelings about ourselves are challenged by the world. When this does happen, we most often choose to ignore or distort these challenges rather than learn from them. We automatically channel our emotional energies into defense. Next, we will explore how this emotional self-defense system works and how we communicate to get the emotional support we need, despite its distorting effects on our perceptions of the world we inhabit.

Self-Defense, Games and Self-Talk in Communication

Our sense of self and the presentation of aspects of ourselves to others during conversation — our "face" and situational identity — are infused with emotional energy. We don't just communicate with words and gestures about topics of conversation, we communicate our feelings about them, about ourselves, and about the others involved in the conversation. We can't help engaging in this type of emotional communication and in picking up emotional feedback signals from others about us. It happens automatically.

As pointed out in Chapter 5 on perception, we seem to be driven by a need for **consistency**, that is, we need to be treated by the world in ways that are consistent with our sense of self. If this doesn't occur, the emotional aspect of our self-concept — our self-esteem — will be threatened. Such a threat is felt as a kind of "psychic pain," which Freud called anxiety. Fundamentally, we are anxiety avoiders. Moreover, this need to maintain internal and external consistency for our self-concept and support for our self-esteem is so strong that when our perceptions, thoughts and feelings about ourselves are challenged by the behavior and emotional reactions of others, our cognitive unconscious takes over and automatically provides us judgments that permit the conscious mind to ignore or distort these challenges rather than learn from them. When faced with contradiction, our automatic response is to channel our emotional energies into self-defense. This suggests that we often don't "live in the real world" but only in the world that we create to sustain a consistent set of feelings about ourselves.

Avoiding Anxiety: Defending Ourselves Against Reality

In the following section, we will explore how our emotional self-defense system works: how we automatically communicate to get the emotional support we need because of its distorting effects on our perceptions of the world, and, more importantly, how we can become more conscious of our emotional reactions and manage our communication responses in a challenging world.

Freud and the Defenses

In his work, Freud was struck by how much suffering seemed to be caused by his patients' inability or unwillingness to accept some of the realities of their lives. He noted how they had unconsciously developed ways of not seeing what was really happening. He called these mental processes "**defenses**." They had developed a variety of automatic thoughts and verbal responses to questions that permitted them to avoid dealing with painful realities and fabricate "reasons" to explain why they didn't have to, or couldn't, change their behavior.

Communicating Around Our Anxiety and Guilt[7]

We use all of our defenses as a way of reducing anxiety by distorting our perception of reality. In the short run they can be valuable in helping us manage sudden life crises or deal with irresolvable conflicts, by giving us time to work things through.

Everyday Defense Mechanisms

- **Denial** — prevents us perceiving threatening events or behavior. It can temporarily reduce stress. "It's not happening to me."
- **Avoidance** — we simply stay away from situations or people that will trigger anxiety. "I'm not going there."
- **Rationalization** — we come up with reasons to explain away our fears — excuses. "It's not my fault."
- **Intellectualization** — we use more complex, detached analysis to avoid feelings that threaten us. "The world is going to hell, not me."
- **Projection** — allows us to attribute our own feelings to others. We avoid taking responsibility for our feelings. "You made me."

Defenses become dangerous when we use them like drugs — too often, for too long — and we become dependent on them for our reality. The trouble is that when we try to defeat reality, reality always wins and when we overuse the defense mechanisms to distort reality in our everyday talk, we undermine the possibility of ever reducing our uncertainty about what's going on, who we are to each other in that moment, and what's going to happen next.

The problem with talk is that it is fluid and changing and doesn't always provide the answers we want. To make things even trickier, others are using *their* defenses to deal with any of our responses that can generate anxiety, while we are using *ours* to do the same thing. Furthermore, our cognitive unconscious is always "on" — looking out for any hint of anxiety-inducing change — and our self-feedback loops are constantly working to help us adjust our talk to any perceived changes. Even in our best moments, talk can be an emotionally risky business. So, how do we manage to get around all of this risky uncertainty? If we were trying to be "real" all the time, we would constantly have to deal with our anxieties; so we manage everyday talk by using a different kind of communication.

Defensive Communication

Originally developed as an approach to therapy, **Transactional Analysis** (TA) is built on a model of internal emotional states and interpersonal communication. It looks at the connections between what is going on inside of us emotionally and what comes out of our mouth and is displayed in our nonverbal behaviors. TA essentially provides a model of defensive communication — insight into how we are able to communicate every day without necessarily being authentic, that is, really being ourselves, and telling our truth honestly while accepting others' truth in the same way (even when we don't believe what we're hearing). TA shows how we can be defensive and still have a "good" conversation.

Transactional Analysis (TA)

TA was made popular in the early 1970s in a series of best-selling books by psychotherapist Eric Berne.[8] He promoted TA as a way to improve communication through better understanding of the relationship between our internal emotional states (ego states) and our behavior toward others (transactions). TA also considers the ways in which people pass their time (time structuring) in what we will call "C.O.N.N.E.C.T. talk," and the interpersonal communication roles people learn to play over and over again, as scripts in their lives. The reason that I'm reviewing this model is because it is an easy and memorable way for people to look at their emotional expression. In Chapter 4, we asked you to think about and name your emotions and then talk about them. This is easiest to do before we talk. What TA does is allow you to "hear" your emotions *while you're talking*. Each of the Ego states about to be described has their own vocabulary and paralanguage. I have found that people can quickly learn to accurately assess each ego state and the emotions it entails. They get conscious about what their emotions sound like when they hear them through the model of Berne's ego states.

The Ego States

According to Berne, an **ego state** is "a consistent pattern of feeling and experience related to a consistent pattern of behavior."[9] An ego state cannot be directly observed but can be inferred from a person's behavior. Perhaps unsurprisingly, Berne's model echoes Freud's three-level model of the mind. Unlike Freud, however, Berne was not interested in exploring the unconscious urges of the Id, using the specialized approaches of a psychoanalyst, but rather in providing an easily understood method for people to discover the overlearned behavioral habits of their childhood, which reside below the level of consciousness but show themselves through the operations of the conscious self — which he calls the ego.

Parent Ego State

Berne's argument is that we don't have to be a **parent** to have this ego state. We only have to have had a parent. As Mead argued, somewhere between the 24th and 36th month, the child literally incorporates the voice and behavior of the parent into its mental state in order to take the role of those significant others so that it can manage its own behavior. It becomes the home of all the **rules** — the "shoulds" and "oughts" we learn as we grow.

The Ego States: A Model of the Emotional Mind

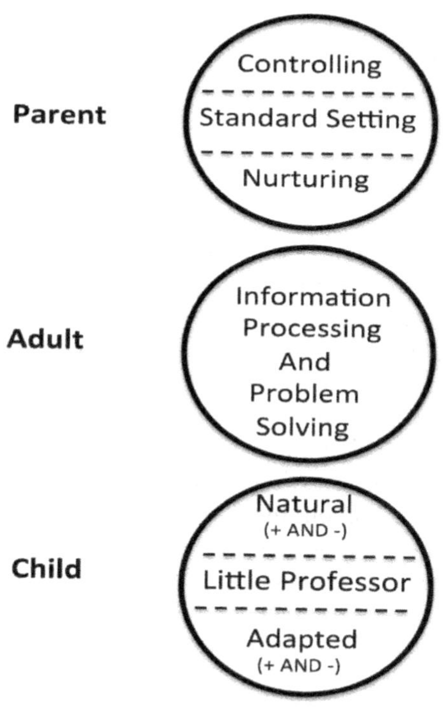

In the Parent state a person acts and sounds parental — setting standards, making moral judgments, controlling, or being comforting and nurturing. As indicated in the diagram above, these different modes within the Parent have open boundaries between them, represented by the dotted lines. Nurturing parents can also sound controlling.

The Parent ego tends to speak in three types of voices:

- **Controlling** parent — this is the one that tells us what to do, when to do it, how to do it, how we ought to be.
- **Nurturing** parent — the opposite side of the controlling parent tells us that they love us, they think we're wonderful, we're the best thing that ever happened to them. They support us and make us feel good.
- **Standard setting** (coaching) parent — this is the instructive parent who says, "Good boy, try again," and "Good girl, I'm sure you can make it."

Child Ego State

The Child ego state comes from having been a child. From the **natural child** we get all our spontaneous energy, our humor, our creativity and fun. This is the part of us that laughs, and runs and plays and jokes — the part where all that good energy comes from. The flip side of all this positive energy, however, is something negative. The natural child is where rebellion comes from. It's where the child who throws a tantrum and says, "You are not the boss of me" comes from. This is the home of teenage rebellion.

There is also an aspect of this state called the **adapted child**. This is the child without which no society could operate. This is the child who happily follows the rules, shows up for school every day and pays attention. This child takes orders, obeys. That's the positive side. The negative side of the adapted child is also the whiny child.

In the middle of this state is the **little professor** child who seeks attention by telling you everything they know, even if they are not asked (whether they are two or fifty-two years old).

Adult Ego State

The **Adult** ego state is the one that we use when we are trying to deal with what's real in the moment — being rational and thoughtful information gatherers trying to find out what's going on. It also acts as a mediator between the demands and judgments of the Parent and the wants and fantasies of the Child. The Adult is the ego state that asks good questions and rationally connects the information from the present world with that found in the other two ego states. It is the voice that describes without prejudice or judgment. We use the Adult problem-solving voice when we get together with friends and say, "How are we going to do this?" This is Adult problem solving without which we couldn't manage the world at all.

The ego states represent the "emotional positions" we take in every discussion. Our emotions are communicated through our nonverbals while we are talking. As we said earlier, we learn packages of words and nonverbal behavior to help us create, sustain and manage meaning with others. The table on the next page lists the common word choices, vocal tone and nonverbal gestures that cue us to the ego state a person is reacting from while we are talking with them.

Typical Behaviors Associated with Each Ego State[10]

Ego State	Common Verbal Expressions	Characteristic Voice Patterns	Body Language Clues
Critical Parent	That's nice, bad That's cute, good You should You ought You never Be quiet, good Don't you Ridiculous You must	Judgmental Admonishing Critical Condescending Loud Disgusted, sneering Scheming Comparing Demanding	Points or wags finger Frowns, squints Feet apart, hands on hips Slaps, spanks Serious looking Arms crossed, closed posture Foot tapping Looks up in disgust Pounds table
Nurturing Parent	Uses words that are Reassuring Comforting Consoling Loving Supporting	Soft Concerned Soothing Encouraging Sympathetic	Arms open Palms outward Holds hands Hugs, holds, kisses Cradles Smiles, touches, strokes, nods approvingly
Adult	Asks questions: How What Where Who Why It seems to me Let's see what we find The solution is I wonder	Modulated Appropriate Corresponds to feelings Controlled, calm Straight Confident Nonjudgmental	Relaxed Stroking the chin Finger pointing to head Looks up (as if in search of answers) Brow wrinkles when thinking Supporting head with hands Attentive
Natural Child	I wish I want I hope I can't I won't Wow Gee, Whoopee	Loud or quiet, depending on mood Laughs Cries Rages Giggles	Showing off Rolls, tumbles Walks freely, easily Posture open, ready to swing into action Flops easily and comfortably on chair or floor Skips
Adapted Child	Compliant words Yes, OK You're right I'll do it I'm wrong Defiant, rebellious No, Make me I won't I don't care Other expressions: Help me It's your fault	Annoying Placating Repetitive Sweet Angry Defiant Loud or soft Total silence	Showing off Pouting Fights aggressively Withdraws timidly Chip on shoulder or Passive conformity Teary-eyed Looks innocent

Transactions

The predictive power of the TA model of communication lies in a fundamental axiom: *how* we say what we're saying (vocal tone, facial and bodily gestures) not only communicates our emotional state to another, but also *automatically evokes* an emotional response to us in the other. Any interaction between people can be seen as a transaction in emotions between their ego states. What matters is which emotions are being evoked in the moment.

Time Structuring

According to Eric Berne, there are six different ways people can allocate or "structure" their time: withdrawal, activities, rituals, pastimes, authenticity and games.

Withdrawal means avoiding other people either physically or perhaps psychologically, such as by daydreaming, for example. *Activities* center on things that realistically have to be done: work or caring for a family. *Rituals* are patterned, low-content transactions, such as, "How are you?" "Fine, and yourself?" *Pastimes* are ways of occupying longer periods of time, by simple information and opinion exchanges ("Ever been to . . . ?") or by gossiping — a common game called "Ain't It Awful." This exchange is intended to be complementary and the mutually expressed emotions usually come out of the critical parent ego state ("kids today . . ." or "the world today . . .") or the child ("you can't trust anyone . . ."). In fact, research on how people sustain their relationships indicates that regularly "trashing" a third party is a common way of keeping people connected.[11]

Authenticity means open, genuine sharing of thoughts and feelings with one another. Since authenticity usually involves taking risks, people tend to avoid it by engaging in withdrawal, activities, rituals or pastimes, or by the more insidious method of playing games.

Games

Berne argued that all recurring transactions between people can be categorized as (1) complementary — the first speaker's ego state emotions evoke the same state in another as in the pastime exchanges mentioned above; (2) crossed — where one person is speaking from the Adult ego state while the other unconsciously replies from either the Parent or Child ego state; or (3) ulterior — where the surface transaction seems to be Adult to Adult but beneath the surface the complementary Parent-to-Child emotions are at work. He calls these "games." They represent the most intriguing and potentially most destructive ways we have of structuring our conversations and time together.

Berne identified a variety games that are played from different ego states. For instance, a classic game is played by people with formal power in a situation — bosses and subordinates, for example. It's called "**Yes, But**." The boss begins a conversation in what sounds like the Adult ego state seeking a complementary response. The exchange typically begins with three phrases: "There is a problem. . . . I need your input . . . because. . . ." These are among the most powerful words for engaging others in conversation. But, as subordinates make suggestions each is met with a critical "Yes, but" from the boss, who argues that each new idea is unacceptable. On the surface, this appears to be an Adult-Adult exchange, but when bosses never accept any suggestions and subordinates run out of ideas, they win the game, having proved how much smarter they are than their staff, and maintaining their personal (parental) power over them.

This game can also be played from the position of the adapted child ego state. This is played between equals. What appears to be another Adult-Adult exchange is really a game because the help seeker always has a "Yes but I can't do that" for every suggestion offered. They really don't want help. Their payoff is that their "whiny" child gets attention. We have all seen such "game playing" in our lives.

In theory, games can easily be stopped if either party refuses to "play." This is easier to say than to do, however, since the games people play are related to their fundamental ways of experiencing themselves and others. Berne refers to those basic ways of experiencing as "scripts," because they serve as the basis for interpersonal roles that people play on a recurring basis.

Scripts

Scripts represent, in a sense, a programming of a person's behavior. The script develops out of a person's previous experiences in interaction with other people. Childhood experiences exert a strong influence in forming a script for an individual. A person who, as a child, was repeatedly told, "You'll never amount to anything" is likely to relate to people differently than one who was told, "You'll be a success." In general, scripts fall into four different categories, depending on the basic view the individual has toward self and toward others.

1) ***I'm Not OK, You're OK***

   In this class of scripts, individuals see others as being well adjusted and effective but sees themselves as inadequate. These people feel powerless compared to others, and tend to withdraw or become dependent on others.

2) ***I'm Not OK, You're Not OK***

   People with this perspective think poorly of themselves as well as of other people. To them, nothing seems worthwhile. They tend to put down both themselves and others. Attempts to support or help them are usually met with refusal, since the would-be helper is seen as "not OK."

3) ***I'm OK, You're Not OK***

Here the person looks positively upon themselves but sees others negatively. This is a position of distrust, suspicion, even contempt. This person finds fault with others and pushes them away but when close relationships are sometimes formed, the script then turns out to be, "Come close so I can let you have it."

4) ***I'm OK, You're OK***

This is the perspective of a person who is potentially realistic and fully functioning and who avoids playing games and is able to solve problems constructively. This person feels positive about self, wants to progress and develop. They feel confident about forming close relationships with others.

The aim of **Transactional Analysis** is to provide a framework that enables people, through improved understanding of the emotional basis of interpersonal behavior, to increase their likelihood of discovering and using authentic talk. It is impossible to say just how much time people spend playing games and otherwise being inauthentic, but it is safe to say that in only a few relationships are the parties always talking from the "I'm OK, You're OK" position. We can all improve.

Everyone has all three of the **ego states** (and, most often without being conscious of it, all of us play emotional games). At any point in a conversation, a person's behavior will come out of one of them, and none of them is necessarily better or healthier than another. What matters is the conversational context in which they are being expressed. To be effective communicators, we need to learn (1) how to notice the shifting ego states in every conversation, and the emotions they evoke in us, and (2) how to talk effectively about these emotions. This will be reviewed in Chapter 11.

Understanding Our Self-Talk

For a more complete understanding of why we use particular ego state "voices" in external conversation, we need to understand our **self-talk** — the voices that talk inside of our head before we ever open our mouth. Additionally, we need to understand our own self-talk so we can find ways of periodically reducing the internal dialogue that is constant in all of us. The "I" and "Me," and all our ego states, are chattering all the time. We are always internally referring to ourselves, and to our behavior and our reactions to the world around us.

Without conscious intervention, the internal circle of communication between the different parts of ourselves — "I" is always talking to "Me" about "my" behavior — never stops. Everybody does it, and how we do it is critical to explaining the way we talk to other people and whether or not they get our message.

The Content of Self-Talk

There are five general **categories** of self-talk: (1) evaluation of ourselves and others, (2) internal problem solving, (3) resolution of internal conflict, (4) planning for the future, and (5) emotional release. In this section we will focus on the first two and how they affect others.

We're always evaluating ourselves and other people in these ongoing internal conversations. "That was great!" "That was terrible." "Joe needs to lose some weight." "Mary is really looking good." And, of course, we talk to ourselves when we're facing choices in our life, or when we're trying to solve problems. "Should I quit school and get a job so I can travel? Or should I get my degree so I can get a better job with a pension?" We talk to ourselves, the different parts of ourselves, and from different perspectives, to sort out our thoughts. And we struggle over the choice between difficult alternatives. This is the "devil" and "angel" debate that happens when we're trying to resolve internal conflicts. Of course, we also talk to ourselves in order to deal with our emotions. We can talk ourselves down from a high, or hot, emotion and use our rational mind to deal with our nonrational emotional reactions. We can put our emotional reactions into perspective before we say or do something rash.

Through this self-talk, we are always building and sustaining the narrative of our self — "I know who I am" so "How do I fit in here?" How we talk to ourselves is vital — it affects our moods and feelings and our reactions to the world around us. Sometimes our self-talk helps us work things out, but its constancy is also a distraction from the reality around us. As someone who has used various practices to still the mind in my adult life, I can say with confidence that it remains a constant intention — but only a momentary achievement. However, I continue to practice because of the side benefits: a calmer body (reduced muscle tension, lower blood pressure) and enough reduction of the noise in my mind that sometimes insights about my world magically appear. But nothing less than years of meditative practice in a distant monastery will enable us to stop the talk in our heads, so we have to take a much more practical approach to this automatic process. If we can't stop it, at least we can become more consciously aware of what we're saying to ourselves. The value in doing this is nicely summarized by Braiker:

> Becoming aware of exactly what you are saying to yourself about yourself can help you understand why you react the way you do to events and people in your life. It can also give you a handle on controlling your moods, repeating your successes and short-circuiting your shortcomings.

The Effects of Self-Talk

Just as "the how" of our talk with others affects how they get our messages, the way we talk to ourselves is critical. What we say to ourselves, the words we use and the emotions behind those words, represent the ego state voices we use when we speak to ourselves. And if we don't consciously choose otherwise, the **inner voice** becomes the voice we use to respond to others. Talking to ourselves in the voice of critical, controlling parent ("What a jerk!")

because we think we've done something stupid is likely to make us just as unhappy as if someone else had said it. This reaction will not only affect our mood but it will also show in our external behavior.

We can also make ourselves feel better by choosing another way of talking to ourselves ("It was a small mistake. I'm not the only one to screw up.") Even though we slipped up, our mood is not affected so negatively and we might actually learn something from the situation. By talking to ourselves in our Adult voice, we can manage our feelings and reactions, if we choose to. The difficulty for most of us is that this choice is extremely hard to make. We most often see our thoughts, and our automatic emotional reactions to them, as unstoppable. They simply happen, and when our lives don't go as we expected, the negative emotional quality of the self-feedback loop can create within us a "spin cycle" of emotions driven by sadness, fear, anger or disgust.

As we look back at previous chapters and review our "natural" habits of mind in communication — involving feelings, perception, and cognition — we see that our reactions are fast and, in difficult situations, our "natural" responses are schematic (automatic, fast and certain) and they often don't provide us with the "good information" we need to respond effectively. We have said that this natural, low-effort, automatic style of perception and thinking works fine for well-structured situations, but in difficult situations — where our feeling reactions dominate — it has a high probability of being inaccurate.

Why? Because in situations where our self and our self-esteem might incur damage, our cognitive unconscious is already preparing our bodies to be hyperaware and reactive — remember in Chapter 3, we said that the cognitive unconscious seems to know what's going on before our conscious mind "gets it." In this biochemical reactive process, our access to real choice through slower, more effortful thought is diminished as our feeling reactions take over. And when we do react externally, our "natural" responses tend to be self-protective, judgmental and controlling. This is not very effective if we're trying to deal with a difficult communication!

Now, give some thought to the following two questions:

1) Since our natural responses can make a difficult situation worse, can we learn to manage our responses consciously?

2) Can we somehow "wake ourselves up" in the process — subdue our automatic emotional reactions, and manage our next words?

The answer is that we can. It takes time and lots of practice, like any good life skill. If we can interrupt the automatic processes, we can learn to avoid saying the first, worst thing out of our mouths. This gives us time to utter our "second thoughts" — the next, better things that we need to say in order to take control of our behavior in the situation. To be successful at this, we need to manage how we talk to ourselves when things don't go well. So let's talk about our inner talk in difficult moments.

Not Part of Presentation

Self-Talk and "Trouble"

The way we talk to ourselves becomes especially critical when we have to deal with what we call "**trouble**" — when we or somebody else has made a mistake, or we feel ignored, criticized or put down. It's easy to feel good and talk to ourselves positively when we feel supported, and if nothing is going wrong in the moment. It gets trickier when we (or our sense of reality) are somehow challenged. At that moment, the way we talk to ourselves can mean the difference between healing and hurting ourselves, and those around us.

The problem is that our affect appraisers instantly recognize the threats in difficult situations and tap into our deepest emotional memories by engaging the emotions of fear and/or anger. This doesn't help our perception and thinking processes.

Selective Perception

Self-talk is shaped by **selective perception**; that is, what we choose to see in a situation and what we don't see in a situation. We use the same tools in selective perception that we use with interpersonal perception. We look at the world from inside ourselves, and leave out anything that contradicts what we want to say or hear — whether it's positive or negative self-talk. The difference is it's much harder on us when it's negative.

"Allness" Thinking and Labels

When we perceive ourselves to be under pressure, we tend to make "**allness**" mistakes in our thinking — one extreme or the other — and use those kinds of labels: "I'm a loser" or I'm great." Such allness statements can be quite damaging (for us) when we use them negatively. We reinforce our emotional reactions to whatever it is we've perceived in the situation by the way we talk to ourselves.

Negative Self-Talk and Self-Esteem

Negative self-talk is based on selective perception and if we have poor self-esteem we tend to select out, or discount, any of the positives in a situation to maintain a consistent view of ourselves. If something good happens to us, we might say, "Oh, I was just lucky! Anybody could have done it." If somebody points out that we actually did get something right, we'll say, "It was an accident. Somebody must have made a mistake. I never get anything right." This process can work in just the opposite way to reinforce feelings of positive self-esteem. We focus on the positives in a situation and we own our behaviors.

Selective perception is reinforced by perceptual accentuation, where we focus on what we want to see. If we have low self-esteem, we tend to focus on those behaviors that we think of as negative and talk to ourselves accordingly. This is called the confirmation bias. We believe information that confirms our already-held beliefs.

By focusing on "bad stuff" happening, we reinforce our "I'm not OK" position (and protect our self-esteem!). Evolutionary biologists theorize that this process is about survival. They contend that if we focus on the negative outcomes, we'll learn from the situation . . .

how to avoid or deal with it in the future. But it turns out we rarely learn from focusing on the bad stuff. In fact, doing that just gets us down emotionally so we react negatively the next time. Instead of learning from our mistakes, we tend to ruminate on our negative feeling reactions to the situation. We make ourselves sadder but not wiser.

Learning from Our Mistakes: Not So Much

In one experiment, undergraduates were given a test. Some didn't do so well but all the participants were asked to meet with the experimenter one week later. At that time the researcher asked them what they'd been thinking about since the test. Some had moved on and had put the test behind them. Others, however, kept trying to figure out what went wrong, ruminating on their mistakes.

When given a second test, those who had put it behind them did better without any further preparation. The ones trying to learn from their mistakes, however, got a poorer score, because they felt de-energized, distracted and couldn't focus. Emotionally, they were back at the site of their first failure.

Self-Talk and the Inference Ladder

Self-talk, and how we apply our words to the thoughts and the feelings that are in our head, is also affected by where we are on the **inference ladder**. We tend to be high on our inference ladder — far away from the facts — when we talk to ourselves. It doesn't matter whether it's good talk or bad talk. If we use good talk — "I'm doing a great job!" — this is a high inference-ladder judgment. Whereas when trouble happens we make the same sort of high inference-ladder judgments — "I never get it right. I'm a loser." Our mind leaps up the inference ladder, driven by positive or negative emotional reactions. Often these judgments have little to do with external reality.

Another risky self-talk practice is **mind reading**.[12] Couples are especially good at this. We're mind reading anytime we tell people — either in our mind or to their face — what they think and what they feel. "You don't really love me. If you loved me you would . . ." is classic "conclusionary" talk fueled by our emotional reactions to them.

Again, in times of trouble, **fortune telling** is a common form of self-talk (Braiker calls this negative fortune telling). "I failed the exam. My life is over. I'm doomed to fail over and over again!" We provide ourselves a perverse form of comfort by predicting the future from our past behavior. The only problem here is that we can talk ourselves into a self-fulfilling prophecy. If we emphasize only our failures, we begin to act as if we were a failure. All of this is self-induced and is a part of what happens inside our head when we're under pressure and deep in emotion-soaked judgment high up the inference ladder.

Emotional Reactions and Reality

Our **emotions** can shift our perceptions — accentuating some over others — and cloud our judgment. If we are feeling bad at a particular moment, we assume the situation must be bad. Research reviewed in Chapter 4, on how emotions affect thinking, tells us that we frequently allow our emotions to help us make choices. If our emotions at a particular moment are negative, they may create in us a negative judgment even though the situation we are in may be neutral. As stated earlier, our emotions drive our inner talk and can directly affect our decision making under two opposite extremes:

- When we are not under any particular pressure, in everyday, normal situations, and
- When we have way too much to do and are under tremendous pressure.

In both of these situations, we tend to look inside, at our emotional reactions, rather than look at the facts to help us decide how to act. When we're not under pressure, we simply go with our feelings at the moment. When we're under pressure, our cognitive unconscious calls up deep emotional reactions to help us decide in an instant. Practically speaking, our emotions drive our thoughts because we haven't chosen to wake up and think through what we're going to do in the next moment. As we react emotionally, our thoughts and conclusions about what's going on tend to become much more personal. We blame others or ourselves (or take credit) for things that may not be under our control.

Over time, these high inference-ladder, emotionally driven judgments can reinforce the worst forms of interpersonal communication and create real problems in our personal relationships. In difficult moments, our emotional reactions — our feelings — drive our problem-solving processes, too: "I'm feeling bad so the situation must be bad" or "I'm feeling fearful, so they must be out to get me." And our solutions become a series of what Book and Stein[13] call "Major musts" — "I must or you must do something for me to be happy" — and "Absolute shoulds" — "The world should be different; you should be different" for me to be happy.

The trouble with extreme answers framed this way is that there is little room in our mind — or if we say them out loud, in the other person's mind — to negotiate an improvement in the situation. We need to learn to manage our reactions and our self-talk in order to become effective communicators, particularly in difficult situations.

Where We're Going Next

In the next chapter we will outline essential concepts and skills that will permit us to think differently about talk; allow us to interrupt an emotional hijack and slow our internal reactions; and give us time to think more clearly about the reality we helped to create so we can choose to make it better.

END NOTES

[1] Wilson, T. (2002) *Strangers to Ourselves: Discovering the Adaptive Unconscious*. Cambridge, MA: Belknap Press of Harvard University Press, p. 69.

[2] Wilson, p. 87.

[3] These next two sections are an overview of the theory of G. H. Mead, as summarized in Wood, J. (1992) *Spinning the Symbolic Web: Human Communication as Symbolic Interaction.* Norwood, NJ: Ablex Publishing, Chap. 7 and 8.

[4] Goffman, E.(1967) *Interaction Ritual: Essays on Face-to-Face Behavior.* New York: Doubleday.

[5] The H. S. Glenn quotes are from the narration of a TVO video series *Journeys to Self-Esteem*. His model of the three beliefs can also be found in Glenn, H. S. (1998) *7 Strategies for Developing Capable Students*. Rocklin, CA: Prima Publishing.

[6] Langer, E., Rodin, J. (1976) "The Effects of Choice and Enhanced Responsibility for the Aged: A Field Experiment in an Institutional System," *Journal of Personality and Social Psychology*, 34, 191–198.

[7] Summarized from Falikowski, A. (2002) *Mastering Human Relations* (2nd ed.). Toronto: Pearson Education, Chap. 3.

[8] This section draws on Fisher, D. (1981) *Communication in Organizations*. St. Paul, MN: West Publishing Company, Chap. 7, which reviews concepts from Berne, E. (1967) *Games People Play; The Psychology of Human Relationships*. New York: Grove Press; James, M., Jongeward, D. (1971) *Born to Win: Transactional Analysis With Gestalt Experiments*. Reading, MA: Addison-Wesley Publishing Co.; and Harris, T. (1973) *I'm OK, You're OK.* New York: Avon.

[9] Berne.

[11] Gottman, J. (2002) *The Relationship Cure: A 5 Step Guide to Strengthening Your Marriage, Family and Friendships*. New York: Three Rivers Press.

[12] The concepts of mind reading and fortune telling are taken from Braiker, H. (1989) "The Power of Self-Talk," *Psychology Today*, December, 23–27.

[13] Stein, S., Book, H. (2006) *The EQ Edge: Emotional Intelligence and Your Success* (2nd ed.). San Francisco: Jossey-Bass.

CHAPTER EIGHT

FUNDAMENTAL SKILLS FOR EFFECTIVE COMMUNICATION

Effective Communication

Our fundamental purpose in all talk, as the definition of IP communication states, is: "Acting together to create, sustain and manage shared meanings." How else can we answer the three key questions to our own satisfaction? We are always in the process of trying to evoke images in the head of another person that are similar to those in our own head, while they are trying to accomplish exactly the same thing with us. We are driven to collaborate. If we can't create and sustain common meanings, we aren't able to understand each other.

In simpler terms, we are effective communicators when we give each other "good" information about what's going on inside our heads. In Chapter 1, we named the elements of "good information" but given what we've said about the inference ladder and the norms for conversation, the elements of "good" information need a more detailed description:

- Accurate (our best effort at describing what's going on),
- Truthful (our words are congruent with our thoughts and perceptions),
- Relevant (our words follow from what was said by the other), and
- Understandable (we use appropriate language and congruent nonverbals).

As we said earlier, we communicate this way so that both people in the conversation can make an informed choice and act from internal commitment, rather than on the basis of manipulation or coercion.

All this may seem pretty straightforward, but in that communication space just beyond the many everyday, well-structured encounters we've described earlier — where we discover unexpected differences or disorder or expected disagreement — the common purpose for talk and our effectiveness as communicators can be put at risk because of the natural, automatic operations of our mind. Consider the conclusions that can be drawn from the analysis of the three previous chapters on the mind's role in communication:

The "Natural" Processes Behind Our Talk

Our **emotions** — the pre-conscious biological reactions to incoming stimuli — emerge out of our cognitive unconscious and energize our perception creation and our flight up the inference ladder of conscious decision making. They are automatically externalized in our nonverbals but can also be consciously displayed for short periods of time. In situations where we confront unexpected differences, disagreement or disorder, however, they are mostly out of our conscious control.

When our **perceptions** of ourselves, and the world around us, are threatened, our first, automatic choice is to defend the way we see things. Changing our perceptions is a last choice.

When our **cognitions** — our thoughts — about what we see are challenged, we automatically move up the inference ladder into our more abstract labels — judgments and beliefs — to defend ourselves.

In summary, it appears that most of the internal processes that enable our communication — the "**natural acts**" of emotion, perception, cognition — are automatic, schematic and fast. They reinforce our need for certainty and, as they seem to flow naturally from within us, we behave as "energy savers" and "anxiety avoiders" in predictable situations. Because they are automatic and nonconscious, however, these same natural processes have a high probability of generating inaccurate or inappropriate responses in ambiguous, complicated or confronting situations. In such difficult moments, our natural acts can instantly shift us from the purpose of creating and sustaining shared meanings to creating and reinforcing differences, by compelling us to respond to others in ways that are self-protective, judgmental and controlling. Sometimes we just naturally make things worse.

To be truly effective as communicators in unexpected or complex situations, we need to shift the way we respond from our repertoire of "natural" acts to a set of "unnatural" acts. **Unnatural behavior** in this case would be conscious, flexible and focused on shared meaning. The "unnatural" acts that allow us to be effective communicators involve (1) three critical abilities (mindfulness, appreciation and metacommunication) we need to possess, in order to (2) enact the five values of the humanistic model, which represent the conditions for effective communication.

Three Critical Abilities

Mindfulness

Mindfulness, an ancient concept in Buddhism, brought into contemporary psychology through the work of Langer,[1] means being consciously aware of what's going on in the moment. Since we seem to live most of our lives in a semi-conscious state of overlearned reactions and/or high inference-ladder judgments about how things ought to be instead of how they are, mentally "coming into the moment" is a real challenge. We can do this by overcoming *static evaluation*, by seeing the other and the world around us in new ways, using new categories, and by being conscious of the power quality of first impressions to limit our perceptions of others.

Mindfulness means "waking up to what's going on within and without us in the present . . . right now!" Our cognitive unconscious, which always operates in the "here and now," allows us to act without having to think too much about things in typical situations. For example, we drive while thinking about other things or while talking on the phone. In fact, we often look at our cell phones throughout the day. We've invented and fallen in love with a technology that says it connects us, when in fact it's just another way of disconnecting us from the moment we're in by taking us away to some other moment — the one on the screen.

Psychologist Ellen Langer described mindfulness as "a flexible state of mind in which we are actively engaged in the present, noticing new things and sensitive to context," which she distinguishes from mindlessness, where we behave "in ways that made sense in our past but have little to do with the present moment."

Langer's research suggests that to be mindful we need to do three things:

1) We need to re-create categorical labels we have for the people in our memories.

We tend to store information about people under one or two labels that are easy for us to recall but that limit the ways we can think about them. As an exercise, think of your partner in terms of all the roles he or she plays in daily life so you can develop a wider variety of categories for them to fall into. This exercise opens up the possibility that you'll think of them in new ways.

My favorite example of this process involves men who think of their partners as mere "housewives" and treat that as a limiting category until they discover — usually while contemplating divorce — the wide variety of roles their wives play, services they provide and jobs they do, and how much it would cost to pay for their replacement.

2) We need to be open to new information and points of view, particularly when they challenge some of our favorite stereotypes.

Accepting (rather than ignoring) new information helps us to reconsider long held but perhaps out-of-date views. Being open to new views and being willing to see our own and others' behavior from another perspective may reduce the number of times we use the self-serving bias to explain reality: if something is a problem for me, it's not my fault, it was the situation. If it's a problem for them, it's their fault.

3) We need to awaken to our dependence on first impressions.

This means truly breaking through an automatic mode of perception. Try to treat first impressions as tentative, as hypotheses to be revised, accepted or rejected when we have more information. Although the unconscious makes up our "mind" for us almost instantly, in most situations we need to pause, get more information — or at least wait until we've shared a conversation — in order to see who the other really is.

When we pay attention for only a moment to what's in front of us, we leap up the inference ladder and create a "single clue" judgment. Remember the "door" story on perception in Chapter 5 . . . fewer people noticed the "changed" person they were talking to in mid-conversation when the person was dressed in hard hat and boots — he was no longer an individual but a construction worker.

The implication of Langer's suggestions is that if we intentionally observe and consciously describe the reality of a moment or of another person to ourselves in some detail, we are less likely to judge it. We can tell ourselves what it is . . . not what it ought to be. Mindfulness is about pausing . . . looking again . . . waiting for one second longer . . . and being patient. An attitude of mindfulness helps us suspend our need to attribute motivations — to mind read. We can challenge our belief that we know what's going on when in fact we are only assuming.

When we become mindful and slow our thinking, and temporarily suspend our judgmental categorization, we can stop acting as if our mental inventions are real and ask people what they really mean or intend. Then we can come up with a shared agreement about the immediate reality. It'll make us far more effective than if we only act on our own reality. And it will make it easier for us to appreciate the other. Mindfulness is about staying focused on the present and open to new information. Appreciation is about how to evaluate this new information.

Appreciation

Appreciation means being aware of our response patterns (mindful) and of the context in which we are interacting (including any cultural differences), and choosing to respond appropriately in different contexts. It also means being open to ideas, opinions and experiences that we may not share, and being able to hold them in our mind without judging them harshly or denying them away, while still being able to present our own views and ideas.

Appreciation is the "values" side of mindfulness. The values represented in the appreciative mindset are found in three essential meanings of the word:

- To have a full understanding — "I appreciate your situation,"
- To value and honor the other — "I appreciate you," and
- To add value — something of worth appreciates in value.

In fact, let's think for a moment about how our talk would change if we consciously committed to fully understanding a situation before we acted or spoke — for the second time. What if we spoke after exercising wise judgment based on a more complete perception and understanding of the worth of the other and the situation we're in, while valuing and honoring those individuals as we spoke? And what if we could express or simply display a sense of admiration, approval or gratitude for another — with nothing more than the way we chose to talk or listen to them?

Wouldn't both of these "what ifs" automatically enable us to achieve the third meaning of appreciation, which is to increase the value or worth of every situation we enter? Appreciation is a way of looking at the world that focuses our mind on what's working, not what's failing. It's not a glass half empty (pessimistic) or glass half full (optimistic) view of life. It's a positive, problem-solving view. The appreciative mind sees the half-full glass and wants to know why it's half full, how did we get this far, and what can we do to add more and do better.

The appreciative mindset allows us to see the useful, desirable or positive aspects that already exist in the current situation or in the people present and know these can be revealed, evoked or realized, if we ask the right question, that is, make an appreciative inquiry.

The Power of an Appreciative Question

Here's a story that shows what I mean: I was asked to join a meeting by a general manager who was struggling to get a group of department heads to make some creative choices about managing the effects of a diminished budget. During the meeting, the group was in a dark mood — tension and even fear were hovering around the edges of their opening small talk. (Remember what we said about mood and decision making in Chapter 4 — a somber mood supports analytical thinking but people need to be positive to be creative.) The boss started the meeting, restated its purpose, and then introduced me as someone who might help with the tough decision making.

My intervention was easy. I said: "Before we get on with the agenda, I want you to take a moment and think about something that went well in your unit this week . . . something that not only worked the way it was supposed to but worked far better than anyone thought. It could be an event you were directly involved in or that you heard about."

I gave them a moment to recall this, and then said: "Before we talk about today's agenda, could we go around the table and have each of you tell us about that something that really worked for you and/or the people in your unit this week? And, please, could everyone give each speaker your full attention while they're telling their story."

By the end of the "go around" the mood was radically altered. People were smiling and even chuckling out loud at several of the stories. In fact, it seemed easier to tell a more positive story as they went around the table. By the time they got to the agenda, the mood of the room had shifted by 180 degrees and within minutes of starting the formal agenda, people were responding more openly and positively to the questions before them. Several people told me later that it was the best meeting they had had in weeks and they felt they were finally getting somewhere. So an appreciative question — about what's working, what we can call on that has worked in the past — that is mindfully asked and answered — works like magic.

So, when managers ask me about the quickest thing I can recommend to shift their folks toward an appreciative mindset, I recommend starting off recurring meetings with the question: "What went well for you this week or this month?" Of course, I also remind them that this is much easier to do when everyone is mindful and present-focused in the situation.

Appreciation requires an "other-oriented" view of talk. It compels us to get past our natural focus on ourselves. If we are going to fully appreciate others, we have to get out of our own way long enough to communicate attentiveness and interest in what they're saying. An appreciative view includes valuing and honoring the other while they are talking by showing them:

- Respect — giving them time to finish a thought, not interrupting to take over the discussion.

- Consideration — asking if it's a good time to talk instead of just starting in.

- Direct acknowledgment of their value by:

    - Asking for their input: "What do you think?" "How do you see it?"
    - Legitimizing their feelings: "I'd feel that way, too."
    - Asking for clarification where appropriate. This keeps the listener focused on understanding what's going on from the other's point of view.

Metacommunication

Mindfulness is essential for another way of talking to become more effective. **Metacommunication** is the ability to talk about the quality of the communication occurring between us, while we are in the midst of that communication. Instead of simply talking about a topic, or about each other, why not talk about the process of talking itself? Metacommunication is communication about communication. Sometimes metacommunication means describing how we perceive or feel about the moment of communication ("I'm beginning to feel pressured here." Or, "What's really going on?"). It can also include "naming the game" when someone says something to us that is positive but they say it in a way that sounds negative. "Damning us with faint praise" is a classic example. We may need to say, "That sounds like a criticism to me. Am I right about that?"

Metacommunication represents *mindful talk about the talk* occurring in the moment. This is where we choose to publicly acknowledge "what's going on" between us — the way we are talking to each other — so we can say the "next better thing." We can learn to metacommunicate about our perceptions of the conversation when we say things like, "When you said that I didn't understand, can you tell me what you meant?" or "When I said I felt hurt, what I meant was . . . ," or we can comment on the whole conversation: "I don't like the way this is going. Could we try to . . . ?"

This is particularly helpful in difficult situations because it slows down the automatic reaction process and helpfully redirects our thinking to the process of talking, while shifting our thinking away from each other for a moment. It can "wake up" the other person to the process in which they are unconsciously participating.

Also, our metacommunication compels us to be one step removed from our immediate reactions. It can help us move back down the inference ladder in our thinking and get closer to what's "real" between us — i.e., my description of something, or asking a question about "What's going on?" or what just happened, momentarily moves us away from a high-inference exchange of defensive judgments. Metacommunication works best, of course, when we are already talking to each other in ways that allow each of us to be open with the other and feel supported as we share our points of view. DeVito[2] offers six guidelines for effective metacommunication below.

Guidelines for Effective Metacommunication

1. ***Give Clear Feedforward (I'd like to talk about . . .).*** Feedforward lets people know what's coming . . . provides a kind of schema that makes information processing and learning easier.

2. ***Confront Contradictory or Inconsistent Messages.*** At the same time, explain messages of your own that may appear inconsistent to your listener.

3. ***Explain the Feelings That Go with the Thoughts.*** Often people communicate only the thinking part of their message, with the result that listeners aren't able to appreciate the other parts of the meaning.

4. ***Paraphrase Your Own Complex Message (What I'm trying to say is . . .).*** Similarly . . . paraphrase what you think the other person means and ask whether you're accurate.

5. ***Negotiate Meanings.*** If you have doubts about another's meaning don't assume; instead, ask, even in the middle of a conversation . . . this is particularly important in intercultural situations.

6. ***Talk about Your Talk Only to Gain an Understanding of the Other Person's Thoughts and Feelings.*** Avoid substituting talk about talk for talk about a specific or problem.

Mindful, Appreciative Metacommunication Is Possible

We know how people do this because of a classic piece of research by social psychologist Jack Gibb.[3] He observed, recorded and analyzed people speaking in small groups over an 8-year period. In his research, he was able to define the *six* key dimensions that underlay a climate of openness in conversation — an atmosphere where people feel appreciated and supported by the others in the conversation — where they can speak without feeling they have to defend themselves. We will look at *three* of the six dimensions of supportive (appreciative) versus defensive behavior developed by Gibb.

Defensive Talk

Defensive talk occurs when people feel threatened or anticipate a threat. Although people can still focus on a common task or subject, they use a substantial amount of their energy to avoid or mitigate "a perceived or anticipated attack." If uninterrupted, say by a piece of metacommunication on the part of one of the people involved, defensive talk can create a downward spiral where it engenders defensive listening in others, which, through facial, postural and verbal cues, is feedback to the original defensive speaker who then becomes more defensive in their speech.

Supportive (Appreciative) Talk

On the other hand, supportive talk can create a climate of open discussion, where people tend to read less negative feeling into the exchange because their tendency to project their fears and concerns onto the other is not being stimulated (they feel more valued). As the talk becomes more supportive, each person is more able to focus on the structure, and the cognitive (as opposed to the emotional) meanings of the messages being sent.

Supportive talk permits people to be open and receptive to their own experience in the moment, freer to examine each other's assumptions, and deal with genuine differences more competently (seeking fuller understanding) — from their Adult ego states rather than critical Parent or Child. Mindfulness requires openness to the present. Appreciation is harder to call up in a defensive climate.

Three Dimensions of Supportive/Defensive Behavior

Here are three ways we can commit to creating an open, supportive climate, even in the midst of difficult exchanges:

Description versus Evaluation in Our Talk

Description is about giving and asking for information, and presenting events, perceptions or feelings in ways that do not imply that the receiver should change his or her behavior. For example, describing our feelings and how they relate to the other ("When I hear you say this, I feel . . .") instead using the language of **evaluation** (judgment) — i.e., praising, blaming or passing judgment on the person or their thoughts.

Recalling the inference ladder: we often speak in judgment, without noticing this critical difference, by saying, "This is all your fault . . ." or "You made me feel. . . ." When we speak like this, we cause the other to close down and be defensive and we give away our power.

Equality versus Superiority

Equality involves the demonstration of mutuality in talk — trust and respect, participative decision making, de-emphasizing status and power — as opposed to **superiority**, which communicates dominance and lack of willingness to enter into a shared problem-solving relationship.

In an equal relationship, disagreement and conflict are seen as attempts to understand differences rather than as opportunities to put the other down. Disagreement requires problem solving not winning and losing or showing the other up.

In everyday talk, equality is also shown by not making "You ought" or "You should" statements. These neither appreciate nor support another. They put the listener in the one-down position while we speak from our "standard-setting Parent" or, if we're angry, our "controlling Parent" voice. The only voice that communicates equality is the "Adult" voice, in which we can ask questions and speak descriptively, acknowledging the other's thoughts and contributions before expressing our own. This works to embody a sense of equality in our talk because the Adult voice is the only one of the three to evoke from the other the same voice, rather than bringing out the opposite emotional ego state. Saying "I see," "I understand" or "That's right" lets the other person know we're listening and understanding.

It's also important to avoid correcting the other if their mistake is of little consequence. Correcting someone shows we think of the relationship as unequal — that we know more than they do — that we have the right to correct them — and this can embarrass the other person.

Provisionalism versus Certainty

Provisionalism means approaching each conversation with a tentative, open-minded attitude and a willingness both to hear opposing points of view and to postpone taking sides on an issue. It means being open and mindful in the way we assert our views. This is in contrast to **certainty**, which means acting as if we already have the answer, being dogmatic, needing to be right.

As an example, let's compare these two assertions:

4) "It seems to me that she's having trouble in her relationship. Maybe she's too focused on herself."

5) "It's obvious she just doesn't know the first thing about caring in a relationship. She's such an egomaniac."

The first statement is provisional: it invites further discussion. "Seems" is a statement of perception not judgment, and "maybe" opens the door to other possibilities.

The second statement is essentially an "allness" statement — spoken in way that is completely certain, as if there's nothing else to be said. People who speak as if they know everything, who always have the answer, are rarely appreciated. We become defensive with such people pretty quickly and tend to hold back our opinions rather than subject them to the critique of a know-it-all.

A Humanistic Model of Communication

This model provides a set of conversation ideals that can be enacted if we stay mindful and appreciative — supportive — in our conversations with others. It is an effort by DeVito[4] to combine the work of a number of communication researchers (including Gibb's works on support- and defense-evoking communication) into a clear statement of the conditions for effective communication. In essence, this model summarizes what we need to achieve to be truly effective communicators. In a practical sense, it suggests that effectiveness means talking to people in a way that will encourage them to listen to us from our point of view, not just theirs, and at the same time make them feel they can reply to what we have said honestly, accurately and relevantly, using words and nonverbals we will understand. The model is summarized as follows:

A Humanistic Model of Interpersonal Effectiveness	
1. Openness	Willingness: • to self-disclose and for disclosure to be reciprocal • to react honestly to messages received • to own one's thoughts and feelings. Speak in I-messages — "I think . . ." "I feel . . ."
2. Empathy	• Try to feel what the other is feeling from their point of view • Try to "take the role of the other" in your head • Listen actively while they talk. Reflect back your perceptions of their feelings in your words.
3. Supportiveness	3a. Description versus Judgment • Describe what happened — don't evaluate • Describe how you feel — don't blame • Explain how this relates to the other person 3b. Provisionalism versus Certainty • Have an open-minded attitude • Be willing to hear opposing views
4. Positiveness	• Try to state the positive rather than restate the negative • Instead of "I hate it when you . . . ," say, "I like it when you . . ." • Compliment where appropriate • Use open acknowledgment not silence
5. Equality	• Give the other person unconditional positive regard vs. acting in a superior way. No "should" or "ought" statements. • Share speaking and listening — show respect by taking turns • Conflict is for solving problems, not winning.

For Mindfulness and Appreciation, First Self-Regulate

To display the fundamental skill of mindfulness in difficult situations, we need to employ the third aspect of emotional intelligence (EI) — **emotional self-regulation** (described in Chapter 4). This means that in difficult situations we need to lower our level of emotional arousal before we can effectively deal with our thoughts and feelings and notice what's going on around us. When we are highly aroused, it is harder for us to manage our thinking and what we are likely to say to others. To be mindful we need to calm ourselves.

John Gottman's[5] detailed physiological and psychological studies of people reacting to others in difficult communication situations indicate that as two people start to struggle, their heart rates rise above 100 beats per minute in the span of a single beat. They enter a state of Diffuse Physiological Arousal (DPA). Once that happens, they find it almost impossible to speak in a rational fashion. Gottman argues that the intense emotion interrupts their access to the left-frontal lobe of the neocortex where rational thought lies, so they fall back on exactly the kind of judgmental, schematic, "emotional" thinking described in Forgas's AIM model — our emotions tell us what to think and say.

Gottman measures heart rate as part of his couples' therapy. His patients wear a finger monitor attached to a biofeedback device that measures the heartbeat. It has a little beeper on it that sounds when the person's heart rate reaches a certain threshold, say 95 bpm (beats per minute). Then he tells the couple that the beep is a warning. It says that one or both of you is now heading toward the place where your next reactions will be automatic and mostly contemptuous and critical (100+ bpm). This represents the point where the limbic brain begins a hijack, where mindful talk will be replaced by fear and anger reactions, which in turn will undermine your relationship. He then teaches people to "soothe" themselves in such situations, as outlined in the box that follows:

Soothing the Emotions — Avoiding a Hijack

Step A. Take a Break. Introduce a "withdrawal ritual" into your relationship.

1. Leave the situation. Give your body a chance to calm down.

2. Don't rehearse distress-maintaining reactions to what just happened.

3. Then take step B — use the mind to continue to soothe the body.

"When you are feeling tense and find yourself going into DPA, use the repair attempt in which you tell your partner you want to take a short break to calm yourself down. Here's what to do during those times."

Step B. The Self-Soothing Process.

1. Get control of your breathing — do six breaths a minute.

2. Notice areas of tension in your body and intentionally contract and relax them.

3. Let the region (of tension) become heavy, to feel as if you are weighted down and leaden.

4. Imagine the region becoming comfortably warm — getting the blood flowing there begins the deep relaxation.

5. Think of a personal image that brings all four steps into focus and memory whenever you need them, e.g., imagine yourself on the beach. . . .

From Calmer Reactions to Cooler Thoughts

Once we start the soothing process, Gottman argues that we need to stop rehearsing "distress-maintaining" thoughts. As we mentioned in Chapter 7, Stein and Book[6] argue that we need to shift our thinking from absolute "shoulds" and "musts" ("I must/should . . . or he/she/they must/should . . . in order for me to feel OK") to "I would prefer it if . . . ," because the extreme "allness" thinking behind "must/should" interpretations of situations reinforces the intensity of our emotions, making our feelings stronger and less manageable. Shifting our interpretation from "shoulds" to preferences gives the left frontal lobe of our neocortex (the rational, "just-say-no" part of the brain) the time it needs to create a more realistic view of the situation rather than the one surging up out of the "hot-button" emotional memories of our limbic brain.

Information from the left frontal lobe doesn't suppress our reactions but it does help to create a change in intensity from "hot" to "cool" feelings. Stein and Book argue that shifting how we name our perceptions from absolute "must and should" to "I would prefer" statements could change the intensity of:

Hot Feelings of . . .	**To Cool Feelings of . . .**
Anxiety or Fear	Concern
Rage or Anger	Annoyance, Irritation
Despair	Sadness
Remorse	Regret
Self-hate	Self-disappointment

In other words, as we momentarily calm our reactions and move our cognitions from intense, absolute judgments like “You jerk . . .” or You should . . .” to calmer descriptions such as “I would prefer it if . . .” we are essentially shifting our ego state from either angry Parent or Child to the Adult ego state. As you remember from Chapter 7, the Adult ego state is one of information seeking and problem solving, where we ask questions (in our mind and of others) in a calm and relaxed way and speak to ourselves, and others, nonjudgmentally. In difficult or ambiguous situations the Adult is the best emotional position to be in to be effective.

Self-Management: Inner Talk First, Then Outer Talk

We can’t choose the emotions we feel. Often, we only notice them after they are already happening. We can, however, control the way we talk about them inside our head and express them to others. When we are confronted emotionally and trying to calm ourselves and move to our Adult ego state, one of the most effective things we can do to help ourselves is to ask ourselves several good questions.

The “I Wonder” Question

When bad things come at us, the brain automatically encourages several organs to release the appropriate hormones to prepare us for a fight or flight response. Yet neither of those extreme reactions is appropriate in most of the situations we have to deal with. To slow our automatic reactions, we need to consciously engage the rational part of the brain.

The best way to do this is to ask our selves a **rational question**: “I wonder what’s really going on?” Our rational brain will then automatically respond, “I don’t know. But they seem to be taking this badly” or “I don’t know. Have they always been like this?” This little conversation originates in the left frontal lobe of the brain — which is where we want the brain to be operating in a difficult moment — instead of in the automatic, unthinking limbic section. Since it begins from the position of curiosity and openness, the “I wonder” question tricks the brain into answering. Most importantly, as we initiate this conversation, the reactive hormonal release commands of the limbic brain slow down.

More Questions

After a difficult situation has passed, we often tend to grind on it, lower our mood and set ourselves up to respond poorly to the next problem that comes along. To stop this longer process, there are three categories of questions developed by Seligman[7] that will help us to avoid the spin cycle of anger and fear that continues after we’ve made a mistake or done something we didn’t want to do.

Pessimistic versus Optimistic Thinking

Duration of the Event

"Will this last forever?" Or
"Will it just be limited to this specific time during which I happen to feel bad?"

Scope of the Event

"Will this affect my whole life?" Or
"Will it be limited to this little part of my life that I am upset about at the moment?"

Responsibility for the Event

"Am I completely to blame for this happening?" Or
"Was my behavior only a part of how this happened?"

Why should we ask ourselves these questions? Because if we don't ask them, answer them realistically, and actively dispute our automatic negative thoughts, every little thing that happens to us can become devastating — especially if we think it's going to last forever. It's called "catastrophizing."

When we ruminate about a problem moment in detail, we believe that we gain a kind of illusory control over it. The paradoxical result is that it gains control over us. The more we keep focusing on the worst aspects of a situation, the longer it lasts and the wider its effect on our life. By asking, "Will this last forever?" and "Does it affect every aspect of my life?" and answering "no" to both questions, we take a step toward reducing the continuous spin cycle of fear that keeps us perceiving the world as a bad place and ourselves as a bad person.

Still More Questions

To manage the problem of "over responsibility" for problem moments in interaction, some of the other questions we ask ourselves can force our mind back down the inference ladder to the level of the "data" about what might actually be happening in the situation rather than focus on our judgments and fears about what has happened. When we are emotionally aroused, we think there is only one view of the situation — the view from the top of our highly judgmental inference ladder. We think it's the correct view and, in a difficult situation, it's usually the one that makes us feel the worst. To reduce this effect, try asking the following questions.

We often forget the fact that we've been down this road before; we've reacted similarly and made similar mistakes. We react automatically to the moment, not from the lessons of our experience. Using our clarifying questions forces our mind to think about what actually has happened rather than simply reacting to it.

More Clarifying (and Calming) Questions

- Is there any objective data that would clarify the situation for me?
- Is there some other way of thinking about this situation?
- Is there some other way I could look at this situation?
    - For instance, if I were an outsider, would I see it the same way?
    - What would the outsider say?
    - If I were the outsider looking at the situation, what advice would I give me?
- What would happen if I expressed my fears to somebody I trusted?
    - What would they say?
    - What advice would they give me?
- Other questions we can ask to gain perspective in a situation are:
    - Have I ever been here before?
    - Have I ever felt the same way?
    - Have I been wrong about these feelings in the past?

Disputing Our Own Fears and Beliefs

To overcome our automatic thoughts, we need to argue with ourselves. That's what **disputing** our fears and beliefs is. If we could think that something else might be going on; if we could look at it in a different way; if we had some other data; if we remember that we've been here before and we made the wrong moves back then, we can slow down our automatic, negative-feeling reactions. In the process of disputing our negative responses, we have to act to change our talk and our actions for the future. We need to engage our emotional intelligence (EI) in situations that evoke our automatic negative thinking — change the way we act and talk — and enact the fourth element of EI — self-management.

Self-Managed Expression

Self-management involves the last element of EI, that is, how we manage the expression of our feelings in ways that positively shape the emotional context of our communication with others. Self-managed talk allows us to either (1) describe our feelings instead of simply acting them out (see the emotional expression suggestions list in Chapter 4) or, if our feelings are not the subject of the discussion, (2) discuss a difficult topic in a way that permits us to be descriptive rather than judgmental. Self-managed talk is built on the emotional nonverbal displays and word choices of what is the Adult ego state in the

Transactional Analysis model of emotions and talk. When things get complicated, this is where we need to go in our head.

When we choose to speak as mindful, appreciative, other-oriented communicators, we radically increase our chances of being effective, even in difficult moments. In fact, using appreciate questions can shift difficult communication situations into more positive and manageable interactions.

Having begun with a mindful and appreciative approach to communication, we can build and maintain the necessary open climate between us if we speak descriptively and as open-minded equals to the other person. And whenever necessary, we can metacommunicate — talk about the ongoing talk — to slow down the process and re-engage everyone's mindfulness about the present moment.

Where We're Going Next

To achieve self-managed expression as mindful, appreciative communicators, we need to be capable of making choices about what to say when, in order to be effective. Remember, effective communicators give and get good information so that by the end of a conversation each person involved gets at least something of what they wanted and there is a level of positive emotional connection between them. To achieve this sometimes difficult and often complex goal, and to make conscious choices about our talk, we need to understand *the effects* of our words and nonverbals on others in particular contexts or situations. This is essentially the pragmatic approach to interpersonal communication and it is the basis for the "Three Mode" model of talk we will be introducing in the next chapter.

End Notes

[1] Langer, E. (1989) *Mindfulness.* Reading, MA: Addison-Wesley Publishing Co.

[2] DeVito, J. (2001) *The Interpersonal Communication Book* (9th ed.) Toronto: Addison Wesley, Longman, Inc., pp. 132–136.

[3] Gibb, J. (1961) "Defensive Communication," *Journal of Communication,* 11, 141–148.

[4] DeVito, pp. 137–142.

[5] Gottman, J. M. (1999) *The Marriage Clinic: A Scientifically-Based Marital Therapy.* New York: W. W. Norton and Company.

[6] Stein, S., Book, H. (2006) *The EQ Edge: Emotional Intelligence and Your Success* (2nd ed.). San Francisco: Jossey-Bass.

[7] Seligman, L. (1998) *Learned Optimism.* New York: Pocket Books. In a recent edition of a text on emotions and health, Seligman is quoted as saying: "If you always go around thinking, 'It's my fault, it's going to last forever, and it's going to undermine everything I do,' then when you do run into further bad events, you become at risk for poor health."

CHAPTER NINE

A PRAGMATIC MODEL OF TALK AND C.O.N.N.E.C.T. TALK

A little more than twenty years ago, in an effort to share my knowledge of communication more effectively, I developed a pragmatic model of human communication that describes three general modes of talk. Each of these modes appears automatically or can be chosen in two of the most common situations we are likely to face in our daily round of living.

I was inspired to do this by a much earlier book that works at the same level my model does — clarifying how people speak in different ways in a conversation. The book was *Straight Talk* by Miller and colleagues[1] and was the first I had ever read that gave the reader specific advice about how to talk in different situations. I have built upon their basic idea of Control Talk and have added two new ways of describing the other types of talk we use every day. Moreover, I have created acronyms of the names of each mode that are intended to capture not only their style elements and the conversational flow they represent but also make them easier to remember.

For each mode, I describe when it is likely to be used, or may simply appear, and what goal or purpose it serves in a conversation. I then integrate specific tips into the description of each mode so they can be remembered more easily. My goal is to get us to notice which mode we're in and whether that style of talk is appropriate for the context and likely to be effective. If not, I believe we can learn to consciously choose another more appropriate mode.

My model begins with a fundamental assumption that the first goal of all interpersonal communication — beginning at birth — is to make connections with others. We said in Chapter 1 that in overcoming our basic uncertainty about who we are and how the world around us works, we need — we are driven — to communicate to build relationships with others and then to influence them to get what we want. The first two modes in my model of talk — C.O.N.N.E.C.T. and C.O.N.T.R.O.L. talk — do just that.

A Pragmatic Model of Talk: The Three Modes

To be self-managed communicators, we need a model of talk that permits us to think about the effects of our words and nonverbals on others in particular contexts or situations. The IP model represents the universal processes that are essential to face-to-face talk in all situations — every time one person talks with another. The model of talk discussed in the rest of this and following chapters, however, is derived from the IP model but is about the pragmatics of communication — the behavioral effects of our communication on each other. It builds on the model of universal processes that make talk work but argues that people also make conscious and non-conscious choices about what to say and how to say it in particular situations or contexts.

It is called the **"Three Mode model"** of interpersonal communication because it describes three ways of talking to each other and the effects each has on people when they find themselves in one of two types of situations: (1) when they are simply trying to make a relational connection with another person (start, build or maintain a communication relationship) and (2) when they are trying to handle a "problem" with another person.

In this model, the word "problem" represents two types of communication issues: (1) a topic that both parties see as separate from the conversation itself because they think they are communicating quite effectively in the situation — talking "the problem" through, or (2) the nature of the talk itself becomes a problem; that is, the *way* we talk to each other makes one or both of us feel misunderstood or unappreciated. In either case, we are dealing with differences that one or both of us feels need to be bridged so we can re-connect.

The first mode of talk in the Three Mode model is called **C.O.N.N.E.C.T.** talk. It describes our most common way of talking to each other in the most common situation we deal with every day — building and/or maintaining relationships. C.O.N.N.E.C.T. talk also reflects the deepest needs we try to fulfill by talking — the discovery of ourselves, and the world, through the eyes of other people.

The second and third modes represent what we do in the other common situation in which we can find ourselves — problem solving. The second mode is based on *our automatic or non-conscious reactions* to "problems." It is called **C.O.N.T.R.O.L.** talk. The third mode is based on *our making conscious choices* about what we'll say and how we'll say it in a problem solving situation. It represents self-managed communication and is called **D.I.A.L.O.G.U.E.** talk. C.O.N.N.E.C.T., C.O.N.T.R.O.L. and D.I.A.L.O.G.U.E. are acronyms where every letter describes a particular behavior that is part of the overall mode. The following flowchart illustrates the connections between these three ways of talking.

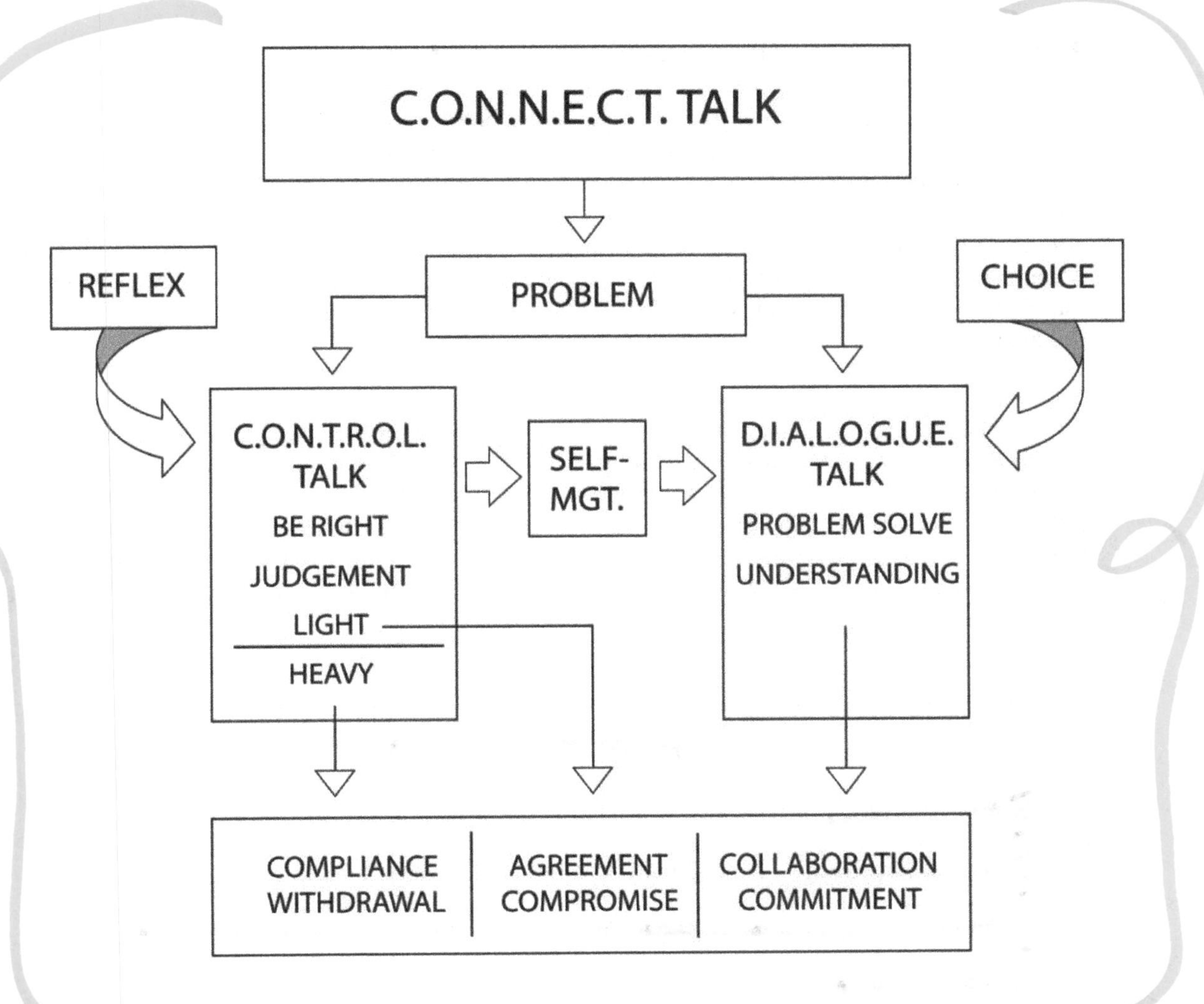

By emphasizing the word C.O.N.N.E.C.T. compared to the other descriptors in the diagram, we are trying to show that this mode of talk is not only the first but also the most common kind of talk that we do. The chart also shows that when "problems" occur in communication, we tend to make a reflex or "natural" choice to move to a form of problem solving called C.O.N.T.R.O.L. talk. This type of talk is driven by our need to be right in difficult situations. If, however, we can slow our reactions and be more mindful of what's going on, the model indicates that we can consciously choose to do D.I.A.L.O.G.U.E. talk, a self-managed form of expression and problem solving that is driven by a need for mutual understanding rather than a need to be right. Each of these types of talk will be discussed in detail.

Automatic, Fast and Certain: C.O.N.N.E.C.T. Talk

(Relationship talk)

Most of the situations we find ourselves in every day are highly structured and for them we have well-learned habits of talk. We don't have to think very much before we talk in these moments. Most of us know how to greet strangers; ask for help in public places; purchase goods and services; pass time talking with acquaintances; carry on everyday conversations with friends and family members. Our talk is mostly automatic, fast and certain: based on deeply learned habits of performance and an unspoken, shared agreement that in these situational contexts (unless something unexpected happens) our sense of self is not at stake.

The kind of talk we use in these everyday situations is called C.O.N.N.E.C.T. talk. It's about starting momentary or potentially lasting relationships and/or maintaining them. It can be superficial or deep but is seen generally as an unthreatening, often pleasant, kind of talk based on shared information, understanding and predictability in the situation. The highlight box below outlines not only the key types of C.O.N.N.E.C.T. talk but also the conversational norms we follow when we engage in it and the effects it has on everyone engaged in the conversation.

C.O.N.N.E.C.T. Talk

C. Courtesy Rituals — Greetings, procedural exchanges, politeness, kindness, patience.

O. Open Expression — Friendly, relaxed, comfortable sharing of information, opinions.

N. No Negative Judgment is expected, thus no defensiveness or intent to manipulate.

N. Narrative Form — We tell stories about events, ourselves and other people (we gossip).

E. Emotional Reciprocity — As we talk we expect appropriate emotional responses from others.

C. Collaborative Process — We take turns in the roles of speaker and supportive audience.

T. Trust-Inducing — We get to know each other. We build credit in our emotional bank accounts.

The CO.N.N.E.C.T. acronym is intended to capture both the elements of connective talk and the general flow of it in our lives. Beginning with the first "C" we start new relationships or recognize continuing connections with the courtesy rituals provided by our culture. These are deeply learned forms of speech and styles of delivery for speaking to strangers or friends. Once we know people better, we are able to share information openly because we don't expect negative judgment — our "face" is not on the line — and, most often we share through narrative — by telling stories about our lives — our mind is wired to do this.

Following the "norms" for conversation reviewed in Chapter 2, we enter into C.O.N.N.E.C.T. talk conversations anticipating reciprocity and collaboration from our listeners. We expect them to communicate complementary, supportive emotions as we talk and to take turns in the conversation by sharing their stories. We believe that connective talk is supposed to build trust between us, so in the early stages of relationships we share information about *us* to allow them to know us better, while in established relationships, we share in ways that demonstrates our care for *them*. It's called "building credit in their emotional bank account." Let's look at the key elements of C.O.N.N.E.C.T. talk in more detail.

Courtesy Connection Rituals

One general example of C.O.N.N.E.C.T. talk is the bus stop conversation. When we say to the person standing next to us, "What do you think about this weather?" we expect them to say, "It's really cold!" This little exchange does something important; it lets the other know that we are a "normal" member of the society, that is, we know which pleasantries to exchange when we meet a stranger in an odd spot and we're standing next to them.

Most of us, most of the time, know the rules for effectively connecting to others — to seek information and get what we want. We tend to make the request in one of two ways: with a tone of neutral civility or politeness in our voice or with a hint of friendly enthusiasm. It's the schema — situational script — we learned growing up.

This is particularly true of what I call procedural rituals. These happen in everyday life when we make contact with complete strangers to acquire a service or product. As noted in Chapter One, these are highly structured interactions that we, and the people with whom we are connecting, are expected to perform easily. Remember, our exchange in a clothing store:

> "Hi, how much is this top? I don't see a tag."
> "$16.99."
> "Great. Here's a twenty."
> "Thanks. Here's your change. Have a good day."
> "You too."

The sales clerk's proffering of a "thanks" and a wish for us to "have a good day" is a cultural requirement essential for the smooth completion of the exchange because we expect these rituals to end in a way that leaves our emotions in a state of calm acceptance, even momentary happiness.

We've also deeply learned that cool, brusque or rude behavior in such situations not only hinders us in getting what we want but also triggers off in us a deep sense of uncertainty about "what's going on" and "what's going to happen next." We expect others (and they expect us) to enact the norms of ritual connection in a smooth, and at least civil or polite, way because that's what "normal" people do. By the way, if you think this form of pleasantly polite ritual doesn't matter, think about how often your mind returns to a moment of ritual breakdown. Moreover, consider how easily you recall and tell the story of being treated badly to anyone who will listen—you gossip. Psychologists[2] argue that gossip is a symbolic way of punishing the offender by destroying their reputation. Not only is it personally satisfying and connective (the listener instantly feels the need to reciprocate with their own gossip) but the pervasiveness of gossip acts as a warning to potential non-cooperators, essentially sustaining the larger social and moral order of the community.

Recognition and Connection

The archetypal version of ritual recognition talk is the "Hi, how are you?"–"Fine" exchange. We've grown up learning that this exchange is "throwaway talk." We think it doesn't mean anything but, in fact, it is the basic building block for beginning and sustaining all of our social connections. Most of the time there is no real information exchanged. This greeting is not about how you are, but who you are. (In a simple but important way, it answers the question "How am I being treated here?")

When we walk down the hall at work or in the mall saying "Hi" or "Hi, how are you?" to people passing by, we are saying, "You are a person who has the kind of relationship with me that needs to be recognized when we enter each other's space." If they say, "Hi, how are you?" to us, we feel the need to sustain our connection and at least nod our head or murmur a "Fine" because, at minimum, we have a visual acquaintance with them and are likely to see them again. To not complete this ritual act might be interpreted as communicating something negative about the relationship.

To confirm this possibility, using a ritual closer to home, think for a moment about what you say when you come home at night. Assuming there's someone at home when you arrive, what do you say? "Hi. I'm home" "Anybody here?" "How was your day?" "What's for dinner?" These are the type of ritual greetings everybody uses when they come home. (Even if you only have a pet to greet you — don't you say something?) Now I want you to think for a moment about what would happen if you walked in the door and said nothing. Don't look angry — have a neutral face — but don't say a word! What do you think would happen? Isn't it likely that the person who is usually there would think something odd was going on, that you were in a strange mood, or that something was wrong?

Like many other rituals, the words of greeting don't literally mean what they say; they have deeper meanings, so "Hi, how are you?" is to be followed by a "Fine. You?" Not by anything else. We don't expect the other to respond with "I'm terrible. Let me talk to you about my disastrous life." A ritual exchange isn't supposed to encourage that.

Ritual Greeting Gone Wrong: A True Story

There's always a gathering at the ground-floor elevators between classes in the biggest building on campus — the Ross Building. Some years ago as I was waiting to go up to my office, I saw and overheard the following exchange: a female student was waiting for the elevator and a classmate appeared. The waiting student said, "Hi, how are you?" and the arriving student, also female, said, "Terrible, let me tell you what happened."

The waiting student looked a bit stunned and a little horrified. This ritual "Hi" was going to get serious. Even more interesting to see was that as the second woman leaned forward to tell her more and more bad stuff, the first woman kept gently backing away. But most remarkable was what happened next: a third woman came up and said "Hi, how are you?" to the complainer, who automatically turned and responded "Fine," and then, without taking a breath, went back to complaining to the unlucky first woman. Resulting lesson: "Hi, how are you?" is a deeply learned ritual with built-in expectations.

Rituals aren't throwaways — they mean things to people. The central function of courtesy, procedural and recognition C.O.N.N.E.C.T. talk is to demonstrate our ability to play appropriate social roles as a member of our community.

Some C.O.N.N.E.C.T. talk exchanges can involve deeper issues around emotional concerns in personal relationships. This is the kind of sharing we do with people with whom we are already deeply connected. Most often, however, C.O.N.N.E.C.T. talk is used to create and sustain social connections in a more general and less intimate way. Most often it is simple "small talk" involving commonplace exchanges of opinion and information about everyday events, at work or in our personal lives. And if we know the other well enough, it can also involve playfulness and humor. The most important commonality that runs through all the varieties of "small talk" we can perform is our certainty that our "face" is not at risk when we are talking. And, despite its demeaning name, small talk (speaking about "nothing of importance") serves two important social functions: self-disclosure and the structuring of time.

Small Talk for Self-Disclosure

Small talk allows us a safe way to show how another person can get to know us better. As we move from discussing general topics to disclosing more personal information, our listeners move from their first impressions of us to something more lasting. Small talk can act as a relationship audition. It is a performance, where we can show different aspects of our "me" — our different selves — and see if something connects.

The early stages of small talk tend to focus on sharing demographic or biographical information — our name, what we do, where we come from, our marital status — or information cued by the situation — the weather is always good for starting a conversation, at least in North

America. We start with "name, job, location" because they are unarguable; they belong to us, so they are accepted. Small talk is not about creating differences, it's about finding similarities as a basis for connection, so at first we cover a range of subjects and keep it superficial because (1) it makes it easy for the other to reciprocate information at that level, and (2) it's easier for us to discover "what works" for the other.

We build up a situational identity in the discussion of a variety of subjects — restaurants, TV shows, clothes, personal interests and hobbies — and when they seem to connect, we add additional emotional energy — put our "face" on the line in the conversation. People discover how we identify ourselves. Then they can decide whether they'd like to continue their connection to someone who acts and thinks like us. And if our early exchanges are reciprocated, satisfying us that we've found subjects that connect us with the other, our disclosure can deepen. So for instance, instead of simply telling someone what our job is, we can go on and tell them how much we hate it and that we're looking for a new one. This is far more revealing of our internal state and it tends to emotionally deepen the relationship.

Berger's[3] research indicates how this process works. He offered 200 suburbanite adults a chance to imagine they were observing a 2-hour conversation between two people meeting for the first time. They were asked to place 150 pre-selected statements on a time line covering two hours and divided into 15-minute segments. They were also asked to leave aside any subjects that would never be raised in the two hours.

As predicted, the first 30 minutes were filled with simple descriptors of the person: where they were born, the schooling level of their children, etc. Midway through this process, we find personal values statements about family — "I'm trying to give my children all the things I never had" — or about the public behavior of particular categories of people. And by the end of this imagined discussion, people were sharing their feelings about themselves and their spouses.

Typically, at the midway point of the disclosure process, when two people find that their value statements seem to connect positively, one of the most common exchanges that can occur is a form of pastime talk we described earlier as "Ain't it awful" — a sharing of values by complaining about the behavior of some third party. This is very connective. Remembering our ego states and the indirect expression of emotion in conversation, this talk is usually carried out in the whiny Child or critical Parent voice. "Ain't it awful, how kids today . . ." or "Those idiots at city hall. . . ." We discover a common interest in blaming somebody for something and we're off. John Gottman's[4] research on relationships and talk has demonstrated that trashing a third party during a struggle between a husband and wife is a terrific way to take a break from their drama and rebuild the connections between them. By the way, statements that never occur in the first 120 minutes included descriptions of a person's salary, sexual experience, or fears about a partner's infidelity.

How Small Talk Structures Time

The first stages of sharing small talk referred to above are also used to structure time in two different social situations known as "pastime talk." The first situation requires sharing among people who are strangers, brought together by a common circumstance and who are not likely to meet again (unless they choose to) — cocktail parties, long plane flights, or the distantly connected relatives at the same table at a wedding reception. And the second situation occurs where people meet who know each other and exchange information to deepen their positive connection — family and friendship gatherings. In these situations, small talk seems to be socially required and the process of engaging in it is just as important as the content exchanged.

> **Pastime Talk at the Table**
>
> As a witness to Italian family small talk, I can't tell you how often I sit in amazement as all the relatives of our family sit around the table during and after lunch or dinner and continue to talk to stay connected — sometimes for hours. They re-spin the events in their current lives — but more interestingly, from their past lives — into a detailed tapestry of stories, comments, jokes and banter — for the sake of togetherness. This happens every time we eat together, and it seems to work every time.

Fundamental Assumptions and Performance Style of C.O.N.N.E.C.T. Talk

The essential assumption behind C.O.N.N.E.C.T. talk is that it's about sharing information — not about criticism or competition. Of course, other people can express different opinions, but there is no intention to challenge those already expressed. As indicated in the "C.O.N.N.E.C.T. Talk" summary highlight box, no one expects a debate — it's small talk. Appropriately, our voices sound relaxed, even when giving opinions, as an indicator that what we say is not to be taken too seriously. The goal is to build or sustain a positive emotional connection between two or more people. For C.O.N.N.E.C.T. talk to happen, both (or all) parties to the conversation need to agree on this fundamental goal and assumption for the style of talk to work.

The table on p. 174 re-states in more detail both the assumptions inherent in C.O.N.N.E.C.T. talk and the "style elements" – its forms of speech and non-verbal behavior.

Overall, the various forms of ritual recognition and small talk are safe ways for us to demonstrate our:

1) Need for connection — to sustain and strengthen our relationships.

2) Competence as normal everyday speakers.

C.O.N.N.E.C.T. Talk	
Assumptions	**Style Elements**
• *Basic agreement, or agreement to disagree* • *No tension, expectations clear* • *Bids for connection* • *Build "emotional bank account"* • *Can turn toward, away or against a bid*	• *Small talk: chatty, sociable, casual* • *Simple descriptions of events, or of yours and others' actions, preferences, opinions, beliefs* • *Joking, story telling* • *Voice tone — friendly, relaxed*

C.O.N.N.E.C.T. Talk Reveals Our Communication Competence

Ritual C.O.N.N.E.C.T. talk, or small talk, is the talk that occupies most of our time and space every day. It's how we demonstrate communication competence. Everyday talk about nothing much in particular is how people learn about us. It allows us a low-risk way to enter into new interactions and a low-cost way of sustaining relationships we already have.

Talking about the weather allows us to talk with people from any kind of social or professional background, as long as we observe the rules of interaction, and enact the appropriate behaviors and forms of address. Others watch us to see how competently we employ our verbal and nonverbal skills and how we adjust our talk to whatever space, or place, or time they are in. They watch to see if we are following the content norms for "normal conversation" (described in Chapter 2) and whether we are paying attention to the context. In the box on next page is a list of context considerations, created by Knapp and Vangelisti,[5] to which competent speakers would pay attention in making C.O.N.N.E.C.T. talk.

Ritual and small talk show our communicational competence. We know the rules for these common types of exchange as well-socialized speakers. We know when to start, stop, when to continue, what topics to speak to, and the appropriate style in which to speak. If we can enter and leave these communication moments, and sustain others' face while doing so, people not only think of us as normal — appropriate — but also as likeable and trustworthy. When we can't or won't engage in small talk in socially "required" situations, or we can't adhere to its rules, we are usually met with some level of sanction — puzzlement, frustration, rejection, even reprimands. And after repeated failures, we are often avoided.

Some Context "Rules" for C.O.N.N.E.C.T. Talk: People Notice When They Are Broken

- When communicators are physically close, listeners expect more personal messages; less personal … when physical distance is greater.
- When a relationship … is intimate, there is a greater demand for messages of affection; strangers are expected to supply messages that reflect less affection.
- When the listener's self-image is highly involved in the message, there is a greater demand for complimentary messages — "I'd like to go out with you . . . I really would . . . but I . . ."; when the listener's self-image is not at stake, undramatic messages are called for . . . [small talk].
- When the speaker perceives the listener as highly ego-involved in the topic, there is a greater demand for respectful message sending . . . ; if listener's ego-involvement is perceived as low, nonpretentious messages are required. . . .

The positive side of small talk is that we think it's easy for people to do. Most of us learn the rituals early in life and can at least begin the process with people we meet. The negative side of this assumption is that when a person doesn't find it easy to carry off, the people they meet can make a lot of negative assumptions about them.

Ineffective Small Talk Sends the "Wrong" Message

A group of employees are just hanging out and they are complaining about their socially inept boss:

"He's a cold fish."

"Yeah. The other day I saw a picture of this little boy on his bulletin board and I said, 'Cute kid. Is that your son?' And he goes, 'No.'"

"And that was it?"

"Yup. So I'm wondering, who is that kid?"

(Somebody else jumps in.) "He's just so out of it, and to think how pumped we were that he was coming to lead this team with his high-powered reputation."

"He's smart all right but what good does that do us? We haven't even launched our site yet."

"That's because he has zero people skills. Have you seen the way the other managers avoid him?"

And around they go — up their inference ladders; judging his ability to lead, worried about their team's success. All because (they later admit) they don't know him. They don't know him because he seems unable to participate in ordinary C.O.N.N.E.C.T. talk. An important point: when people don't know you as an individual they will make inferences about you without thinking about it, and more of these guesses are likely to be negative rather than positive. This is the *negativity bias* in action. Evolutionary psychologists argue that as a species we are wired to pay attention to the negative aspects of our situations first, so we can protect ourselves. This is also what Professor Wiio meant by his third law of communication: *if a message can be interpreted in several ways, it will be interpreted in a manner that maximizes damage.*

And that's the third function of C.O.N.N.E.C.T. talk: to audition for new relationships — to find new connections through the reciprocal disclosure of information about ourselves, in increasing depth, over time.

It turns out that the functions of "small talk" are not that small after all. They help us display our humanity but, as the research described below indicates, they do so in a way that is not obvious on the surface of these ritual exchanges. It seems that the content of the talk is not as important for building or sustaining connection as the way we respond to each other's talk in these moments. As John Gottman's research, reviewed in the next section, powerfully demonstrates there's more to C.O.N.N.E.C.T. talk than words.

Emotions and C.O.N.N.E.C.T. Talk: Building Relationships One Bid at a Time

Whenever we enter into ritual talk with another, whatever the topic, we are also telling them how we feel about them and how we feel about ourselves — in a low-risk situation. In his book *The Relationship Cure*, John Gottman[6] describes this type of everyday sharing as "emotional bidding." He argues that any exchange of information is "a bid" and that relationships are built and maintained not just by revealing important things to each other, but by the *way* we respond to each other as we share those little tiny bits of information. He argues that this "**bid and response**" process, makes the difference because we build our relationship with somebody one bid at a time.

And what are those bids? They are very ordinary topics of C.O.N.N.E.C.T. talk like, "What do you think about the weather?" "What do you think the kids will want to do this summer?" "Do you think we need a new television set?" These are the real building blocks of relationships. Moreover, the topic is not as important as the bid response: the way people react to what we say. So, two radically different exchanges: "Will you marry me?"–"Yes!" and "Pass me a beer"–"Sure, no problem" contain the same emotional message — acceptance. Gottman describes three types of responses to our bids for connection as follows[7]:

1) "Turning toward" bids,

2) "Turning against" bids, and

3) "Turning away" bids.

Gottman and his colleagues spent many years studying the dynamics of friendships, parent-child relationships, adult siblings, and couples in all stages of marriage and child rearing. Much of the data supporting the following definitions and conclusions on emotional bidding came from observing couples who volunteered to spend a weekend together at the family research facility on the University of Washington campus. The researchers learned that people typically respond to another's bids for connection in one of three ways: they turn toward, turn against, or turn away. By correlating these three types of behavior with the status of their relationships ten years later, Gottman and his colleagues were able to show how each of these types of behavior affected people's connections over the long term.

Turning Points: The Choices We Make in Responding to Bids

1. **Turning toward.** To "turn toward" one another means to react in a positive way to another's bids for emotional connection. One person makes a funny comment, for example, and the other person laughs. A man points to an impressive car as it passes by, and his friend nods as if to say, "I agree. That's quite a car!" A father asks his son to pass the ketchup, and his son does so in a kind, accommodating way. A woman muses about a vacation she'd like to take, and her co-worker joins in. He asks her questions, adds his opinions and lends colorful details to a trip they imagine together.

   In relationships where people consistently turn toward one another's bids for connection, long-lasting relationships, deep in good feelings for one another, are developed over time. In this situation, people also seem to more easily use humor, affection and interest in one another during conflict. This allows them to stay connected emotionally, solve problems and avoid the negative feelings that can undermine relationships.

2. **Turning against.** People who turn against one another's bids for connection might be described as belligerent or argumentative. For example, if a man fantasized about owning a passing sports car, his friend might reply, "On your salary? Dream on!" Turning against often involves sarcasm or ridicule. In one instance in our marriage lab, a wife gently asked her husband to put down his newspaper and talk to her.

   "And what are we going to talk about?" he sneered.

   "Well, we were thinking of buying a new television," she offered. "We could talk about that."

   But his next response was just as mean: "What do you know about televisions?" he asked. After that, she said nothing at all.

   Gottman notes that married couples in the study who regularly displayed "turning against" behavior did not divorce as soon as those whose style was for one partner to turn away. In the end, however, most of them did divorce.

3. **Turning away**. This pattern of relating generally involves ignoring another's bid, or acting preoccupied. A person in these instances might comment and point to that impressive sports car, but his friend wouldn't bother to look up. Or he might look up and say something unrelated, such as, "What time do you have?" Or, "Do you have change for a five-dollar bill?"

   In one poignant example from our marriage lab, the wife apologized to her husband for a mistake she made in preparing dinner that night. She raised the issue three times during the course of the evening, obviously wanting him to let her off the hook. But all three times the husband met his wife's comments with silence and looked away. In effect, he's saying "I'm not listening to this. I don't care what you said." Very undermining and frustrating for the one on the receiving end.

. . .

In their studies of marriage, Gottman and his colleagues found that turning away as a habit is truly destructive. Couples who displayed this pattern of interaction often became hostile and defensive when they discussed an area of continuing disagreement. This typically resulted in early divorce. The lack of any response leaves people very uncertain, and we have discussed how we deeply dislike uncertainty. Studies done on the dynamics of parent-child, adult friendship, adult sibling, and co-worker relationships showed that "turning away" also undermines these types of relationships.

All this is may appear to be meaningless on the level of topic content, but Gottman argues that bids are the essential building block of all relationships. They each contain essential components of emotional information that can weaken or strengthen connections between people.

C.O.N.N.E.C.T. Talk as Relationship Maintenance

If our bid is not requited in a momentary relationship – people don't give us what we need – we can walk away. Our "face" might be a little dented but at least we have someone to blame. The real issue emerges in continuing relationships. C.O.N.N.E.C.T. talk is critical to maintaining relationships. The inability to respond at all, or to respond critically to what are simply ordinary requests for connection, is a prime determinant of whether the relationship will last another twenty minutes or another twenty years. If people begin to be negative in the way they respond to one another, it doesn't take very long before they stop talking at all. People will not persist if we don't respond in the way they intended us to. This leads to the third kind of bid response, the **unrequited bid** – we ask for a positive response and are ignored. Once or twice ignored and people tend to give up. And when they do this, they break the emotional tie. When that happens, the relationship is over emotionally. As an example, in Gottman's book *Why Some Marriages Succeed or Fail*,[8] he states that husbands headed for divorce disregarded their wives' bids 82% of the time. Husbands who stayed married did this only 19% of the time.

The frequency of bids also matters. That is, more small talk is better than less. *Not* talking about "nothing in particular" actually means something. We have to learn that sometimes it's necessary to talk about the weather, to "turn toward" the other, because when we respond appropriately, it keeps the connection alive and lets them know that a relationship is happening, even if it's only for that moment.

Gottman argues that for the relationship to survive, the bid ratio needs to be 5:1, that is, five positive bid-responses for every negative bid-response. When this pattern is sustained, he argues, we are building credit in each other's emotional bank accounts. This is an emotional cushion we can fall back on when things don't go well. People have emotional memories, and if their overall feeling is, "This is a good relationship," they provide room for the other to fail them occasionally — room to forgive.

In long-term relationships — marriage or workplace — Gottman says the data are clear. When the ratio of "against or ignore" bids relative to positive bids slumps to 2:1 or 1:1, people may still be in a relationship but they have little going for them emotionally. In fact, they are most likely struggling over their connection to each other. When married couples with these negative patterns face major issues, they don't have much emotional credit to sustain them through the hard times and they are far more likely to quit the relationship. When employees face the same patterns of negative response to their bids as married couples, they soon feel misunderstood and disrespected, and they stop trying. They are more stressed, produce less and, if they can, they will quit their job.

The frequency of bids matters. To maintain a relationship we have to keep trying to positively respond to the way people bid for our attention. It doesn't take very much. Very small talk can have a very large impact. If we stop responding, our relationships begin to wither.

The most interesting "breakthrough" in family therapy in recent years is to require a disintegrating family to eat together, at the same time, at the same table, at least twice a week, without using any of the technology that keeps them disconnected — TV, cell phones, computers, etc. They also have to talk to each other — not about anything significant, just small talk. The families who did this, as well as occasionally working together to maintain their living space, reported significant improvements in their lives. They seemed to have reawakened their caring for each other. For families or pair relationships, the connective dynamic seems to be the same. At the end of the day, there have to be substantially more positive moment-to-moment exchanges between people than negative, if the relationship or the family is going to last.

When C.O.N.N.E.C.T. Talk Disconnects Us

In a C.O.N.N.E.C.T. talk situation, we begin by thinking it's easy to be pleasant because there's nothing much at stake here, just the harmless exchange of ritual words. But, as Gottman's research shows, it's not so easy to be pleasant if the other person returns our bid with a response that is critical or rude, or simply ignores what we said.

Our first reaction may simply be to stop talking. We may be taken by surprise and feel that criticizing their "bad behavior" may not be worth the effort in a situation based on an unspoken agreement that either this relationship doesn't matter much (it could be a bus stop conversation) or the relationship to the other is already established and this is an ignorable mistake because the talk is supposed to be about reinforcing the relationship.

It seems that our choice either to ignore the others or defend ourselves against their negative responses to our bids for connection doesn't so much depend on what they say or how they say it as much as it does on whether their response arouses anxiety in us about the nature of the relationship. If their responses suddenly arouse anxiety about our presented self ("disconfirmation of face") and/or about the continuity of the relationship (disconnection from the other), then we become deeply uncertain about the answer to key question number two: "Who am I to you and who are you to me in this situation?"

Where We're Going Next

Our quick and automatic response to such an ambiguous situation is likely to be a shift to C.O.N.T.R.O.L. talk. The emergence of **differences, disagreement, and disorder** — the 3 D's — in a conversation instantly raises the issue of whose definition of the situation is right. One of the goals of using C.O.N.T.R.O.L. talk is to make the other see that our definition of our self and the situation is "right." It is our emotion-based response to talk that seems to call both the relationship (intentionally or not) and our face into question. When the latter happens, we seem to be driven to save it, or at least defend it.

Maintaining face is important. It's the central emotional force behind the axioms from our model of communication: we exchange selves *and* messages, not just messages. Once a perceived threat occurs, we can't ignore the fact that our "face" is out there (communication *is* irreversible). So we almost always respond automatically by using C.O.N.T.R.O.L. talk. In the next chapter we will analyze how this mode of talk operates and how effective it is in particular situations.

End Notes

---

[1] Miller, S. et al. (1981) *Straight Talk.* New York: Signet.

[2] Haidt, J. (2006), The Happiness Hypothesis. New York: Basic Books, Chapter 3.

[3] As cited in Knapp, M. L., Vangelisti, A. L. (1996) *Interpersonal Communication and Human Relationships* (3rd ed.). Needham Heights, MA: Allyn and Bacon.

[4] Gottman, J., Declaire, J. (1999) *The Marriage Clinic*. New York: W. W. Norton.

[5] Knapp, & Vangelisti, Chapter. 6.

[6] Gottman, J., Declaire, J. (2001) *The Relationship Cure: A 5 Step Guide for Building Better Connections with Family, Friends, and Lovers.* New York: Crown Publishers.

[7] This excerpt summarizes and quotes Gottman, & Declaire (2001), Chap. 1–2.

[8] Gottman, J. (1995), *Why Marriages Succeed or Fail: And How You Can Make Yours Last*. New York: Simon and Schuster.

CHAPTER TEN

THE FIRST MODE OF PROBLEM-SOLVING TALK: C.O.N.T.R.O.L. TALK

Problem Solving in Conversation

The final two modes of talk deal with situations where conversation has become difficult. The basic agreements that underlie C.O.N.N.E.C.T. talk have suddenly disappeared, or were not expected in the first place, and communicators are struggling with the 3 D's (difference, disagreement or disorder) in their relationship with another. In these types of situations we have two ways to proceed when problems loom large: (1) our natural and reflex reaction called C.O.N.T.R.O.L. talk, or (2) our mindful, self-managed approach called D.I.A.L.O.G.U.E. talk. This chapter will discuss the form, effects and expected outcomes for the first of these modes of talk: C.O.N.T.R.O.L. talk.

C.O.N.T.R.O.L. Talk

Our natural response when conversation begins to break down, that is, when differences, disagreements or disorder appear (with or without warning), is a mode of talk called C.O.N.T.R.O.L. talk. I have converted the word CONTROL into an acronym (see pp.

188 and 205) that represents a series of intentions and speech forms that I think are the natural (unmindful) responses to what happens when we confront difficult communication.

C.O.N.T.R.O.L. talk occurs in difficult situations because it's a natural, reactive reflex. It happens because it's what we know how to do. We are socialized into C.O.N.T.R.O.L. talk the way we are into C.O.N.N.E.C.T. talk — through the observation and imitation of those around us as we grow up, and with their instruction when we don't know what to do, or we somehow "get it wrong." Contemporary approaches to parenting often focus on engaging in age-appropriate problem-solving talk with a child to encourage the development of self-control, but even the most encouraging parents have limits to their patience. And when those limits are reached, their default position is "demand or command" C.O.N.T.R.O.L. talk. These words come from the critical Parent voice often enough that both the students in my undergraduate classes and the middle-aged managers in my leadership workshops begin their analysis of the Parent ego state by first remembering commands: "No!" or "Stop that!"

There is also a more general cultural schema we internalize as we grow up. In Chapter 1, we called it talk as contest. We learn to take a competitive approach to finding solutions to problems (if you win, I lose). We see this as normal and in a culture like ours a tendency to debate and to find a "winner" pervades our difficult conversations.

Our personal experience and this internalized cultural schema complement our sense of emotional investment in a conversation: We need to defend our face — our sense of "rightness." Our face is tied to our self-esteem and our need to be seen as competent, valued and influential. So we feel the need to argue to protect our self-esteem and avoid the psychic pain of not being "right" in the moment.

Just as we overlearn our language deeply enough to speak it without thinking, we engage in C.O.N.T.R.O.L talk in the same way. This doesn't mean that we can't stop and think about how to deal with communication problems differently, and how to engage in problem solving in a mindful and flexible way. We can. It's just that mindful speaking is most often not our first choice — automatic C.O.N.T.R.O.L talk is.

In all talk, as asserted in the IP model of communication, there are always three levels of meaning at work in every conversation.

- Level one concerns the words we use to discuss a shared topic of conversation.

- Level two is represented in the way we speak — our gestures and vocal tone, for instance — which reflects the quality of our relationship to the other.

- Level three is also represented by our nonverbal communication but is centered not on talk, but on the quality of our emotional reactions to the other.

On the surface, we talk to each other about a shared topic of conversation, while beneath the surface our *ways* of talking about the topic reflect both the quality of our relationship as well as our emotional reactions to them and ourselves. In C.O.N.T.R.O.L. mode, the latter levels — relational and emotional — are simply closer to the surface. We are no longer just discussing a topic of conversation; we are also reacting to the way we're being treated while we are talking. The C.O.N.T.R.O.L. mode of talk has emotional elements built into it concerning our face — our sense of self in relationship to the other person or to the world.

And, as we noted in the previous chapter, C.O.N.T.R.O.L. is about being right. If our rightness concerns our views on the topic, we feel the need to change the other's mind to get their agreement. If it's about the way we are being treated in the conversation, then we will feel the need to defend our face and get the other to show respect for us, or at least demonstrate concern for our feelings. In most difficult conversations, our need to be right concerns all three levels. No matter what level of communication is involved, C.O.N.T.R.O.L. talk is about having to change other people's behavior to make us feel better in this particular moment. It's also about getting our views of ourselves and of the world recognized before we will pay attention to anybody else's views.

When C.O.N.T.R.O.L. Talk Appears

As mentioned in Chapter 9, C.O.N.T.R.O.L. talk can sometimes just blossom in front of us and take us by surprise during ordinary C.O.N.N.E.C.T. talk conversations when somebody suddenly says something rude or out of place and we are offended. We may feel that our "face" and our sense of self are threatened, and so we respond. There are, however, socially acceptable forms of C.O.N.T.R.O.L. talk required for recurrent situations where there are recognized differences between people that don't involve a threat to their conversational face. **Light C.O.N.T.R.O.L.** talk — including various forms of rhetoric and persuasion — is seen as one appropriate way to sell people things, teach them, coach and manage them.

Light C.O.N.T.R.O.L. can also occur when we are trying to reach agreement about problems that are at "arm's length" to us and the other person. While we are trying to persuade them to agree with us, they respond with their own light C.O.N.T.R.O.L. in order to deflect our arguments and change our mind. This kind of exchange can be described as a discussion or a debate, but underneath, it is simply a kind of competition to see who wins. It is called **competitive light C.O.N.T.R.O.L.** and is worthy of notice because it happens so often and also because it contains the potential to escalate into our worst form of talk. If people using competitive light C.O.N.T.R.O.L. begin to take the resistance of the other personally (their feelings begin to take over their thoughts), they can move into using **heavy C.O.N.T.R.O.L.** talk. When that happens in a conversation, problem solving is no longer the point. We just need to make the other person wrong. What ensues is a struggle over truth, intentions and fixing the blame using various forms of personal attack. Heavy C.O.N.T.R.O.L. will be discussed in detail later.

Assumptions and Style Elements of C.O.N.T.R.O.L. Talk

As with C.O.N.N.E.C.T. talk, the use of C.O.N.T.R.O.L. talk is built around a series of assumptions about a situation and what we should be doing in it. These general assumptions and style elements of C.O.N.T.R.O.L. are summarized in the following table:

C.O.N.T.R.O.L. Talk	
Assumptions	**Style Elements**
• *I need to be right.* • **I must manage you** *and the situation to maintain my face* • *If I persist — you will change your opinions, beliefs, behavior.* • *My story is obvious and is* **the** *truth.* • *My truth is based on* **real** *data — my data.* • *I have access to* **all** *the data I need.* As **C.O.N.T.R.O.L**. turns **heavy:** • *I know what you really meant.* • *You are to blame.*	• *I talk from judgment.* • *I use* **"you-messages"** *to tell you your story — how you ought to feel, believe, think.* • *I ask questions only to probe for agreement and/or understanding of* **my** *story.* • **I listen for Leverage**— *only for agreement with me or for weakness in your story.* • *I offer little or no acknowledgment of your story; only when you see my side.* • *I offer support only when you agree with me.*

In a difficult situation, our first assumption is that we need to manage the other when we don't get the response we want in conversation. Intentionally or not, our face has been challenged and we need to manage the others and their responses so our face will remain intact and be reconstructed to make us feel OK. The second assumption is that if we keep on pressing our point of view, they *will* change. We don't change; they change — because we're the one who is right.

Notice that the next assumptions are the same premises underlying the inference ladder (see Chapter 6). This is what happens in our conscious mind when we start to get into deeper disagreement with people. Our emotions drive us up our ladder of inference and we begin to talk as if we are thinking, "What is wrong with you? I am telling *my* truth here and it should be obvious to anyone in the room. My truth is based on real data, which (of course) are my feelings." As our emotions take over our thinking, it simply shuts down. We speak from high-level judgment, as if we know everything we need to know and, most importantly, we know who is to blame.

Light C.O.N.T.R.O.L.: "On the C.O.N."

C.O.N.T.R.O.L. talk operates at two levels, the most common of which I call light C.O.N.T.R.O.L. We will discuss the second level, heavy C.O.N.T.R.O.L., later in this chapter. **Light C.O.N.T.R.O.L.** is the effort to convince the other of our point of view when we are in disagreement. Light C.O.N.T.R.O.L. is the kind of persuasive talk we typically use, without thinking about it, when people act differently than we expected; or don't agree with our views; or we don't get what we want.

In fact, light C.O.N.T.R.O.L. is such a natural response that Flick[1] calls it conventional discussion. It's what we've been socialized to do. You disagree with me; now I need to persuade you to my point of view (the tennis game starts to gets "serious"). But when C.O.N.T.R.O.L. talk is overused, we become obsessed with proving a point. The difficulty is, once we start down the road to being right and getting someone to agree with us, that becomes *the* point. It's not about understanding them. It's not about being clear where they are. It's all a matter of getting them to agree to what it is that we have to say. As a result, we radically reduce the chances of building mutual respect and creating mutually beneficial outcomes.

When faced with the 3 D's we naturally use conventional discussion (C.O.N.T.R.O.L. talk) to resolve issues, and instead of deeply shared solutions, we end up with surface compliance by the other (just to get us to stop or go away), or compromise agreements. To get either of these, we often endure arguments, stalemates dominated by diatribes, even violence. At the community level, we have made efforts in the past twenty years to resolve some of this. For instance, in divorce litigation, many jurisdictions (including Ontario) now require that before couples go through mediation before they go to divorce court. A mediator attempts to get the two parties to talk to each other and seek common understanding instead of verbally beating on each other and seeking one-sided victory.

Flick summarizes the key elements of conventional discussion as follows:

Conventional Conversation	
Premise	There is only one right answer — usually one's own.
Goal	Win, be right, sell, persuade, convince.
Attitude	Evaluating and critical.
Focus	"What's wrong with this picture?"
Behavior	Listen judgmentally; interrogate others; defend our assumptions, faith.
Role	Devil's advocate or truth slayer.
Outcome	Debate

Criticism versus Complaint / Active versus Passive

In light C.O.N.T.R.O.L. mode, summarized in the table on next page, we always begin from a position of critical judgment — which takes the form of either criticism or complaint. In the **active** form of light C.O.N.T.R.O.L., we begin with a direct criticism of the other person. "You are wrong." We tell them directly they have the wrong idea; are thinking, doing or saying the wrong thing; and, most importantly, should be accepting our idea. Then we give the *new* information they need to know to see "our rightness"— our "facts" and point of view. Our intention is to make sure that they change their mind.

<table>
<tr><th colspan="2">Type</th><th>Active</th><th>Passive</th></tr>
<tr><td rowspan="3">L
I
G
H
T</td><td>C.</td><td>Critical Judgment
• I criticize you directly
• "You are wrong.</td><td>Critical Judgment
• I complain about your action
• You made me. . . ." "I don't like what you did. . . ."</td></tr>
<tr><td>O.</td><td>Offer New Information
• Tell them more of your story - Use active influence and compliance-gaining talk
• Ask questions to probe only for agreement and/or understanding of my story
• Listen for leverage — only for agreement with my story or for weakness in their story</td><td>Offer Old Information
• Tell them more of your story - Use passive influence and compliance-gaining talk
• Ask questions to probe only for agreement and/or understanding of my story
• Listen for leverage — only for agreement with my story or for weakness in their story</td></tr>
<tr><td>N.</td><td>Negotiate Change in Other
• Get them to agree with my views and save my "face"
• No or low acknowledgment of their story
• No or low support for them</td><td>Negotiate Change in Other
• Get them to agree with my views and save my "face"
• No or low acknowledgment of their story
• No or low support for them</td></tr>
</table>

C H O I C E	**T.**	**T**ry C.O.N. again **T**erminate the Conversation **T**ake it personally. Threat feelings arise. Escalate to heavy C.O.N.T.R.O.L.

The **passive** form begins from a position of complaint. So rather than saying, "You are wrong!" which is a criticism, we say, "I don't like what you did." The next step is to repeat old information. Working from passive light C.O.N.T.R.O.L. we try to "guilt" the other into changing. We give them enough of the "bad" stuff from their past to realize their "wrongness" now, and decide to change. Passive or active, it's still a matter of negotiating change in them.

As Flick asserts in her analysis of conventional discussion, C.O.N.T.R.O.L. talk begins with our idea that there is "something wrong with this picture." So we create some combination of three critical judgments. Either they are: (1) incorrect (wrong idea but think they know what they are talking about), (2) incomplete (they don't know enough and that's why they don't agree), or (3) inappropriate in their behavior (socially, ethically, morally). We then persuade them to our idea — by showing them their incorrectness and by giving them new information (our perspective or advice). We teach or we begin to moralize, telling them how they *should* think or what they *should* do. We induce guilt or shame by reminding them of their errors, unkept promises or inappropriate behavior.

After we have given them all of that, we may also offer them positive inducements to change — praise or rewards now or in the future. We make "if-then" promises: if you do what I want, then you can have a new TV, or get an A or go to heaven. We believe that if we make the reward high enough, they won't notice the fact that we are trying to push them in a direction we want them to go, and that *they* need to change so that *we* will be okay.

In small ways and large, we do this all the time. We seek to negotiate change in the other. We ask questions, but only to seek clarity of understanding of *our* information. In C.O.N.T.R.O.L. mode, I don't care much about you. What I care about is: are you listening to me? Do you agree with me? Are you making the change?

We do listen in these kinds of situations, but only to gain leverage. We don't listen to their story; we only listen for weaknesses in their story. In the end, we don't need their information or their story to succeed. We simply need to know if they got ours. If our C.O.N.T.R.O.L. works, the victory comes either in agreement with our viewpoint or in some sort of compromise acceptance of our views (or change from their views toward ours). Most importantly, they have to give up some or all of their position so that we can see they have become more correct, complete or appropriate in their views and behavior.

Power

C.O.N.T.R.O.L. talk is about exercising power to influence the other. Power in a relationship can be categorized in terms of its sources: positional power, personal power and relational power (the power of least interest).

1. **Positional power**: Often C.O.N.T.R.O.L. talk comes out of the fact that people have socially distinct roles that are recognized as having more authority and power than others. This is often called **legitimate power** or the power of formal authority. For example, teachers have light C.O.N.T.R.O.L. power over students, managers over employees, and in some situations, doctors over patients.

2. **Personal power**: This has to do with your persuasive abilities and your personality. It's about your ability to present yourself persuasively as a person, not whether you are in a position that allows you to tell other people what to do. Lots of people who have positional power have very little personal power. Forms of personal power include:

    a. **Referent power** is the power we have over people because they identify with us and want to be like us (e.g., the power of a celebrity "role model"). It is also present in the kind of power that persuasive speakers momentarily have over audiences.

    b. **Reward and coercive power** has to do with whether we are able to reward or punish people and, therefore, more or less likely to be able to exercise C.O.N.T.R.O.L. talk over them, depending on the situation.

    c. **Expert power** allows some people to control situations because they know more than everybody else.

    d. **Information power** is based on whom we know, that is, the network of information we can pull together.

3. **Relational power — the principle of least interest**: This happens in relationships between equals. In every long-term relationship there is always the lover and the beloved. And the beloved has less interest in the relationship because the other is doing more psychological work to maintain it. This gives the beloved a kind of psychological edge. The person with less interest in the relationship is also less controlled by the rewards and punishments offered by the other. Generally, for the one with less interest, being right is far more important than maintaining the relationship. For the other person it's just the opposite.

Light C.O.N.T.R.O.L. and Personal Power

Light C.O.N.T.R.O.L. talk is a form of personal power that can use all of the other forms to persuade and convince. It can be both rational and emotional. Success is a matter of how much information we can put together and how much emotional persuasion we can use to make ourselves right so the other will accept our argument. In everyday conversation, information structured with some rationality and presented with the emotions of enthusiasm (the emotions of joy, anticipation, acceptance in Plutchik's model) is often the most persuasive. In other words, we engagingly state why, in our view, their behavior or their talk has to change.

As we have seen so often in our lives as friends, lovers, employees and parents, light C.O.N.T.R.O.L. as persuasion doesn't always work. There are two main reasons for this. One, even though we may have the forms of power described (legitimate, referent, expert, etc.), we may not have the competence to pull our information together in a persuasive way in order to effectively use these resources to gain the compliance of the other. Two, we are often trying to influence another person in the *wrong* situation. Since we automatically use light C.O.N.T.R.O.L. every time we face the 3 D's (it's an automatic reaction based on our deep learning of the forms of conventional discussion), we don't realize that it works best only when we have legitimate power over the other.

Legitimate Power, Light C.O.N.T.R.O.L. and Everyday Rhetoric

Light C.O.N.T.R.O.L. as persuasion works well when the other person has:

- Far less power than we do, or recognizes our authority to speak,
- Less knowledge or insight than we do and needs or wants what we have, and
- Little to contribute in the situation (or at least it feels that way).

The basic influence tactic in these types of situations is the use of rational persuasion — the use of logical argument and new information — accompanied by appropriate appeals to values and emotions. It is the basis of talk for teachers, preachers, coaches, sales people and managers: for anyone in a position to know something we don't, that we might like to know or need to know, and are willing to accept direction on.

Control talk for rational persuasion or teaching begins with a tacit critical judgment of the other person in the situation — their knowledge or perspectives are somehow incomplete — and our teaching will fill this void. We help them change by giving them more information. Or, they may have lots of information but their ways of thinking about it simply lead them to the "wrong" answers or reactions. Usually this situation requires a little more effort on the part of a teacher, coach or manager. Simply giving the other(s) more data is not enough. We need to help the other construct new ways of framing information and essentially change the way they think. To do this we need to use more than facts and logic. We need to appeal to their values and their emotions. In fact, the more elegantly we can combine rational arguments — supported by appropriate data with appeals to the other's positive values and feelings about a subject — the more likely we will be able to engage them emotionally to change the way they think. Also, remembering what we said earlier: feelings are contagious and the feelings we display, as we present our data, will be picked up by the other(s).

In an article in *University Affairs*[2] I analyzed the relationship between emotions and the "facts and logic" approach to large-lecture delivery. I argued that in addition to presenting a well-structured talk, lecturers could be far more effective if they found ways to communicate two important things:

1) Their love for the subject (after all, they have dedicated their adult lives to it), which means telling their students how enthusiastic they are about the field and why this particular information is so important, and

2) Their care for the students. By this I mean not only by using language levels and metaphors that are more likely to connect with the students, but also by paying attention to the effects of their words on a few students in the first rows of the lecture hall. So, for example, they can repeat a point if they see looks of confusion appear.

My research data showed that students notice these efforts and respond positively to them. A similar effort could improve the quality of doctor-patient interaction. Doctors could show their care for their patients by simply paying attention for a moment longer to what patients are trying to tell them. Many doctors don't do this.

Roter and Hall[3] in their book *Doctors Talking with Patients/Patients Talking with Doctors* review what are now widely accepted studies on the first 90 seconds of an appointment — right after the doctor asks the question, "So what seems to be the problem?" In studies done 15 years apart, they found the same results. Around 70% of doctors interrupted the patient's opening statement after only 15–20 seconds to follow up on the first problem described. Without thinking about it, in order to exercise their expert power and legitimate authority, the doctors essentially "silenced" their patients.

The studies also revealed that the issues raised in later parts of the conversation (if that was permitted) were just as important and sometimes vastly more important than the first thing the patient said. But in the C.O.N.T.R.O.L. talk approach of most doctors, these issues never came out, or came out only in a haphazard way. For instance, on the way out of the office, the person might turn in the doorway and nonchalantly say: "So this lump under my arm is going to be OK, right?"

For most doctors it was a matter of controlling their appointments in terms of time; they didn't want to encourage endless small talk. So the researchers looked at the 30% of patients in their study who were allowed to continue their first statement without interruption. It turned out that their remaining statement took no more than 2.5 minutes. (Keep this in mind when you have your next doctor's appointment!)

In summary, whatever position of authority the speaker happens to be in, the process of persuasive light C.O.N.T.R.O.L. is the same. It begins with some level of judgment about the other, moves on to providing more or different information than they have now and is intended to create some sort of change in them. In the case of academics, it could be: "Know this; it will be on the exam." In the case of doctors, it could be something like: "You have to follow this regimen exactly." And for car salesman: "Here are the keys to your new car."

Active Light C.O.N.T.R.O.L. Tactics

Rational argument doesn't always work by itself, even if presented with enthusiasm, so as part of our persuasion we use emotion-based, compliance-gaining tactics. When we expect or encounter resistance from the other, we often move beyond facts and appeal directly to values, feelings and higher commitments. The table below gives an overview from DeVito.[4]

Compliance-Gaining Tactic	Example
Pre-giving. Pat rewards Chris and then makes a request.	Pat: I'm glad you enjoyed dinner. This really is the best restaurant in the city. How about going back to my place and . . . ?
Liking. Pat is helpful and friendly in order to get Chris in a good mood so that Chris will be more likely to comply with Pat's request.	Pat: [After cleaning up the living room and bedroom] I'd really like to relax and bowl a few games with Terry. Okay?
Promise. Pat promises to reward Chris if Chris complies with Pat's request.	Pat: I'll give you anything you want if you will just give me a divorce. You can have the house, the car, the stocks, the kids; just give me my freedom.
Threat. Pat threatens to punish Chris for noncompliance.	Pat: If you don't give me a divorce, you'll never see the kids again.
Aversive stimulation. Pat continuously punishes Chris and makes cessation of the punishment contingent upon compliance.	Pat: demonstrates hysterical reactions (for example, screaming and crying) and stops only when Chris agrees to comply.

Positive or negative expertise. Pat promises that Chris will be rewarded for compliance because of "the nature of things" or punished for noncompliance for the same reason.	Pat: If you follow the doctor's advice, you'll be fine, or If you don't listen to the doctor, you're going to wind up back in the hospital.
Positive self-feelings. Pat promises that Chris will feel better if Chris complies with Pat's request.	Pat: You'll see. You'll be a lot better off without me; you'll feel a lot better after the divorce.
Negative self-feelings. Pat promises that Chris will feel worse if Chris does not comply with Pat's request.	Pat: You'll hate yourself if you don't give me this divorce.
Positive or negative altercasting. Pat casts Chris in either the role of the "good" person or "bad" and argues that Chris should comply because a person with such qualities would comply.	Pat: Any intelligent person would grant their partner a divorce when the relationship has died, or Only a cruel and selfish neurotic could stand in the way of another's happiness
Positive esteem. Pat tells Chris that people will think more highly of Chris (relying on our need for the approval of others) if Chris complies with Pat's request.	Pat: Everyone will respect your decision to place your parents in an assisted living community.
Negative esteem. Pat tells Chris that people will think poorly of Chris if there is no compliance.	Pat: Everyone will think that you're paranoid if you don't join the club.
Moral appeals. Pat argues that Chris should comply because it's moral to comply and immoral not to.	Pat: Any ethical person would return the mistaken overpayment.
Altruism. Pat asks Chris to comply because Pat needs this compliance (relying on Chris's desire to help and be of assistance).	Pat: I would feel so disappointed if you quit college now. Don't hurt me by quitting.
Debt. Pat asks Chris to comply because of the past favors given to Chris.	Pat: Look at how we sacrificed to send you to college.

To summarize the active light C.O.N.T.R.O.L. tactics: the persuasive strategy of pre-giving is one of the most commonly used. Research has found that if you give somebody something free up front, they are more likely to do what you want when you ask for it.[5] Promising a reward is also widely used. We call it the "if-then" tactic — if you do this, then I will give you a reward or you will be a better human being. Besides telling them they will feel better about themselves, or others will feel good about them, sometimes we simply assert that they *are* good and smart and kind (positive altercasting) and as result are likely to do what we want, before we ask for the change. Finally, if none of that works, we can tell them that the change is "just the right thing to do."

On the negative side, we can, among other things, threaten them with direct punishment or the loss of good feelings about themselves and the criticism of others. These are all natural, everyday communication techniques we use to persuade people to our point of view when they don't want to go there.

Passive Light C.O.N.T.R.O.L. Tactics

When we resort to the negative compliance-gaining tactics, we are using passive light C.O.N.T.R.O.L. This approach asserts: "If you don't do this, the world will turn against you. Other people will say things that make you feel bad or they will think less of you." There is also the "you owe me" tactic of calling in past favors. "You have to do this for me now because I helped you in the past." The idea is to make them feel guilty. If we can't get our way by simply asking or persuading, we can use these kinds of negative emotional techniques. They rarely get us what we want, but we use them anyway.

On the "C.O.N.": Active Light C.O.N.T.R.O.L. in Action

The following conversation between an employee (Jim) and his manager (Bob) is a good example of active light C.O.N.T.R.O.L. Bob needs to fill a supervisory position quickly and he needs to convince Jim to accept the job, despite any misgivings Jim might have about the offer.

When this example of light C.O.N.T.R.O.L. is shown as a short video in classes and seminars, there's always a ripple of knowing laughter at the end. It seems to say, "Bob got his way and Jim is in trouble." It turns out both those conclusions are true.

On the "C.O.N."	
Bob:	Jim?
Jim:	*(Comes out in the hall from a computer area.)* Good morning, Bob
Bob:	Can you come by and see me after the staff meeting tomorrow morning?
Jim:	Sure.

Bob:	Good
Jim:	Oh, listen, if it's about that problem with scheduling, I think I'll have it figured out by then. I've been working. . . .
Bob:	No. No. I'm sure you can work that out. I want to talk to you about the possibility of taking over computer operations. Ken's leaving in a week, you know.
Jim:	Yeah. I heard something about that. *(Sigh.)*I don't know what to say.
Bob:	*(Enthusiastically.)* It's a great opportunity. I think you can handle it.
Jim:	All right. (*As if to himself.*) All right. I'll think about it. I'll talk it over with Betsy tonight. *(Tentatively.)* It's a big step.
Bob:	Piece of cake for a guy like you. You think it over, and talk to your wife like you say, and come by and see me after the meeting. OK?
Jim:	Sure.
Bob:	See you then.

	The Next Day (Knock on Bob's Door)
Bob:	*(Seated behind his desk, looks up.)* Come on in Jim. Sit down. Like some coffee?
Jim:	*(Sits down in front of Bob's desk.)* No thanks. I never touch the stuff.
Bob:	*(Gets up, walks around his desk and sits on the edge of it looking down at Jim. Holding a paper in his hand toward Jim.)* OK now, here's the deal. You'll be over the dozen or so people we have in the computer operations center. I have a job description here for you, but basically just keep things moving and iron out any problems when they come up.
Jim:	*(Folds his arms tightly across his chest.)* That's pretty different from what I do now.*(Voice sounds uncertain.)*
Bob:	*(Seems to pay no attention to Jim, continues to talk enthusiastically.)* You'll coordinate the weekly departmental reports, covering all the financial activity in the section. Those reports come directly to me. As far as salary goes, it's a great jump for you, plus benefits and the possibility of further increases. So what do you say? *(Hands him the paper.)*
Jim:	*(Sighs deeply. Takes paper but speaks up.)* Well, first of all let me say one thing. I really appreciate you considering me. I'm flattered and, of course, the money is a big temptation. But after thinking it over, I feel like I'd be going over my head into something I'm not sure I could handle. I know my limitations, and besides, I like what I'm doing now.
Bob:	*(Speaks warmly.)* Come on. Don't be modest. Of course, you could handle it. If you start next Monday, you'll have a full week to break in with Ken before he leaves. No problem.
Jim:	*(With nervous intensity.)* I'm not so sure. Handling 12 people sounds like a lot. I have enough trouble getting out the report I have to do now, much less one for a whole section.
Bob:	*(Upbeat.)* We can teach you those things. I've got great confidence in you with

	all the work you've done here in the last 3 years. What does your wife say? Did you talk to her about it?
Jim:	*(Somewhat quietly.)* She wants me to take it, you know, because it's a step up the ladder, but I don't know.
Bob:	*(Smiling.)* And there's the extra money. What does your wife say about that?
Jim:	*(Smiles in response.)* Well, sure we can use that with the new house and the kids and all.
Bob:	*(Upbeat.)* See, this will put you on the right track. No one has to be told how to spend money.
Jim:	No, that's for sure.
Bob:	*(Firmly and positively.)* Good, then we've agreed. Tell you what, I'll arrange for you to see Ken Carpenter today. He'll give you information on computer operations. Read it this weekend and you can start on Monday, and if you have any problems just let me know.
Jim:	*(Looks a bit surprised, then smiles.)* Thanks Bob.
Bob:	*(Smiles back.)* You're welcome. That's what I'm here for.

Bob simply never acknowledges Jim's uncertainty — never notes his obvious nonverbals of concern — and responds directly to Jim's negative assertions with his own opposite judgments. He essentially tells Jim his own story — how he's going to be fine; he's right for the job and can learn it in a week. He also uses several compliance-gaining techniques. He's helpful and friendly; promises Jim a great future; casts him into the role of accomplished manager to stimulate positive self-feelings. When that doesn't seem to work, he shifts the discussion to Jim's wife, implying that things might not go so well with her if he turns down the offer. Most importantly, he never asks Jim a single question about any of his concerns and uses his positional power to assert an agreement that actually doesn't exist in the moment. Jim was right, he doesn't last a year in the new job. He couldn't keep up with the work and manage the staff at the same time.

Light C.O.N.T.R.O.L. in the Workplace

As we have said, light C.O.N.T.R.O.L. works well when the other person (1) has far less power or knowledge than we do; (2) really needs or wants what we have; or (3) feels they have little to contribute in the situation. In other words, the very situation described above between Jim and Bob, as Bob the boss, with the position, information and reward power in the situation, uses persuasive light C.O.N.T.R.O.L. to get what he wants — a position filled within a week by somebody he thinks can do the job. In fact, the regular use of this kind of light C.O.N.T.R.O.L. talk is built into the structure of most workplaces in our society.

The Competitive Light C.O.N.T.R.O.L. Loop

There are times in formally structured organizations, in families, or in friendship relationships, when the automatic light C.O.N.T.R.O.L. response doesn't get us what we want because the other person has about the same power or knowledge as we do, and feels they have something to contribute. So, when we try to exercise light C.O.N.T.R.O.L in essentially equal relationships, the other may feel that we are imposing our views on them; trying to tell them what to do or how to think and as a result they resist by using light C.O.N.T.R.O.L on us.

C.O.N.T.R.O.L. Talk and the Structuring of Organizations

These conditions are present in almost every major form of organization in our lives. When we are confronted with creating goal-driven predictability in the behavior of a group of people over time — building an organization — we use various forms of coordination and control techniques based on a common structural form: the **hierarchy.** This is a rank order of socially recognized positions, with varying levels of legitimate authority, decision-making power and status attached to them. This structure is often shaped like a pyramid, so that there are relatively few positions at the top of the hierarchy, whose occupants hold most of the authority, power and social worth, and an increasing number of positions below them occupied by those with more limited forms of power, authority and status who oversee the actions of those with even less. This isn't the only structure that organized human behavior takes, but it is one of the most common forms developed when large numbers of people need organizing.

The first condition for the effective use of light C.O.N.T.R.O.L. (people with more power and knowledge talking to those with less) is built into the hierarchical form. It is seen as one appropriate way to manage others' behavior. The second condition — people accepting our persuasive C.O.N.T.R.O.L. because they want what we have — is also built into this organizational form. Whether or not they agree with them, those further down the hierarchy often accept what their managers say in order to present themselves as people who could manage if given the chance because they covet the additional status, authority and power that a higher position would bring.

What emerges are the **3 D's** (differences, disagreement and disorder) and the competitive light C.O.N.T.R.O.L. loop — with each of us trying to "out-C.O.N." the other to win, to be right. Flick calls this a debate: while I am trying to persuade you to change, you respond by trying to persuade me to your position as well as by attacking my position. Our language rapidly becomes argumentative, even inflammatory, as it shifts from the reality orientation at the lower end of the inference ladder to the sweeping judgments at the top. As each of us resists, the other feels the need to make "allness" statements.

When C.O.N.N.E.C.T. talk goes awry, or when persuasive C.O.N.T.R.O.L. talk suddenly feels threatening, people are often taken by surprise and their negative emotions are aroused. This is an "emergent problem" situation. For example, when one person undermines the unspoken agreement about playful sharing of similarities in C.O.N.N.E.C.T. talk by saying something that is heard as critical, when it was perhaps meant to be humorous, or expresses an opinion that seems "out of place" in this type of conversation, the unexpected differences create a problem.

When C.O.N.N.E.C.T. Talk Turns into C.O.N.T.R.O.L.

You're an adult member of the family, married with kids, great job, held in esteem by other family members, except until one of them reminds you at a Thanksgiving dinner of some odd or unflattering behavior from your childhood. Everyone laughs, but you're embarrassed. They've revealed something from your "hidden" side of your self. You feel your anger rising, and they notice and say, "Hey what's wrong with you? It was funny! Can't you take a joke?"

This is a situation where we instantly feel the need to get them to "see the truth." We display every limitation of the perception and thought processes discussed earlier because our emotions are engaged and our feelings push us into judgment. Their words aren't simply incorrect; they are somehow deeply inappropriate.

Our face and our emotional investment in the conversation is threatened, so to feel better, we need to be right by changing their "wrong" views. We need to get them to back off or back down. Light C.O.N.T.R.O.L. is our automatic response. It's the seventh axiom in action. In difficult situations we need to feel right.

So, instead of laughing, we move into C.O.N.T.R.O.L. talk aimed at defending our self and explaining away what we did as a child, or undermining the other person's assertion by trivializing it: "Nah, you're full of it, that's not what happened. Anyway, how would know anything about it? You were two at the time. Maybe you should have another glass of wine to refresh your memory!"

The climate suddenly gets serious as the tacit assumptions of C.O.N.N.E.C.T. talk evaporate. The other begins a comeback criticism . . . and we move into competitive light C.O.N.T.R.O.L. Whether dealing with unexpected differences — or expecting disagreement before we start — our responses are always the same. They start with a critical judgment ("You're wrong") or a complaint about their actions ("I don't like what you said") and then launch into giving new information, that is, *our* (right) view of the situation to get the other to change their thoughts or actions. If this sounds like rational, persuasive light C.O.N.T.R.O.L. on steroids — it is. Without a third-party intervention to distract the "combatants" with some humor about both of them (to restore the climate of C.O.N.N.E.C.T. talk) things could go very badly.

Unlike the established social situations we discussed earlier where the speakers' use of C.O.N.T.R.O.L. talk is supported by their position or their expertise, we only have our assumptions about the "rightness" of our views to work with in our personal relationships. In addition, if this action-reaction loop continues too long, the emotions behind our words will begin to surface in our conscious mind and our talk can escalate from a discussion or a debate into a fight. In fact, the problem with automatically using light C.O.N.T.R.O.L. every time we run into disagreement is that it too easily escalates into heavy C.O.N.T.R.O.L. when we don't get the agreement we want.

Competitive Light C.O.N.T.R.O.L. Is about Personal Power

The real struggle in competitive light C.O.N.T.R.O.L. is about who's in charge and who needs to be right. When we have no positional power — no legitimate authority with its reward and punishment power — it comes down to our own personal power and relational power — the principle of least interest.

In studies of influence tactics[6] used by couples in making everyday decisions, whoever was least dependent on their relationship was most likely to exercise their personal power in order to win.

Hard and Soft Persuasion Tactics Used in Couple Decision Making

- When couples saw themselves as being equals in the overall relationship – sharing the formal decisions about money or where to live, for instance — they tended to choose the rational persuasive approach (facts and argumentation) to exercise light C.O.N.T.R.O.L. They saw themselves as bargaining and reaching compromises in difficult moments. They used rational persuasion when they weren't expecting much resistance from the other, and when both were likely to benefit from the change.

- When couples described their relationship as having distinct power differences — one person made all the main decisions in the family — the more powerful partner almost always picked hard or negative compliance tactics. It seems that when a person sees themselves as having formal power in an informal relationship, they feel much freer to put their foot down and demand the other's compliance. On the other hand, in the same high-low power relationship, the less empowered person chose positive or "soft" emotional tactics to persuade the other to change.

Emotionally evocative tactics can tip an argument toward resolution when "facts and argumentation" don't work. Below is a list of some of the tactics used by the couples in the study (see DeVito's complete list on pages 193–4).

Negative or Hard Tactics	*Positive or Soft Tactics*
• Threatening them ("If you don't comply, I will reject you.") • Casting them in a negative role, say that of the villain ("Only a stupid person wouldn't give me what I want.") • Promising negative self-feelings ("You'll hate yourself if you don't ...") • Invoking negative esteem ("Everybody we know will hate you."), or • Calling in past favors ("Look at how often I gave you what you wanted. You owe me this.")	• Promising the other concrete rewards ("If you will just . . . I will give you. . . .") • Calling on positive self-feelings ("You'll feel better about yourself if you do this.") • Positive alter casting — that is, casting the other into a positive role ("You can handle it . . . you're a very smart guy.") • Invoking positive esteem ("Other people will think well of you, if. . . .") • Moral appeals ("It's the right thing to do."), or • Altruism ("Look, I really need your help.")

Everyday Debate Is a Form of Competitive Light C.O.N.T.R.O.L.

When we use competitive Light C.O.N.T.R.O.L., we are responding to and enacting the many invisible assumptions our cultural learning has taught us about the "combative" ways to discover "the truth." These include:

- Assuming that there is a right answer and we have it,
- Proving the other wrong or at least seriously diminishing the strength of their argument with our criticism,
- Listening only to find flaws in their thinking and building counterarguments,

- Defending our assumptions as objective truths — from high on the inference ladder, and
- Seeking a conclusion that ratifies our position.

These assumptions place a premium on being right, winning, and in the process of confirming our "rightness" we often feel that we have to disconfirm the other by:

- Trivializing their statements: making light of what they're saying,
- Telling them they don't have enough data, or they have bad data, or demanding proof,
- Ignoring or interrupting them,
- Speaking in a superior way when we reply,
- Discounting what they say, or
- Overloading them with closed questions — make them defend themselves.

When two people are competing for C.ON.T.R.O.L., the sparring can simply go round and round like a hamster wheel until somebody finds a way to silence the other or escape. Below is an example of competitive light C.O.N.T.R.O.L. between a son and his father. As they get caught up in their needs to be right, neither the age differences between them nor the legitimate authority of the parental role matters. It comes down to which of them is more effective in wielding their personal power in the situation.

Competing to Be Right

Son: *(Looking down)* Geez, I am sooo dumb!
Father: You are *not* dumb.
Son: I am so.
Father: You *are* not.
Son: My report card says I'm dumb.
Father: Your report card says you need to work harder in a couple of courses.
Son: No, it says I'm dumb.
Father: It does not.
Son: What about my camp counselor last summer? He said I was dumb.
Father: I talked to him about that. He was only kidding.

Son:	He was not. I am dumb.
Father:	You are not. You're smart.
Son:	No, I'm dumb, but I'm not dumb enough to believe you when you say I'm smart.
Father:	Why?
Son:	Because you're my Dad and you have to say stuff like that. I'm dumb!
Father:	Stands there in stunned silence.

It looks like the son has "outpowered" his father this time. However, you might also notice that this conversation has all the markings of a "Did"–"Did not" childhood spat. The father misses the opportunity to move out of his Parent voice and move into his Adult inquiring voice. He never asks any questions to break the flow of this "tennis match" and discover what's really going on in the mind of his son — and how long he's been feeling this way about himself. Instead he uses what he thinks of as a "nurturing" Parent voice and simply offers — one after another — reassuring but ineffective positive judgments to compete with his son's negative judgments about himself. He doesn't seem to realize he's trying to impose his positive views of his son, on his son. There is little "good information" being discovered by either one of them in this moment and it can only end with one of them being right and the other being "silenced." The son simply finds a clever way to do that to his father.

Moving into Heavy C.O.N.T.R.O.L.

In competitive light C.O.N.T.R.O.L., our exchange of personal power and persuasion becomes intense discussion or debate, but it can escalate into arguing and fighting. This occurs because we begin to take the other's resistance personally and start to feel threatened. We begin to feel righteously angry or indignant.

This righteousness is often framed as: "This person is out to get me rather than just disagree with me. I don't deserve this so I have to do whatever I can to defend myself against this threat to my face." We begin to respond with a different level of argument — **heavy C.O.N.T.R.O.L.** Once the emotions of threat are engaged, we shift from solving the problem at hand to winning at all costs. It moves from a dispute over the facts or the situation, to something much more personal and destructive — the laying of blame. The "psycho-logic" in this situation seems to be: "Since you are actively preventing me from getting my way, and that's unfair, I deserve to be angry and you deserve what's about to happen to you."

Heavy C.O.N.T.R.O.L. is aggressive. It happens because, without our even noticing, our heart rate has climbed to 100+ beats in the span of one beat; our bloodstream is surging with the stress-excitement chemicals of adrenaline and cortisol; and we are on the way to a "hijack." This emotional surge closes off access to our rational thought processes. The only trouble is that by the time this rush is over, we haven't solved the problem that initiated the discussion in the first place. We've simply found someone to blame for our failure to communicate — them.

Heavy C.O.N.T.R.O.L. Tactics

In heavy C.O.N.T.R.O.L. we send **"you are" messages**. Once we've said, "You are," the next thing that comes out of our mouth is a label — a judgment. And, unless we're feeling joyful and loving at that moment and say, "You are wonderful," we're likely to say something negative like, "You are an idiot!" Active heavy control is about **direct attack** — criticism, ridicule and all other forms of negative labeling. The passive form of heavy C.O.N.T.R.O.L. talk is about using **guilt** to control the other by making them feel responsible for our problems. "You made me do this! It's your fault!" The driving emotions and key elements of heavy C.O.N.T.R.O.L. are summarized in the table on next page.

We also use **mind reading** (see Chapter 7) in heavy C.O.N.T.R.O.L. talk. We tell people how they feel ("You don't care") and what they should think or believe. As soon as we tell people what's in their mind, we are high up the inference ladder, far from reality and in judgmental control mode. Moreover, once we get to heavy C.O.N.T.R.O.L. talk, we don't just imply these criticisms in the tone of our voice, we verbalize them.

Another problem with negative "you are" messages is that they are an *indirect* way of talking about our feelings. Instead of saying, "I am really angry at what you just said!" we say, "You're an idiot!" The other person gets our anger, but they get it in a package with a high-powered **negative label**. They notice the label and ignore our anger. They defend themselves and resist us so we hit back harder. This is what heavy C.O.N.T.R.O.L. is about. It's not about solving the problem or resolving our issues, it's about being right and trying to make the other wrong.

The Heavy C.O.N.T.R.O.L. Loop

Through our heavy C.O.N.T.R.O.L.[7] talk we avoid ownership of our messages. We try to make the other responsible for our feelings of upset, anger or fear. The mindful, flexible and effective response to the other's C.O.N.T.R.O.L. would be to step out of the way and not engage, but that isn't our automatic, fast and certain response. Instead, we respond in kind and make things worse. When people attack us, we seem to naturally feel the need to defend ourselves. That's why heavy C.O.N.T.R.O.L. can go so bad so quickly.

H	R.	**R**ighteous Anger	**R**ighteous Indignation
E A V	O.	**O**vert Aggression Put-Downs Mind Reading Labeling Commands Threats Venting Demands Criticism Ridicule Sarcasm	**O**vert Passive Aggression Intense Complaint Disqualifiers Whining Martyrdom Withholding Denial Self-Put-Downs Giving Excuses Procrastination Lying
Y	L.	**L**aying Blame	**L**aying Blame

In heavy C.O.N.T.R.O.L. we also treat communication as a series of "punctuated events" by pretending that communication is simple and that when things go wrong there is only one cause — the other person. In fact, however, we co-create our realities with others. Our responsibilities are mutual. When we are angry and upset, it's hard for us to notice this, let alone accept, so we go for control by punctuating the circle of communication into a linear model of cause and effect. "I did this because you made me."

Heavy C.O.N.T.R.O.L. in Action

This couple's "post-party" struggle is a good example of heavy C.O.N.T.R.O.L. It begins with what Gottman calls a "harsh" startup — a you-message that is spoken with an intensity guaranteed to make the receiver defensive and angry. Things go downhill from there.

Guy: You really pissed me off when you flirted with other guys at the party last night!

Girl: Yeah, well you made me mad when you got drunk.

Guy: I wouldn't have had to drink so much if you'd have paid more attention to me.

Girl: Maybe I would if you'd smarten up. I mean, get serious about school and start acting your age.

Guy: I'll do that right after you quit smoking and spend some more time with me instead of always burying yourself in your books.

Girl: You're just jealous that I'm succeeding in my program.

Guy: Succeeding! *(Chuckling sarcastically)* Journalism isn't a real career.

Girl: At least it *is* a career, which is more than what you have.

Guy: You never do anything but whine and complain! What a bitch!

Notice how each tries to blame the other for their own bad feelings — the struggle for punctuation — as well as the defensive reactions of direct criticism of the other (you-messages), mind reading, disconfirming talk and commands — all in loud voices and in nine lines of talk. The interesting question is, where can this couple go after such an exchange?

In summary, as C.O.N.T.R.O.L. talk turns heavy, the surface struggle seems to be about[8]:

1) **What was actually said**. There is always a tussle about the "truth" — what really happened. Unfortunately, we always start from the position that our version of the truth is the right version. We work from our conclusions and our beliefs, not from what actually happened.

2) **What was meant by what was said.** The issue here is, what is the other's intention? What lies behind their words? The assumption that's always hidden behind our talk is, "I know what you meant." This reaction is so automatic we just assume that our assumptions are facts, and that often gets us into trouble.

3) **Who's to blame?** This is the essential reason behind the use of heavy C.O.N.T.R.O.L. We didn't want to take responsibility for a situation we couldn't control and in which we couldn't get things our way.

Rationally, heavy C.O.N.T.R.O.L. makes no sense at all. The problem that started it doesn't get solved and the other person can't be made to be wrong. They can only be silenced. Emotionally, however, it makes tremendous sense to us. The upheaval somehow releases us from the responsibility for our own bad behavior. The worst thing about

C.O.N.T.R.O.L. talk in general, and heavy C.O.N.T.R.O.L. talk in particular, is that no matter how the drama ends, it undermines the integrative, connective basis of the relationship.

We do all of this because we don't have a natural way of talking to each other that keeps us connected even as we struggle with differences. We don't regularly practice the ideals of the emotionally and cognitively self-managed talk we discussed in Chapter 8. When facing unexpected differences or disagreements, we can't seem to find the right words and behaviors.

Where We're Going Next

There is, of course, something else we could be doing in every **3 D** situation. We need to learn a:

- *Way* of talking that communicates the meta-message to the other that
- *Where* they are in the discussion (a different position than us) will not define
- *Who* they are in relationship to us.

In other words, we need to talk about problems in a way that others won't take so personally — so they will actually listen to us rather than defend themselves against us. We will discuss this third mode of talk, called D.I.A.L.O.G.U.E., in the next chapter.

End Notes

[1] Flick, D. (1998) *From Debate to Dialogue.* Boulder, CO: Orchid Publications.

[2] Kehoe, D. (2008) "*Five Ways to Energize Your Lectures,*" *University Affairs Magazine*, online edition, December 1.

[3] Roter, D., Hall, J. (2006) *Doctors Talking with Patients/Patients Talking with Doctors: Improving Communication in Medical Visits* (2nd ed.). New York: Praeger.

[4] DeVito, J. A. (2001) *The Interpersonal Communication Book* (9th ed.). Toronto: Addison Wesley Longman, Inc., p. 308.

[5] Cialdini, R. (2001) *Influence: Science and Practice* (4th ed.). Needham Heights, MA: Allyn and Bacon.

[6] Kipnis, D., Schmidt, S. (1985) "The Language of Persuasion" *Psychology Today*, April, pp. 40–46.

[7] The "O." descriptors are mostly from *Straight Talk* by Miller, et al. (1981). New York: Signet.

[8] Stone, D., Patton, B., Heen, S., Fisher, R. (2000) *Difficult Conversations.* New York: Penguin Books.

CHAPTER ELEVEN

THE SECOND MODE OF PROBLEM-SOLVING TALK: D.I.A.L.O.G.U.E.

The mode of talk that allows us to deal with interpersonal communication problems, without making the other person (and their conversational face) the problem, is called D.I.A.L.O.G.U.E. This acronym outlines the "being" and "doing" steps we need to take to be more effective communicators when our communication with someone begins to slide into breakdown.

The "Three Mode" Model Revisited

There are times in conversation when we must make the choice to stop and deal with the problem that's right in front of us rather than try to overwhelm the other person with our "rightness."

To illustrate this moment, I want you to think of yourself in a car heading into an intersection to make a left-hand turn. You wait as the oncoming traffic clears the intersection and you begin to complete the turn. The light is turning red so you have to make the turn, but as you move forward, you are suddenly aware of a car that is running the red light. You have a choice here: you are in the right if you make the turn, but if you make the turn, you will be hit. You can make the turn and later, in the hospital, you can claim that you were in the right. Or you can solve the problem right here and now: slam on the brakes and let the other car whiz past you.

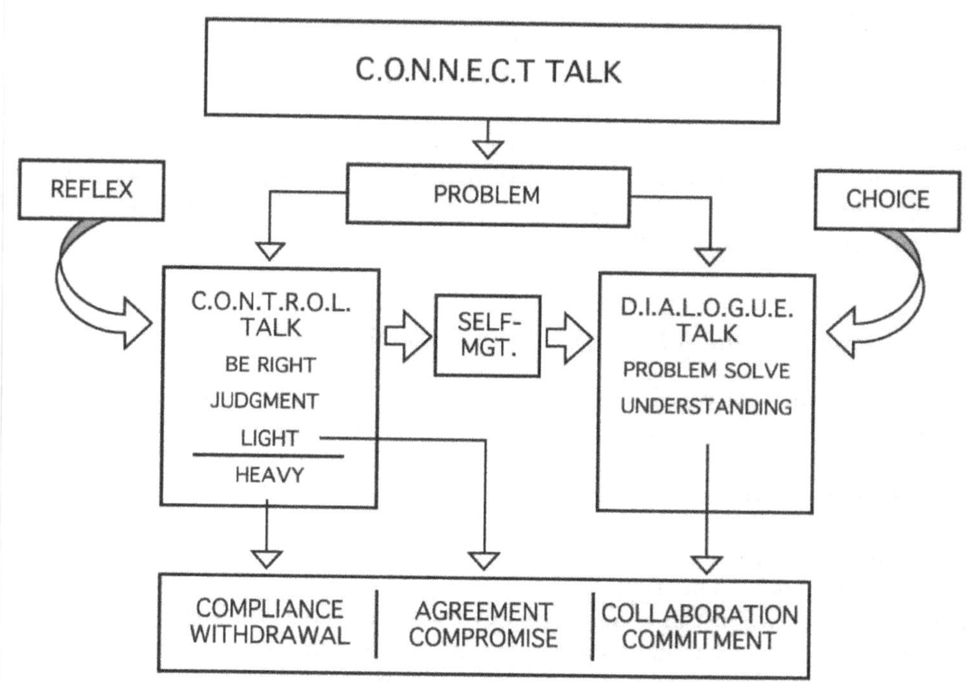

When this happened to me, I would have preferred the chance to solve the problem. I unfortunately didn't get the choice. I was already too far into the turn to avoid the driver that T-boned my car. The light was already red and all the oncoming cars had passed. I don't know where he came from, but the last thing I saw before he hit me (and before I went unconscious) was his face — turned to his right, talking to his passenger. He didn't even notice the light.

If we come into a difficult moment absolutely certain of our right answer, we come destined to use C.O.N.T.R.O.L. talk on the other. If, on the other hand, we come to the moment to discover the answer that lies between us, we can enter into D.I.A.L.O.G.U.E.

As the diagram of the Three Mode model of talk indicates, D.I.A.L.O.G.U.E., unlike C.O.N.T.R.O.L. talk, is driven by conscious choice. On the D.I.A.L.O.G.U.E. side of the model the emphasis is on **self-management** (emotional self-regulation and the use of the three critical skills for effective talk) before speaking. D.I.A.L.O.G.U.E. requires thought before we talk. In fact, we can't use D.I.A.L.O.G.U.E. unless we first choose to be "self-managed" — that is,

- Become aware of what is happening to us and the other in the present,
- Accept what is going on *as it is* without being judgmental about it, and
- Choose to talk appropriately for this situation.

This means speaking and reacting not out of or about our past fears, or out of our need to be right, but speaking to *what has just happened to us a few moments ago and what continues to happen, right in front of us, in this situation.* This may sound like what we already do — it's not. It may also sound straightforward and easy — it isn't.

The Assumptions of the D.I.A.L.O.G.U.E. Mode of Talk

The complexity of D.I.A.L.O.G.U.E. is indicated by its basic assumptions (summarized in the table on the next page). They fall into three categories:

Problem Solving, Not Winning

The assumptions behind D.I.A.L.O.G.U.E. talk are the opposite of those for C.O.N.T.R.O.L. talk. The first and most critical assumption is that when we speak in D.I.A.L.O.G.U.E. we intend to solve whatever problem is at hand, not just save our own face by being right. As the second assumption notes, saving our face is not at issue because we are choosing to manage ourselves, not the other person. In effect, we are getting our emotional reactions to their differences, disagreement or disorderly behavior out of our way.

Fact-Finding, Not Flaw-Finding in the Present

These assumptions overturn the mind's natural tendency to *avoid* dealing with the "facts of the matter" and instead judge others from high atop our inference ladder. By recognizing that there are always two different stories in every situation (not just my story and my belief about your story — which is still only one story), we compel our minds to focus on locating all of the potential problem-solving data available to us in this situation by asking questions and really listening to the other *before* we tell our side.

Mutual Causality, Not Self-Serving Punctuation

Once in the D.I.A.L.O.G.U.E. mode, we "get real" about the interleaved flow of relationship communication. We make the assumption that a part of *what we did or didn't do* in this situation (or previous situations) made some sort of contribution to the problem we now have in the present. It isn't called *inter*personal communication for nothing. It happens between us, so we both must have contributed to the creation and maintenance of whatever reality is being struggled over at the moment. This realization also forces us to move away from automatically blaming the other by managing the "punctuation of events" to serve our own needs.

D.I.A.L.O.G.U.E. Talk Assumptions

- *I need to solve problem, not save face.*
- ***I manage myself****, not you.*
- *We both have to change.*
- *My story is my story — obvious only to me.*
- *Your story is your story — obvious only to you.*
- *I have all the data only when I listen to and understand your story.*

As D.I.A.L.O.G.U.E. deepens, becomes more complex:

- *You clarify your meaning and assumptions.*
- *How did we contribute to this situation?*

As one of the key assumptions of D.I.A.L.O.G.U.E. states, to solve this problem we both have to change, somehow. Despite our childlike urge to blame the other, we are bound together in our relationships, particularly if we have a history. We each have contributed to this moment not only by our present behaviors but also by avoiding doing or saying things in the past that might have changed everything for the better. In those moments we didn't respond because: (1) it didn't seem polite to say it, (2) it might have upset the other person, (3) we were waiting for the right time, and/or (4) we didn't think it really mattered.

This can go on until things get really difficult and then we claim our innocence: "I didn't do anything to deserve this." As theologian Harvey Cox once said, "Not to decide is to decide." I believe that in many instances, inaction is really another form of action.

The Style Elements of D.I.A.L.O.G.U.E. Talk

The D.I.A.L.O.G.U.E. acronym represents all the things we must be and do to engage this mode of talk. The last two letters – **U** and **E** – are how we must "be" in the situation (our frame of mind) in order to engage in effective problem-solving talk. The remaining letters — **D.I.A.L.O.G.** — describe what we have to do to show the other we are using this mode.

The last element — **E** — represents **emotional self-regulation**. Without somehow stepping aside from our emotional reactions to the other's resistance to our rightness and the implied loss of face, we can't make a choice. As John Gottman[1] points out in his laboratory studies of couples in difficult long-term relationships, when couples fight, their heartbeats rise above 100 beats a minute, in a single beat, and they can't access rational thought. The brain's biochemistry cuts off access to the frontal lobes — where the executive decision-making functions reside. He recommends the self-soothing process outlined in Chapter 8. Only then can people be mindful — truly present in the moment — and be able to move to the next element of D.I.A.L.O.G.U.E: **U** — **understand first**.

When we choose to understand first, we think before we talk and pay attention to the other. We appreciate the situation more deeply. So before we open our mouths and say the one thing we'll regret, we mentally take a step back and ask ourselves, "What's really going on here?" This is the moment when we stop being in our own little drama about how unfair life is, how unfair the other person is, and how righteous we are.

In seeking to understand, we may need to metacommunicate — talk about the way things are being talked about in this particular situation. And we need to be flexible — open to hearing things we may not want to hear — and ask ourselves the "I wonder" question. "I wonder why this bothers me so much? I wonder what this is about?" Asking ourselves that question shifts the whole focus of our minds from "I am right" to "I am seeking information about what's going on."

Understanding first moves our mind and verbal expression from judgment ("You are a jerk") to description ("I don't like the way you leave your laundry on the floor for me to pick up"). We begin to shift from being judgmental, overbearing, or frightened and angry to being problem solvers.

This is a commitment to the first step in appreciation. It involves suspending our negative judgment and replacing it with an intention to truly understand the other, even in this difficult moment. When we learn to suspend judgment, we open the door to seeing the other's point of view. We don't get rid of our own judgments and opinions — that's not really possible — but we create a space between our judgment and our overt reactions that allows for listening and for bringing the conscious mind into the "here and now" rather than mindlessly and automatically responding to judgments of the present, based on information we learned in the past.

D.I.A.L.O.G.U.E.
Style Elements

D. Descriptive Language

— Use nonjudgmental language
— Assume as little as possible
— Present the "facts" as you see them

I. I-messages

Nonjudgmental descriptive statements of your:

— Acknowledgment of other or situation
— Perceptions and feelings (I see, I hear, I feel, etc.)
— Desired outcome or what you want to happen

A. Appreciative Questions

— Get other's information, story, perceptions, and views
— Open the door to information flow
— Seek understanding of your information, your story
— Seek confirmation, agreement after you understand both sides

L. Listen Actively

— Listen for their story, meanings
— Periodically reflect other's ideas in your words to show understanding
— Build trust
— Listen for implied offers, partial agreement

O. Open Acknowledgment

— Of their concerns, fears, feelings, etc.
— Of the situation
— In order to build bridges, show understanding

G. Genuine Support

— Affirm other's right to disagree and see things differently
— Support other's efforts to resolve
— Affirm their humanity

U. Understand First

— This is the purpose and mindset of D.I.A.L.O.G.U.E.
— It is the opposite of C.O.N.T.R.O.L. (winning, being right)
— Without mutual understanding, resolution can't be certain

E. Emotional Self-Management

— Key to D.I.A.L.O.G.U.E.
— Begins with awareness of self and others
— Pause and make choice not to react reflexively
— Choose to move from hot to cool feelings

Suspending judgment or evaluation is also a key to building a climate of trust and openness. As people learn that they won't be judged "wrong" for their opinions, they feel freer to express themselves. When people see that we are judging them, they simply stop listening to what we have to say. And unless we temporarily let go of our judgments, we can't come down our inference ladder and ask questions in our Adult ego state, to rediscover the data in the situation — that is, the other's description of what has just gone on between us.

In addition, we start to sound like a person who wants to discuss the problem rather than just simply be right about it. In TA terms (see Chapter 7), this means we are have moved from our controlling Parent or angry Child ego states into our **Adult.** In D.I.A.L.O.G.U.E. the U and E choices give us the emotional space we need to understand what *they* are really trying to say, not just what *we* hear them say; and to try to understand the situation before we enact the first six active elements of the D.I.A.L.O.G.U.E. model outlined in the table above.

The "D" of D.I.A.L.O.G.U.E.: Descriptive Language

When it's our turn to talk, we have to choose words that are nonjudgmental and try to assume as little as possible about the situation. This means talking about the things that we see and hear without labeling them. We have to manage our language because it's actually quite hard for us to simply *describe* things. Unthinkingly, we often use descriptors that are high-powered labels or judgments. Hanna[2] provides an excellent example of the differences between judgmental and descriptive talk C.O.N.N.E.C.T. talk:

Judgmental versus Descriptive Talk

> Pretend you are the listener in the following conversations and assess each one in terms of your reactions:
>
> 1. "People in this neighborhood just don't care about their property. They let their houses run down, and their yards are a disaster. You'd think they'd never heard of a lawn mower! Anyone who owns property should keep it up or just move. . . ."
>
> 2. "I've noticed in the last few months that the houses in the neighborhood look shabbier than they used to. And I haven't seen anyone mow a yard for at least a week. I'm frustrated by it because I take pride in my property and believe that it's considerate to keep my house in good condition."

Hanna argues that although the basic same message was delivered in each situation, listener reaction would be quite different. The first assertion is an "allness" statement, delivered as if it is the final and only thing one could say about this neighborhood. It is composed of (1) mind reading ("People . . . don't care"; "let their houses run down"; "never heard of a lawn mower"); (2) abstract and inflammatory language ("their yards are a disaster"); and (3) commanding judgment ("Anyone who owns property should keep it up or just move . . ."). Whether or not the result is intended, this statement is more likely to close off a discussion rather than open one up. The finality and generality of the statement leaves little room for reasoned response. People would probably think, "I can't win against this, so I'll just shut up." We would describe the first statement as defense-inducing C.O.N.T.R.O.L. talk. It begins and ends with critical judgment, and is delivered to sound certain and superior.

The second statement is framed to support open discussion. The thoughts are presented in a way that sounds more provisional, egalitarian and descriptive and is likely to trigger a reasonable discussion with a listener. This is a moment of **d**escriptive talk using **I**-messages — the **D.I.** of D.I.A.L.O.G.U.E. The speaker describes what they've seen, when they've seen it, and how they feel about it by making statements that start with "I." This kind of talk shows ownership of one's perceptions, beliefs and emotional reactions without trying to impose them on the listener. Descriptive talk leaves space so people they can talk together.

Descriptive I-Messages

In **3 D** situations, we need to speak so that people will listen to us rather than feel the need to defend themselves. To get people to hear our side of the story, we need to avoid making sweeping critical judgments because these tend to inflame emotions, which in difficult situations are already running high. If people don't come down their inference ladders, they won't be able to think clearly, listen fully and speak effectively.

The emotional power of using descriptive language rests on the fact that it tells our truth. When we say "in my opinion," or "as I see it," we are describing the only "truth" we actually know . . . *our* thoughts and perceptions. Implicitly, I-message talk:

1) Keeps us honest. We speak our truth — only about what we have experienced directly.

2) Recognizes others will have different thoughts and perceptions and can challenge us.

3) Restrains our inclination toward mind reading and pretending to describe other people's thoughts, perceptions and feelings as if they were facts.

4) Reduces our need to judge others by telling them how they *ought to be* thinking, seeing and feeling.

You-Action Descriptors

In the discussion of C.O.N.T.R.O.L. talk, we argued that "you are . . ." is the archetypal, judgmental phrase. It can't be neutral because the verb "to be" refers directly to our inner selves — our essential existence. When we use it we are essentially invading another's interior space with our words and, when that phrase is followed by something negative, everyone automatically goes into defense mode. Even if they're not saying a word, they're not listening because they're too busy telling themselves how angry or indignant they are because of what we just said.

The point of D.I.A.L.O.G.U.E. is to speak in a way that allows the other to listen in difficult moments, *without having to defend themselves*. It provides a way to use the word *you* without critiquing their essential humanity — the "you-action" phrase. In difficult moments we need to describe another's behaviors or words by saying "When I see you do . . ." or "When I hear you say. . . ." Notice that you're talking about something that both of you have seen, or heard, but not about their internal state of being — their self, personality, values or beliefs. In D.I.A.L.O.G.U.E. talk you *can* describe what's going on inside of you — you actually know that — but you can't talk about what's going on inside of them because you cannot know that directly (only they can). The most you can do is make a judgment about it from your perspective and that puts you right back into C.O.N.T.R.O.L. talk.

The "I-Message" Framework: Asking for a Change

- Describe the actual behavior you saw or words you heard. Describe what actually happened.
    - "When I see you do . . . or I hear you say. . . ."
- Then describe your feelings about it using another I-message.
    - "I feel . . . about it" or "It makes me feel . . ." or "I get. . . ."
- Then describe how it affects something the other person can see — beyond your feelings. People need plausible reasons to change. We're plausibility machines.
    - "And it affects the kids . . ." or "I can't get my work done . . ." or "We lose money."
- Finally, say what you want to have happen next.
    - "I want you to . . . I need you to . . . do something else." or "I want us to do things differently."

Another useful way of including the word *you* in your talk is to use the phrase "you seem." With this phrase you're describing your perceptions of their behavior in terms of how it is giving you clues about the way they are feeling at the moment. You are not making a conclusive judgment about how they actually are. Like your "you-action" statements, your perceptions of them are open to discussion. From their point of view you may be wrong about how you see them or their behavior, but at least your perceptions can be discussed. They can say without defense, "That's not what I said, or meant when I did that," or "I'm not angry, just frustrated" or any number of other responses that can move your talk in the direction of establishing a mutual understanding of what's going on.

The I-message framework is structured like a formula to make it easy to remember and use. It has a beginning, a middle and an end, and if used this way, it can be effective in dealing with difficult behavior in others, without resorting to you-messages and C.O.N.T.R.O.L. talk.

Judgment versus Description: An Example

Your friend, family member or romantic partner often "loses it" in a particular situation, raising their voice and cursing. Their behavior really upsets you and you want them to stop. You can do this in one of two ways: (1) heavy C.O.N.T.R.O.L. talk driven by your angry Parent voice or your frightened Child — "You jerk! You really make me mad! Stop talking like that!" or (2) D.I.A.L.O.G.U.E. — using the I-message framework and your Adult voice — "When I hear you curse, I get really angry (or frightened, or both). It upsets me so much I can't get my work done and I need you to stop!" (If you have talked about it before, then say so: "I'm really frustrated because we've talked about this before.")

So what's the difference? Heavy C.O.N.T.R.O.L. is quick and to the point, but will certainly not allow the other to hear what you have to say. They will be too busy defending themselves against:

- **Your label** — "You are" messages attack the person's "self" directly. They have to defend themselves, so they deny or distort your message, even if they may be behaving in a way that *they* realize is inappropriate.

- **Your blame** — "You make me mad." "You-blame" messages unfairly make the other, the cause of your unhappiness. Again, they go into defense — with a critical judgment of you " "Don't be so sensitive!" "You-blame" messages also implicitly give the other the power to manage your emotions.

- **Your command** — "Stop talking like that." No one likes to be given orders by someone they think of as an equal, so they will resist changing. Even when a person in a superior social position orders someone to change their behavior, the receiver may only comply for as long as the other can see or hear them.

The I-message framework tries to avoid all of this resistance and defense by keeping the speaker's words focused *on* what can be seen and changed (their behavior) and *off* what can't be changed — their selves, attitudes, motives, and personalities. For instance, when we begin with "When I hear you curse like that . . ." we are describing our perceptions of the publicly noticeable behavior that irritates or upsets us. And when we use "you-action" descriptors that reflect what anyone else in the situation could have heard or seen (the data or facts in the situation), we avoid "you-are" or "you-blame" messages, which are about mind reading or attributing motives that can't be seen. Next, we own our feelings with I-messages that describe our emotional reactions. Finally, we offer an additional reason for the change, and then ask for it. The "voice" in which we say all this matters greatly.

D.I. and the Adult Ego State

Descriptive talk is hard and we have to work at it. Not only do we need to think about how we can describe what is going on without blaming the other person or making them feel like they have been judged, we also need to watch *how* we say it — how we use our "voice." Descriptive language can only sound descriptive if we use our Adult voice (see descriptors in Chapter 7). If we have chosen to be emotionally self-managed in the situation, and are in our Adult ego state, then we use a tone and intensity of voice that is well modulated, calm, engaged and open. It is surprisingly hard to be judgmental when speaking in this manner.

Self-Managed Assertion

There is also a type of I-message called the **assertive** I-message. The differences between an I-descriptive message and an assertive I-descriptive, are ones of context and intensity. Assertiveness is the conscious use of our emotions in communication — a self-managed, but more intense description of our views or rights. It may be called for when the context is one in which the other is in active heavy C.O.N.T.R.O.L. and being aggressive, or in passive heavy C.O.N.T.R.O.L. and refusing to pay attention to what we have to say. Instead of responding with critical you-messages, we can stay in the I-message framework of D.I.A.L.O.G.U.E., but increase the intensity of our voice and repeat the message so they will get it. In an assertive I-message we consciously speak about our emotions rather than unconsciously act them out. This valuable skill will be reviewed in detail in Chapter 12.

The Value of Persistence

This is not to say that your first description of what is going on in a difficult situation will automatically get you what you want in terms of a change, but think of the alternative. If you fall back into using C.O.N.T.R.O.L. talk, you certainly won't get your way and you will likely make things worse. Even when people don't instantly give you what you want, sticking with the D.I. of D.I.A.L.O.G.U.E. won't add fuel to *their* fire. As you persistently speak about your perceptions, feelings and need for change, they won't be able to ignore you by pretending that you're attacking when all you're doing is describing how you see their behavior.

The Next Step

If we speak from the D.I. of D.I.A.L.O.G.U.E., not only do we create a powerful and safe way of communicating for ourselves, but we also create the same for the other. In fact, D.I.A.L.O.G.U.E. talk allows both people in a **3D** situation to deal with the "mixed messages" inherent in all talk by separating out the *content* of the talk (different ideas, viewpoints) from the emotional level of talk about face and relationship. This doesn't mean that the emotional side of our communication disappears. We just don't deny it or try to shift its ownership to the other. We simply describe it as another aspect of the information we are sharing in order to give the other our story. In this process, we come down our cognitive inference ladder to the facts or data in the situation, and either come down from our Parent or go up from our Child to the Adult ego state so our emotional communication is congruent with our words. The D.I. of D.I.A.L.O.G.U.E. can only happen if we commit to the E. (emotional self-management).

To fulfill the second commitment in D.I.A.L.O.G.U.E. — (U.) Understand first — however, we have to get the other to tell their story. By using D.I. we've chosen not to invade their part of the space between us. That's half the job. The other is to encourage them to fill up that space with their thoughts, perceptions and feelings so we can figure out what's really going on and how we can solve whatever problem we're facing. We also have to do this in a way that supports their taking the risk to share openly all of the information appropriate to the situation without attacking or blaming us. We need to get to the heart of D.I.A.L.O.G.U.E. — **A.L.** — by **a**sking questions and **l**istening actively.

The Heart of D.I.A.L.O.G.U.E.

Asking questions and listening actively — A.L. — are called the heart of D.I.A.L.O.G.U.E. because when they are combined effectively into a single process, they represent an *act of communication that engages all of the ideals of effective talk* (see Chapter 8). **A.L.** requires *mindful attention*, an *appreciative mindset* and *metacommunication*, which, in turn, requires emotional self-management and the commitment to seek understanding.

It is called *active listening* because you have to be active *internally* and *externally* — making a *conscious effort* to focus on the other, to do it effectively. It sounds like a lot of work, and it is, but the upside of all the effort involved is that it is the only form of talk that helps you solve problems *and* enhance relationships at the same time. Listening actively creates the conditions for empathy and equality.

The Heart of Asking Questions

Asking questions is the first step in seeking to understand the other. When somebody comes at you, don't react; ask one of the **4W2H** descriptive questions. They are: **what, where, when, who, how,** or **how much** (how often, how big, small, etc.).

These are called **open questions**. Their purpose is to draw out the other person, to encourage them to tell their story. If someone is upset, questions like "What's going on?" or "How come you feel so bad about this?" will give you time to slow down your reactions and give them a chance to tell their story.

When you ask open questions, the other will tell their story in their own way, which may not work for you. So you can follow up with **closed questions**. These are questions that are about specific details and can often be answered in one or two words. Consider them as questions of clarification and confirmation, such as "Did he call before or after you left the house?" or "As I understand it, you said . . . Am I right about that?"

Workshop Story: Police Interrogation

In the midst of my explaining the difference between asking open- and closed-ended questions, a workshop participant, who happened to be with the police, asked me, "Did you know this is a new form of police interrogation?" I said, "No."

"We're learning to do this," he said, "instead of the way we used to interrogate, using very closed-ended, detailed and demanding questions: 'Who were you with on the night of . . . ?' 'Didn't you meet them at this address around 9 PM?' etc., etc. The trouble was that the more we did this, the harder it was for a prosecutor to believe that the accused was telling us their truth instead of responding to our version of reality. We now say, 'Tell me what happened,' and the person rambles on in their own words and we record it. Then we ask closed questions to get some of the details straight, and the prosecutor is much more likely to believe it wasn't a forced interrogation and confession."

I didn't know about this change in police procedures, but his story also interested me because I have regularly used "interrogation" as a negative metaphor for asking questions. The difference between "good" question asking and interrogation is as follows:

The interrogator begins with the presumption of guilt. He already has the confession in his back pocket and just wants you to sign it. He just needs confirmation of his assumptions and judgments about how you committed "the crime." Interrogation is a very high-powered, invasive form of questioning that really demands a confession as the way to make the interrogation stop. For many of us that may sound like our moms when were 15 and arriving home hours later than we were told to be home. Her motives may have been of the highest order and her questions driven by her fear of the worst, but the process is the same. It was an interrogation.

Asking appreciative questions leaves the answers open and up to the other person. It lets them tell their story, their way. We only use closed questions for clarification of their story. One other form of question that helps people get it all out when they're stuck, is a creative door opener: "Is there anything else you can think of?" "Else" gets people to think out loud and frees them to speak "off the cuff" for a moment.

The "Why" Question

You may notice that "why" was left out of the list of questions. The difficulty with asking "**why questions**" ("Why did you do that?") is that most people have a hard time hearing them as neutral, even if our tone of voice is nonjudgmental. People often hear the "why" question as a search for blame rather than information. Although I don't have formal research data to support this observation, I have years of positive results from workshop clients who dropped "why" from their use of questions with individuals and teams at work. They found that the 4W2H questions — particularly "how did it happen" — gave them all the information they needed. So *how* did "why" become an issue? Here's one idea:

The Story of Why: Blaming the Cat

I believe it happens at the moment when children start to move — crawl — around the house. The baby is in the kitchen, looking around for interesting new information. With the parent's attention on something else, the child discovers a container on the floor that has some white stuff in it. The baby touches it and, amazingly, it moves. "Hey, this is good!" Just then a hand appears and moves the container — the cat's milk bowl — and a voice says, "Honey, don't play with that. It's for the cat."

So our intrepid adventurer seeks other unexplored regions of the kitchen floor and the mother turns back to her work. But there isn't anything nearly as interesting nearby and baby heads back to the bowl. As he touches it again, he sees that miraculous movement: "Cooool!" And again, the hand arrives, pushes the bowl a little further away under the kitchen table, and moves the baby to a spot in the corner where there are toys to play with. The voice says more firmly, "I told you not to touch that; it's the cat's milk."

The baby fiddles with the toys but can't quite take its focus off the marvelous thing that it can't have that's now on the floor under the table. Then the phone rings and the mothering one picks it up and turns away for a moment. Our explorer is off once again and gets to the bowl just as the cat arrives. Kitty stops and waits and, as the baby tries to pick up the bowl, something really good happens. The white stuff moves again — right out of the bowl, making a puddle on the floor that the cat starts lapping around the edges. You can put your hands in it . . . it feels neat . . . you can bang it . . . it moves faster . . . and then . . . all hell breaks loose!

> The 800-pound gorilla, mothering other puts down the phone, rushes over and yells: "Why did you do that?" Instantly the baby jumps and learns two things: (1) the negative emotional power of the word *why*, and (2) how to avoid blame by pointing at the cat. (By the way, an angry 800-pound gorilla wields about the same emotional power over an adult as an adult wields over a toddler.)

The Heart of Listening Actively

If we ask a question, we should listen to what the other person has to say. We often don't. We tend to listen to the surface of their talk and give them just enough attention to carry on a "normal" conversation. On the other hand, effective listening is an active, two-step process of giving the other our *undivided attention, and then periodically providing understanding feedback* to show that we get what they are saying. We will explain how to carry out these steps in detail later in the chapter. The general problem is that we are not socialized to do this kind of listening as part of our cultural learning. In our culture, the focus is on the power of talk not the power of listening. In fact, my favorite quote on listening is: "In North America conversation is a game wherein the first person to take a breath is considered the listener." Conversation for us is often simply waiting for our turn to speak because we think speech has the power. In reality, listening has the power.

Overcoming Mental Barriers to Active Listening

Getting beyond our culturally learned schema that talking is more important than listening requires some work: first on our internal barriers to listening more intently, including being positive about the process itself. Our natural or automatic way of listening creates attitude barriers to active listening and we have to choose to overcome them.

Self-focus versus Other-orientation

Our automatic focus is always on ourselves and our own thoughts. Effective listening, however, puts the other at the center of the conversation. We have to be mindful of our self-focus and consciously shift attention outward to the other and what they're saying.

Speaking Rate versus Thought Rate

People speak at around 125 words per minute, while we automatically listen at 6 or 7 times that speed. So we automatically dip in and out of the other's talk and roughly keep up while shifting our attention to others things. We know that when our conscious mind isn't engaged, the cognitive unconscious will be, and the cognitive unconscious relies on our previously learned schema and patterns to do its work. And that's a problem because we don't want to fit what our partner is saying to us into our old patterns. It isn't about us, remember? It's about them. So we need to listen consciously — actively — as if what they're saying were brand new (even if we've heard it before, in other arguments). We need to use "the space" created by our listening speed to our advantage — to summarize and understand what the other has said so far. Also any lack of emotional self-management can seriously interfere with effective active listening. If we hear things we don't like, our emotional reactions and feelings can intrude on our listening. We need to use our self-talk to manage this response, put it aside, and get back to listening to what the other is saying.

Criticizing the Speaker

Criticism can also sabotage effective listening so remember to focus on the message, not the messenger. We judge the speaker as they talk — you-messages pop into our head. So we need to turn off our judgmental self-talk and go deeper than surface appearances by asking ourselves questions like: "What are they really talking about" or "What does that mean?" Our listening rate gives us time to do this. It's a matter of keeping our focus on the content of the talk not the speaker, and listening to more than the words.

Giving Them Our Undivided Attention

All of these mental barriers can get in the way of the first of the essential processes of active listening — give the other our undivided attention. We need to work at this process in a way the other can see.

> **The Attention Experiment**
>
> A psychology professor in a small seminar taught six students the behaviors of paying attention. A guest lecturer was invited and began to lecture. The students behaved in the typical nonattending ways — looking down, checking their notes, gesturing to each other. The visiting professor continued to lecture — head down, eyes on his notes, monotone voice, and paying no attention to the students. At a pre-arranged signal from the host professor, the students started physically paying attention in the ways they were taught. Within 30 seconds the speaker made his first hand gesture; 30 seconds later his speaking rate increased and he become more lively and engaging. This continued for several minutes and then, at another pre-arranged signal, the students stopped paying attention. After several awkward attempts to re-engage them, the speaker returned to his monotonic style. Their undivided attention made all the difference.

Using the body to demonstrate attention:

- Lean toward the speaker, even if only slightly. This communicates involvement — compared to leaning back or sprawling.

- Face the other with your body. Your right shoulder lines up with their left, with your eyes at approximately the same level.

- Open body position: uncross your arms and, if appropriate, legs to indicate readiness to receive.

- Appropriate body movement: active listening is active. People feel very uncomfortable talking with someone who seems highly controlled and literally unmoved by their words.

- Slight movements of the head and hands to indicate encouragement are important — e.g., head bobs — less when they're talking and more when we're providing feedback. Move in rhythm with the speaker.

- Avoid distracting movement such as nervously shifting position, drumming your fingers or fiddling with your cell phone.

- Positive eye contact: start with their eyes but move to look at their face. No one likes to talk to people whose eyes are darting away from the exchange to other people, or the rest of the room. It indicates inattention, even lack of caring.

Encouraging them to continue:

- Ask them an open-ended question — "What's on your mind" or "Want to talk about it?" — to open the door. Once we're physically paying attention, we have to encourage them to keep talking.

- Facial expression: a smile to start always helps. Let your face communicate an inner state of what researchers have called "relaxed alertness." Relaxed — "I am comfortable listening to you and accept you" — and alert — "I am intent on listening because what you say is important to me.

- Paraverbal and verbal encouragers. Paraverbals are the "hums," "ahs," "uh huhs" that must be inserted periodically to show you are paying attention. Verbal encouragers are short interjections to encourage more talk: "Yeah," "Tell me more," "Right," "I see," "And then . . ." "Go on."

We can ask the right question to get them started, fake the right position, even the right look and still be doing something else in our head while they talk, but we have to be truly paying attention to put either the right sound or the right word into the exchange to encourage more talk. So, that's what we do.

Giving Understanding Feedback

The second, and perhaps most critical aspect of listening actively, is the art of periodically reflecting back to the speaker in your own words the content and/or feeling the speaker has communicated in order to show your acceptance and understanding. You can do this by:

Paraphrasing content:

- Restate it in your own words the essence of what you think they have said so far about the topic.

- Keep it concise and focus on the essential details of the content of the speaker's message.

- Useful phrases include: "It sounds like you're saying . . ." "What I'm hearing is . . . , is that right?

- Be sure to ask "Is that right?" and then listen carefully to the answer.

Reflecting feelings:

- Talk always happens at two levels and active listening is only effective if it also happens at two levels.

- If the speaker is communicating their feelings openly, then a direct reflection of them will work fine. Listen for the *feeling words* in their content — *excited*, *happy*, *rejected*, *upset* — and use those to guide your reflection: "You seem pretty happy about all this."

- Often, however, the speaker is talking about something that you can see evokes feelings in them — e.g., they are talking about a problem at work or at home — but they don't name their feelings directly. Infer from the content and from their nonverbals what the feeling could be. If someone complains about their personal life, you can say, "You sound pretty down about this" or "That sounds really discouraging."

- If you're not sure of what feelings they're expressing, ask yourself a question: "If I were in this situation, what would I be feeling?" This can help you frame the other's nonverbal communications to make your reflections more accurate.

- However, if you try and don't get it exactly right — don't worry, they will correct you. Let them. Again: this is about getting good information about them, *not* about you being right in this moment. Encourage them to clarify: "You seem pretty angry about this. Is that it?" "Well not so much angry, just really, really frustrated."

- Reflecting their expressed feelings back to them — as we perceive them — can be truly connective in situations where we are separated by differences.

The Four Don'ts

1. ***Don't give your opinion or advice until they ask.***
   This is not a platform for you to show off your cleverness or experience. Moreover, the other won't be listening until they ask you. Our only talk here should be reflective feedback to show understanding. Wait on handing out the advice until you're asked — and accept that you may not be asked for it! Giving reassurance or comfort when another is talking to you about something truly sad falls into the same category. Our efforts to reassure, without being asked, are actually to make us feel better not the other. A quick "It's gonna be all right" or "You'll get past this" lets us off the hook, and frees us from doing the real work of offering genuine support — attentive and supportive silence.

The remaining three "don'ts" are warnings against intruding on the listening process:

2. ***Don't interrupt to debate them.***
   This is about them telling their story not you being right. Same thing if they correct your reflections — let them.

3. ***Don't tell them what they should be thinking or feeling.***
   This is not C.O.N.T.R.O.L. talk, so don't impose.

4. ***Don't use their story as a "taking off point" for your story.***
   Even though you think it's a way of showing support, it's actually taking over their "air time."

Active Listening at Work: An Example

Looking quite glum, Dave walks over to Joe's cubicle. Joe asks, "What's up?" Dave answers that it's not such a great day, but stops as he sees Joe's eyes go to his computer. Joe apologizes, and Dave excuses himself and walks away. People read nonverbal signals of nonengagement instantly. But Joe likes Dave — Dave's a good guy. So Joe makes a deliberate decision — he turns from his computer, switches off the cell phone, and follows Dave to suggest a quick coffee break. He learns that Dave is panicked about an assignment that seems too difficult. Dave says he doesn't understand how to do the work. He says he's afraid he can't get the assignment done.

Joe could slap him on the back and offer a rote response — "Relax, that'll never happen. Cheer up." But he doesn't. He asks for more details of the assignment, even though he doesn't completely understand Dave's work. It doesn't matter that he doesn't understand because it isn't the work that's the problem — it's Dave's worry and fear about it that's the problem.

Joe tries to put himself in Dave's place — but he doesn't talk to Dave about what he, Joe, would do in the situation. Instead he says something like, "So you're panicked because you may not have enough time to learn the new system and get the report done in time?" He lets Dave know that he's listening — he's keeping Dave at the center of the conversation. Encouraged by Joe's interest, Dave goes further. He confesses that he's afraid he might be fired if he can't produce this report. Again, Joe doesn't tell him to relax, not to worry. Instead, he again keeps Dave's concern front and center. He might say something like, "So you're worried about losing your job. Maybe you're worried that you shouldn't have taken the job."

Dave says "Yes, you nailed it." Then he asks, "What do you think I should do?" Joe might suggest to Dave that he talk to his boss about the situation, or he might ask Dave what strategies he has considered. There are many ways that this conversation can go . . . but most importantly, with a little focused, active listening, Joe got to the heart of Dave's story. He reflected his feelings, paraphrased content several times, and he will go on to provide some very useful advice, but only because David *asked* for it!

Open Acknowledgment

Open acknowledgment is an important part of D.I.A.L.O.G.U.E. — another form of I-message. "Open" means we speak about our recognition of what's going on with someone else. Too often, we notice things but don't say anything, compelling others to mind read. When something difficult happens to them, we sometimes need to say, "This kind of thing has happened before. It's not the end of the world." Your mother said this to you for a good reason. She wanted you to recover quickly from feelings of fear or shame when you screwed up, so you could act to solve the problem.

Open acknowledgments — "I can see how you might think that" or "If I'd been in your shoes, I might have done the same thing" — are simply ways of recognizing the other's humanity (and our own) and keeping the conversation going — even in moments of disagreement. They let people know we can recognize their situation without necessarily agreeing with it or accepting it.

They allow us to get through 3 D moments in a way that keeps the other connected and gives us a chance to negotiate some kind of mutually acceptable outcome. This particular use of descriptive I-messages can really make a difference in a difficult situation. I-message acknowledgments help us stay connected with the other, even in disagreement. I-message acknowledgments are inherently appreciative. They recognize the other positively even when the situation isn't going well. There are four helpful ways to openly acknowledge the other or the situation:

Examples of Open Acknowledgments	
Situational "This has happened before."	***Disarming*** "I'm no expert, but. . . ."
Personal "I was upset." "You seem really upset."	***Hypothetical*** "If I'd been in your situation, I would have done the same thing."

1) *Situational acknowledgment*

The situation has happened before — "It occurs to me we've been here before" or, in a work situation, "Lots of people have this problem early in their career." It's called "normalizing." Everyone believes that they are the first person ever to screw up and that drives them to defend themselves and as a result, not give us good information ("the truth") about what happened. Because we naturally blame situations or others for our behavior when we are in trouble, when someone has made an error and we have to deal with it, we need them tell us what happened without defending themselves. To do this we need to reduce their fear of our critical judgment long enough for them to give us the information we need to help both of us solve whatever problem has occurred.

The great thing about life is that it's pretty repetitious, so this has happened before, either to someone we know, or have heard about, or maybe even to us. By acknowledging this, we free their conscious mind from the fear of our imminent judgment so both of us can talk about it differently this time.

2) *Disarming acknowledgment*

The acknowledgment recognizes that the other may have reasons not to listen to our thoughts on a subject — biases against certain ideas, stereotyped views of us based on our age, sex, occupation, how long they've know us — and we realize this. To be heard, even for a moment, we need to temporarily disarm these mental barriers, so we begin our sentences with phrases like: "Look, I know I'm new here, but . . ." or "Sure, I'm only your kid brother but I think . . ." or when crossing professional boundaries, "I'm no expert, but. . . ."

3) *Personal acknowledgment*

This means talking about ourselves in terms of how "we are" — "I am really happy" — and how "they seem" to be — "You seem really upset." Notice the difference between "you are" and "you seem." "You are" tells them how to feel. It's C.O.N.T.R.O.L. talk. It comes across as a "truth" when it's really a judgment. On the other hand, "you seem" simply expresses our perception of their behavior. Our "you seem" statements are not "truths" about reality. They are our first estimates in a negotiation of a shared reality.

Personal acknowledgment is a vital form of metacommunication. In Chapter 8, it was suggested that we could use personal acknowledgment to clarify our feelings — "When I said I felt hurt, what I meant was . . ." or to comment on our perceptions of the whole conversation — "I don't like the way this is going. Could we try to . . . ?"

In difficult situations, open acknowledgment of our own, or the other's, feelings and perceptions is truly important because it interrupts the automatic process of emotional reaction (the third layer of complexity), slows down our talk and brings both of our conscious minds to bear on what is actually being said in the moment — we become more mindful and "present" communicators.

4) *Hypothetical acknowledgments*

These are usually offered as, "If I'd been in your situation I would have . . . too." This is a great tool for a particular issue in conversations involving disagreement. When we describe what we saw them do or heard them say, they might justify their actions with an explanation about a situation or series of events that caused the behavior we've called into question. So, rather than attack their statement, we can acknowledge their explanation without agreeing with it. Our acknowledgment is simply a way of saying "I'm human, too. I can see how this might have happened." This is preferable to hitting them with a critical judgment about their behavior or about their explanation. Acknowledgment helps us keep the discussion going until we get all the information we need to help them help us solve whatever problem is on the table.

The Wile E. Coyote Problem

The hypothetical acknowledgment solves what I call the "Wile E. Coyote" problem. Remember the Saturday morning *Looney Tunes* cartoon that featured a coyote and roadrunner? The roadrunner is a kind of bird that walks along the edge of roads in the southwest United States. When I was driving in the region I saw them once or twice. They are also called chaparral cocks. They are New Mexico's state bird and they can run fast when they're threatened.

In the cartoon, the Road Runner is the prey and the coyote — Wile E. Coyote — is always out to catch it and eat it. The coyote comes up with ever more complex ways of trapping the Road Runner — blowing it up, running it over — and the Road Runner always avoids the trap. So Wile E. ends up chasing the Road Runner instead. In the cartoon, the bird runs so fast that the coyote is left in the dust. The Road Runner can keep up this speed, even around the hairpin turns on cliff-side roads, but, when Wile E. tries to do the same thing . . . well, instead of zooming around the curve like his prey, he flies right off the turn. But it's what happens next that matters.

Wile E. hovers for a moment, as if he's OK. Then he makes the mistake of looking down. This is when he turns to the camera and goes, "Uh Oh!" and plummets to the desert floor below.

When we're dealing with folks in a difficult situation, the person whose behavior we want to change is always in the place of Wile E. Coyote after a bad turn — they're hovering. And rather than forcing them to "look down," psychologically speaking, by attacking or judging them so they fall into their fears and defenses, we need to stay connected with them and keep the discussion open.

An acknowledgment does imply agreement. In fact you may be saying, "I may not agree with your behavior but I can see how you might have got there." This builds an invisible bridge between you, keeps them focused on the topic not their fears, and prevents them from defending themselves (and not giving you any "good" information). I-message acknowledgments are a very powerful form of talk because they show we're listening.

Genuine Support

The last element of the D.I.A.L.O.G.U.E. model of talk is represented by **G.** — **G**enuine support. There are two types of genuine support: (1) positive, timely, specific feedback (compliments, thanks and appreciative nonverbal behavior) in response to accomplishments, and (2) effective feedback for change.

In order to effectively show that we care for the other person and we genuinely support them, without it becoming ritualized and meaningless, we need to pay our compliments in a specific way, using the I-message construction: "When I see how hard you've worked with the kids over these years, and how well you talk about me even when I'm not around, I want to let you know that I really feel great about that. I love you." We describe in detail the behavior we are about to compliment and openly acknowledge the positive feeling we have before saying, "I love you" at the end. That is what a positive, timely, specific compliment is about. This approach works in every kind of situation, not just in personal, romantic moments. Notice that by describing in detail the behavior we are complimenting, this form of support seems more real than the kind of fake support we use in light C.O.N.T.R.O.L. to get people to change their mind.

I call this the descriptive I-message compliment. For this compliment, we use descriptive I-messages to clarify the reasons we are giving the compliment in the first place. We can then end it with a positive you-message. It too is a kind of formula. Do it in the following order and it works every time:

- "When I see you" (action verb)
- "I feel" (any positive feeling descriptor)
- "I think (or I want to tell you) you are" (positive descriptor).

Provide Effective Support Anytime

- ***In the workplace:*** "When I saw how you all stayed late on Friday to get this order out to the client, I was very impressed. You folks are terrific. Thanks."
- ***At home:*** "When I see how hard you work and then come home with the energy to help the kids and me, I think you're amazing. I love you."
- ***In the midst of a difficult discussion:*** "I know this must be hard for you, it's hard for me, too, but when I see you making an effort to work this through, I want you to know that I really appreciate it." I-message compliments are the appropriate way to show appreciation — even in the tough conversational moments.

To make support work, use I-messages to describe the behavior for which you are about to give the positive you-message at the end. Without the descriptive support, common phrases like "You're great" or "great job" or even "I love you" don't have much impact. In fact, too often they become forms of ritual C.O.N.N.E.C.T. talk.

We often want to influence others and we don't want to use C.O.N.T.R.O.L. talk every time we need to do this. D.I.A.L.O.G.U.E. provides genuine support while asking for a change:

Genuine Support for Change

- Put the other person at ease.
- Use DESCRIPTION and I-MESSAGES to outline why you're having this talk and to express your concern about the behavior you feel needs changing. Avoid sounding judgmental. No you-messages. Use the I-message formula to describe your feelings about it and what you'd like to have happen.
- ACTIVELY LISTEN for and OPENLY ACKNOWLEDGE their feelings about what you have described.
- ASK QUESTIONS. Get their story. Seek their opinion on how things could change; encourage their thinking about the situation and draw out specific suggestions about what might happen.
- GENUINE SUPPORT: Use I-messages to let them know that you respect them and their views and their efforts to reach mutual understanding with you.
- Use I-MESSAGES to offer suggestions when appropriate, building on their ideas where possible.
- Agree on appropriate actions.
- Finish off with recognition of the effort involved in reaching agreement. If agreement isn't reached, then provide support for at least trying. "I guess we'll just have to agree to disagree, but I want you to know that I appreciate your talking this through with me."

It Always Comes Down to One Choice When Problems Arise

In every communication situation where we face "problems" — either those that we know about before we start to talk or those that emerge as we are talking — we always have two choices about how to respond: either (1) *we want to be right* — so we use C.O.N.T.R.O.L. talk, or (2) *we really want to solve the problem*. If we want to problem solve, we pause for a moment, take a breath, manage our emotions and commit to seeking understanding first, using the **A.L.** of D.I.A.L.O.G.U.E. talk.

To Get Out of C.O.N.T.R.O.L.: Ask and Listen

As the following diagram shows, when we are at the **T.** point in C.O.N.T.R.O.L. talk, we make choices about what to do next if our first efforts don't succeed. The first of those choices — "Try Again" — is automatic, but the remaining three require some level of mindfulness. At some point in the repetition of our efforts to get our way, we can become fully mindful and try D.I.A.L.O.G.U.E. To do this effectively, however, we need to go to the heart of the D.I.A.L.O.G.U.E. process – A.L. – asking questions and listening actively. We need to stop our C.O.N.T.R.O.L. talk, and ask about what's going on with the other person – and then, really listen. We need to "understand first."

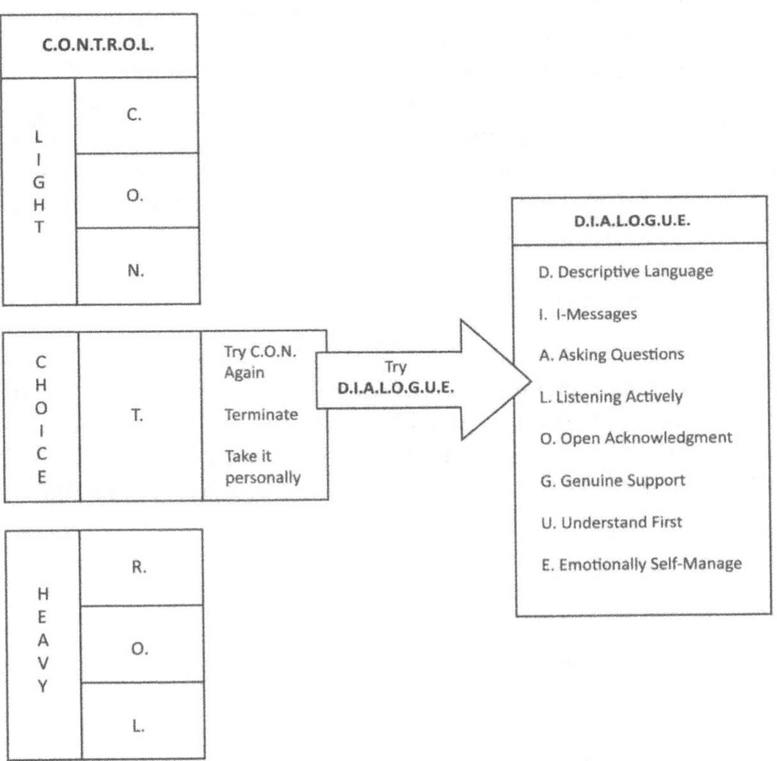

When we are in a **3 D** situation (facing unexpected differences, disagreement or disorder) we need to stop focusing on our story and instead focus on the other person's story. One of the key assumptions in D.I.A.L.O.G.U.E. is that we don't have all the information we need to solve a problem until we know the other person's story, so we have to go to A.L. to get that critical information (as shown in the figure above) and then use O.G. — open acknowledgment and genuine support — to keep the other engaged in the conversation in a way that supports their self-esteem and reduces their need to defend themselves (so they will give us more good information).

In the end, to resolve a problem in face-to-face communication, all the elements of D.I.A.L.O.G.U.E. talk have to be woven together into a seamless flow. With practice, we can do this, but only if we have already committed ourselves to getting out of C.O.N.T.R.O.L. mode and into a truly problem-solving mode, rather than imposing our "rightness" on the other.

If we want others to change, our talk needs to create a "safe" space for cooperation that (1) permits *them* to move in our direction without feeling that their basic sense of "rightness" (about themselves) is threatened and, if appropriate, (2) permits *us* to move in their direction without feeling a sense of loss and threat. This space can be created using D.I.A.L.O.G.U.E., which represents a set of choices about talking in a way that respects the other while accepting our mutual disagreement for what it is, not as a disaster or a threat to us or to them, but a necessary result of each of us being our unique, individual selves in this situation. We talk *with them*, rather than *at them*, in a way that makes them feel that they matter, are competent, and have a say in this situation, even though they disagree with us.

Where We're Going Next

The least effective way to get people to do what we want is by using C.O.N.T.R.O.L. talk. When we're under pressure, intense debate or command may work in the moment but they tend to deepen our differences with others and create conflict in the longer run. In the next chapter, we will review how to use assertive D.I.A.L.O.G.U.E. instead of C.O.N.T.R.O.L. talk to positively affect potentially conflict-filled situations.

End Notes

---

[1] Gottman, J.M. (1999) *The Marriage Clinic: A Scientifically-Based Marital Therapy*. New York: W.W. Norton and Company.

[2] Hanna, S. (2000) *Person to Person: Positive Relationships Don't Just Happen* (3rd ed.). Toronto: Prentice Hall Inc.

CHAPTER TWELVE

D.I.A.L.O.G.U.E. AND CONFLICT MANAGEMENT

The 3 D's Become Conflict

There is always the potential for some level of conflict between ourselves and others. Despite the fact that most people dislike and want to avoid conflict, the **3 D**'s — unexpected differences, outright disagreement, and unpredicted disorderliness — are inherent in our everyday relationships. In the end, everyone is different. We each develop unique combinations of perceptions and beliefs about our selves and the world, and have a particular combination of needs we feel must be met in order to feel safe, happy and effective as individuals. Thus, regularly managing low-level differences and disagreements is a "natural" part of social life. When, however, we enact our deeply learned, reactions to conflict, we often weaken our conscious efforts to deal with it.

Although, we are faced with low-dose **3 D** situations every day (and often conflicted about what choices to make), we define external conflict as occurring when *we come to believe that the actions of another will prevent us from getting what we want or from being the way we want to be.*

The Three Levels of Interpersonal Conflict

There are always three levels of conflict at work in conflict situations: Disputation, Defense of Position, and Destruction of Relationship.

Disputation

Conflict usually begins with talk about our perceptions of the other's behavior, and our inferences about those acts, in a particular situation. This is called **disputation**: we are disputing "the facts" and trying to demonstrate that our perspective on the situation is "right." We might say, "That's not what happened!" or "You're looking at this all wrong." Our dispute is about "who said what" and what's really going on in the situation. We use light C.O.N.T.R.O.L. talk — some form of reasoned argument — to influence the other, and unless the other defers to our view of the situation, disputation can become Defense of Position.

Defense of Position

Our persuasive light C.O.N.T.R.O.L. talk engenders competitive light C.O.N.T.R.O.L. as the other resists our influence with their views and arguments. What usually develops is a more intense discussion, during which disputants begin to emotionally intensify their talk, reinforce their arguments with more supporting perceptions and "facts," and, in classic military terms, harden their "battlefield" positions and defend them more strongly. At this point, we begin to see ourselves as being in conflict with the other.

One way of dealing with the emergence of this kind of intense argument in continuing relationships is to "drop it"; back off from the fight; silently blame the other for their stupidity or insensitivity; avoid another confrontation, but never forget what happened. Thus, unresolved "defense of position" arguments become the basis for many of the ongoing arguments in our personal lives. These "positions" get built into our daily life and we become obligated to defend them whenever they are challenged.

Over time, our unwillingness to re-engage with the other on a key issue gives us external "peace" but at a high emotional price. We begin to think of the other not as someone with whom we can connect and who happens to stubbornly hold a different ("inappropriate") view on an important issue in our lives, but as someone who is committed to becoming separated from us and intends to damage us personally. When this thinking emerges in our personal relationships, we are in serious trouble. We are at the third level of conflict — the Destruction of Relationship.

Destruction of Relationship

At the level of **Destruction of Relationship**, we no longer care about the relationship and "peace at any price" but "victory at all costs." We feel an emotional push to move from fighting over facts and perspectives toward "hot feelings" and extreme thoughts — that the other person has *always* done this to us and has caused us to be very angry. We take the position that this is the ongoing theme in our relationship. We shift to heavy C.O.N.T.R.O.L. talk. We are prepared to sacrifice the relationship to get what we want.

The maintenance of a long-term relationship — a friendship, marriage or work relationship — requires a very special act of commitment not to move to level three. For instance, a married couple may have consciously made that commitment, or they may have gone to position three and unthinkingly decided it was too scary to stay there and were afraid of the changes it might bring. Most often, they automatically hang somewhere between levels one and two — enduring repeated angry "flare-ups." This can be painful, numbing and emotionally disruptive over time. Yet they may hang there for years using rationalizations like "staying together for the kids" or "our tradition doesn't permit divorce." Another couple in the same situation may "face up" to their situation and seek counseling and other forms of support to help them resolve some of their triggering issues and learn to manage their ongoing conflict more consciously and effectively.

We've all known people who have a life position based on conflict that has become so habitual that it's the way we recognize them. They seem to be stuck in a particular moment of unresolved conflict. Why? Because they have never learned how deal with their day-day conflicts effectively. Until we can put self-managed D.I.A.L.O.G.U.E. to work to help get through the "small stuff" it won't become a "natural" part of our conflict resolution style when we are faced with the "big stuff" in our lives and need to build solutions that are wins for us and the other person.

Assertive D.I.A.L.O.G.U.E. for Everyday Conflict

When we have to deal with difficult behavior in others or actions that challenge our expectations about appropriate behavior in a particular situation, we often resort to C.O.N.T.R.O.L. talk — command or demand — to get others to stop. Command as a form of C.O.N.T.R.O.L. talk works in only one kind of situation — a crisis — where someone focuses the thoughts and fears of others by ordering them to behave in a way that will help them get through the crisis. But this is the only situation where one can get away with command without the others involved disputing our right to speak to them in that way.

In non-crisis situations, however, instead of creating change, commanding someone to stop or start a behavior simply creates resistance. To reduce the chances of this outcome if we want another to change, we need to assertively ask for what we want — using D.I.A.L.O.G.U.E. talk spoken in a voice that communicates clarity, courage and calm. There are three steps to successful assertive D.I.A.L.O.G.UE: (1) **Show up**, (2) **Stay in** (3) **Speak out**.

Showing Up In Your Head In The Moment

When someone does something that infringes on our sense of self or fairness in a particular situation, our emotions get aroused and feelings of either righteous indignation or anger instantly appear in our conscious mind. Our mind races into the past to compare this moment to other moments so we can make a judgment: "That's wrong" or "They're wrong" or "This is not fair."

As true as this is, it doesn't help us get "into the moment" we are about to act in. To do that effectively we need take a breath and ask ourselves, "What really happened here?" or "I wonder why they acted like that?" Also, "How do their words and actions impinge on me?" and "What can I say or do about it?"

What we're really asking ourselves is, "WHY do I need to say "No" to what's going on here and ask for a change?" Remember, we said that "why" is not a good question to ask others early in difficult situations, but it's very useful for us when we need to discover what's behind our need to stop something and start something else in a difficult situation.

William Ury, in his book *The Power of a Positive No*[1], argues persuasively that to effectively say "No" to another, we first have to discover our own best interests in the situation, what we value or think is important, so we can say "Yes" to ourselves. We need to focus on the situation in a moment of calm reflection (he calls it "going to the balcony") so we can see the larger things that are part of us. As Ury says: "The real action of standing up for yourself takes place inside of you before you say No."

If we can do this, we can anchor our "No" in a personal value or deeply felt need we want to fulfill or protect. This will give us strength so that when we speak, we'll come across as acting firmly to protect something of value rather than simply preventing someone from doing what they want. Moreover, if we explain our deeper reasons for saying "No," the person may not feel our "No" as a reflection on them.

Consider the example of a work friend who tries to hit you up for a small loan, but, as often happens with "small things," still hasn't paid back the bit of cash he borrowed from you the previous month. How do you say "No" without sounding personal or petty? The answer is by asking yourself why you don't like doing this. If you do, you'll realize that when you lend money to friends, it inevitably diminishes the friendship. That's your principle: so tell them that when you say "No."

> "I'm sorry, I can't do it. I've committed myself not to lending money to friends because I value their friendship. I don't want a few bucks to get in the way."

By doing this, you've made the "No" about you and your values, not about your forgetful colleague's request. So, we need to talk to ourselves for a moment before we talk to them. Ury's exercise about finding the "Yes" in ourselves to strengthen our "No" to them will do two things: (1) it will stop our conscious mind from dredging up past grievances, and (2) it will give us the confidence to say one of the hardest words there is to say without fear or guilt: "No."

Staying In The Moment And Preparing To Speak Authentically

Assertiveness starts with your Adult ego state and involves self-talk focused on problem-solving in the moment, beginning with three questions:

1) "What do I want out of this situation?"

2) "What do I think they want?"

3) "What can I say or do that will get me the outcome I want and preserve the dignity of *everyone* involved?"

The answers to these inner questions are communicated to the other through a firm (not parental sounding) but pleasant tone of voice, direct eye contact, appropriate facial gestures (focused, calm), a confident body stance, and controlled body movements.

Let's clarify what we mean by assertiveness by comparing it to the three other automatic — thus far more common — responses we have to the problematic behavior of others. It's important to understand that assertiveness is different from aggressiveness, passive-aggressiveness, and passivity.

Aggressiveness:

Some people confuse assertiveness with aggressiveness when in reality they couldn't be more different. Aggressive speakers start from a different place emotionally and talk to themselves in a very different way about how to get others to stop doing something they don't like. Aggression flows out of the angry parent or angry child ego states and aggressive responders ask themselves three quite different questions about the situation:

1) "Who do they think they are?"

2) Why should I sit here and take this?"

3) What can I say to put them in their place and keep them there?"

As a result, they are likely to say too much, too loudly to make their point, demanding or commanding others to change their behavior.

Passiveness:

Passive communicators take on a difficult situation from the opposite perspective of aggressives. They see the world from the dependent, adapted child ego state. Their self-talk questions include:

1) "How can I respond without hurting their feelings?"

2) What do I need to say in order to have them like me?"

3) Why do these things always happen to me?"

This kind of thinking results in simply giving in or holding back — i.e., saying and doing nothing — then later ruminating on what we "should have or could have done."

Passive aggressiveness:

Again, this style of response comes out of a very different thinking and acting process than we have outlined for assertiveness. Passive-aggressives work from the offended adapted-child ego state — an aggressively whiny aspect of it. They are judgmental and often angry in their self-talk because they feel unjustly treated and because they know they are not going to act in the situation:

1) "I don't like what's happening here. It's not fair."

2) I think they're trying to get me and I need to find a way to get them back."

3) How can I get even with them after this is over?"

If they do speak in the situation they will make sarcastic remarks or complain to anyone nearby — but never to the person they believe has offended them. Then they will exit the situation, doing nothing to change it. However, they will continue complaining to everyone they meet. They also seem to thrive on negative gossip and spreading rumors about anyone they think has behaved inappropriately.

To summarize, assertive speakers will act directly to change a difficult situation. Unlike passive speakers, who are likely to say nothing, and passive-aggressive and aggressive speakers, who use either passive or active Heavy C.O.N.T.R.O.L talk, assertive speakers will use D.I.A.L.O.GU.E. talk in a way that is clear about what they need to happen in the situation, while still maintaining the dignity of both parties involved.

Speaking Out Effectively In The Moment

Speaking out effectively in the moment means we say what we mean and tell the other the only truths we own in the moment — our perceptions, thoughts and feelings about what happened — using descriptive I-messages, or you-action messages, without directly attacking or criticizing them.

Consider the example of someone who cuts in front of you in line in a store. Aggressive people might raise their voice, be sarcastic, or swear, but they are not likely to change the situation. In fact, this aggressiveness is more likely to compel the line cutter to resist and save face by staying in place. Nobody likes to be ordered about. The downside of this behavior is that the aggressive person's anger will be with them for hours.

Passive people, on the other hand, are likely to stand by quietly and fume inwardly, thinking of all of the things they would like to do, but, of course, doing none of them. They turn their anger inward. That and their self-disappointment will still be with them hours later.

By being assertive in this situation, it's possible both to change the outcome and to feel good about the way you handled it. An assertive response involves the following I-messages to the line-jumper: "I know that the cashiers are really busy today and our line looks short, but we've been asked to stand back a bit and keep the aisle clear. I'm at the front of this line and I've been waiting a while, so your going in front of me is upsetting. Would you please join the end of the line back there?"

You might get an angry (aggressive) response, or be ignored (a passive response), or the person might apologize for unknowingly cutting in front of you and move to the back of the line. What you certainly will get is a strong feeling of self-respect for having kept your cool and tackled the situation in a straightforward way. Whatever the outcome, it's not likely to spoil the rest of your day.

Assertive D.I.A.L.O.G.U.E. talk shows that you have confidence in yourself and are positive, while at the same time understanding other people's points of view. You respect yourself and show respect for others.

Assertive D.I.A.L.O.G.U.E. Techniques

Let's unpack our general statements about assertive D.I.A.L.O.G.U.E. talk and show how we can effectively speak out in the present by

- Telling our truth, and
- Asking for a change.

Tell Your Truth

Telling your truth is the first of the four steps of the I-Message formula for "Asking for Change" (described in the previous chapter) spoken more firmly:

(1) Describe your perceptions directly to the person whose actions are affecting you. Tell what you saw and/or heard, using Descriptive I-messages or Descriptive you-action phrases: For example: "I heard you say . . ." or "When I hear you (say something) . . ." or "I saw . . ." or "When I saw you (do something) . . ." or "When you do that, I. . . ."

- Speak calmly as you clearly describe specific behaviors/actions. Try not to make any assumptions or judgments.
- Be brief, but say what you need to say.

There are two additional considerations regarding what we need to describe:

We often need to talk about the "little" things that happen repeatedly in a relationship and bother us, but about which we never say a word because they seem too small to talk about at the time. However, Daniel Gilbert's[2] research on happiness makes it clear that it's the little hurts in life that happen again and again — but that we ignore each time — that drag us and our relationships down in the end. So, if we're facing the same irritating behavior for the umpteenth time, we need to describe it to the other.

Also, when appropriate, we need to begin our description with an acknowledgment of the situation or the other's expressed concerns. In our line-cutting example, our assertive customer began by stating the obvious: "I know that that cashiers are really busy today and our line looks short, but we've been asked. . . ." Then we move on to "you-action" descriptions. Now that we've described the behavior we're concerned about, we need to do the second step, which is

Disclosing Your Feelings

(2) Say how you feel about the situation - "I felt annoyed or unfairly treated . . ."

- Know what you're feeling right now. Don't try to soften it or smooth it over. Accept it. This is when we should pay attention to what our body is telling us in order to accurately name the feeling. The first thing we feel is the thing that needs to be spoken.

- Try to get the intensity right. Say what it is without adding judgmental labels. You are trying to be descriptive of what is rather than speak in inflammatory generalities. For instance, it's one thing to be annoyed or angry but another to be "abused" by someone's behavior. In addition to evoking your feelings, their actions have specific effects that need to be talked about.

Describing the Effect of Their Behavior

(3) Describe the tangible effect their behavior is having on you. Be as specific as you can. Describing the specific effects helps to convince the other.

- Don't end with "it makes me mad." Ending this way could also be seen as a way of imposing your values on the other and is easily dismissed with a "too bad" or "get over it." If you end instead with concrete effects like "my time is wasted" or "it costs me more," or in the case of our line cutter . . . "I'm late and I need to get home to my kids," it sounds more "real" for the other. They might be more able to identify with it than with an internal result — like your anger.

- Describe the overt effect directly and firmly. Put it in terms of a value or deeper need you discovered in your time of reflection ("on the balcony"). This may make it easier for them to hear. But don't hint around it or speak evasively to save face or ease the situation.

Ask for a Change of Behavior

(4) Say what you think needs to happen next, respectfully but without additional reasons. I need you to "stop" something or "start doing" something.

- Stop and look at them with pleasant anticipation. This is a non-verbal encourager that shows that you believe they will do as you ask.

- When appropriate — in a longer-term personal or work relationship — but not in a difficult moment like line-cutting, state the benefits of change or the consequences of not changing.

Assertively Asking For Change: A Summary

Step	Goal	Action
Step 1	Describe a specific behavior of the other person, non-judgmentally.	***When I see you do this. . .*** ***or hear you say. . .***

Step 2	Disclose how you feel as a result, without using the expression "you make me. . ."	***I feel angry, upset. . .***
Step 3	Declare the effects or impact of the person's behavior on you, your principles, values, or the situation.	***I can't focus on my work. . .*** ***I lose time or money. . .***
Step 4	Ask for the change. Describe what you want the other to start or stop doing.	***I prefer you to,*** **or** ***I would like you to,*** **or** ***I need you to. . .***

Using Our Adult Voice

We do all this self-managed, descriptive I-messaging in our Adult voice, not just because it's more likely to get us what we want, but also because it's the only way to tell our truth and stay inside our own space. This prevents them from using our bad behavior as an excuse to continue their bad behavior. It hardly seems fair but when we point out another's behavior as inappropriate by using C.O.N.T.R.O.L. talk — commands and demands in an angry voice — they instantly defend themselves against the way we've spoken to them and ignore what they did to upset us in the first place.

Assertiveness In Customer Service

Let me tell you how we've handled this in some of the customer service training we've done. In their anger, frustrated customers often take out their feelings on front-line service providers — especially in moments when they're trying to return a failed product and get a refund. Every company has a set of rules about this, and questions to be asked before an item can be replaced or a refund given. These procedures often make customers angrier and the front-line employees pay the price.

The front-line service provider usually hears these as personal attacks, because angry customers often make them personal: "Give me what I want or I'll get you fired." So, like everyone else, they feel the need to defend themselves — but we have to ask them not to do that. Because as soon as they respond in kind to a customer, the customer immediately starts to focus on their behavior as the "real" problem, not on whatever they (the customer) might have done or said to get into the difficult situation in the first place.

When a front-line service provider replies to attacks in kind, it allows the customer to shift the focus of their anger to the service provider's "bad" behavior — and for many people this justifies escalating the situation. So in organizations focused on quality customer service, front-line employees are trained to use assertive D.I.A.L.O.G.U.E. so they won't give the customer a reason to let that happen. With practice, they can avoid the tough situation of having their boss called over and taking the customer's side. The employees have to rise above their natural righteous anger and keep acknowledging the customer's concerns in their Adult voice — and offer to do whatever they can to resolve the issue. Anything else allows an ugly customer to get even uglier and then blame the employee for their ugliness.

Besides the basic steps of assertive Dialogue: (1) staying present, (2) speaking up descriptively, and (3) asking for change, we also teach the employees additional techniques that everyone can use in dealing with personal relationship struggles. **Three of these additional assertive D.I.A.L.O.G.U.E. techniques** include:

Repeat As Needed

Repeat as needed is almost inevitable in a difficult situation. When disagreements arise, people don't listen the first time — or even the second time. They simply react. So you have to say it again. Repeating several times what we want to have happen may seem a bit awkward — people are supposed to get the message quickly — but we forget that young children do this all the time, and it works for them! Repeating your request gets the other's attention and keeps them focused. We just have to do it without sounding like a four-year-old or a machine. We need to:

Acknowledge Before Asking Again

You acknowledge their response to your request (if it's not agreement), and ask for the change again. Tell them what you need (or the situation needs) in a short, clear Descriptive I-message — calmly expressed — and then acknowledge their next response. Then repeat your request for change.

By using an acknowledgment to open each repetition, you demonstrate that you are listening to what they're saying, but you can't help them or can't support them in continuing whatever they're doing. The "Ask, Acknowledge, and Ask Again" response permits you to persist in getting what you need to happen without them sidetracking you with their reactions or demonizing you as uncaring.

Acknowledge Their Truth, When They Come At You With Criticism,

When someone behaves aggressively, they expect direct resistance. Try to side step their anger by agreeing with some part of what they say: "Sometimes I'm like that" or "That does happen" or "I can see how you might think that." Note that you are not agreeing with them but only acknowledging that someone could think that way. In this situation, you need to be self-managed — calm and confident — so you acknowledge a bit of truth instead of responding defensively. By offering no return in kind — i.e., no obvious resistance — you can diffuse some of their negative energy and open the door for them to listen to what you have to say next.

As you progress toward some sort of resolution of the situation, you will find these additional connective statements helpful:

Situational Acknowledgement: "I know this has been tough on both of us."

This works well because it re-states the equality between you and the other in this situation and expresses your willingness to see how they might be affected by what's going on. It connects you even in moments of separation.

Blameless Apology: "I'm so sorry this has happened."

This is a simple recognition of what's happened to them. It doesn't mean taking responsibility for their problem but, like a hypothetical acknowledgment, you can see how it would affect you if you were in the same position. You're connecting through a general feeling of supportive regret.

Repeat As Needed and Acknowledge: A True Story

Let me give you an example of how well this can be done. This happened to me and another passenger in a small regional airport. I walked in, early for my indirect — and longer — flight home, to find the airline staff still boarding the direct flight. I, and another man, approached the desk and asked if there were empty seats left and if we could still get on. The ground service employee said: "I do show some empty seats, but the flight has already been called. I'm sorry but I can't get you on it now."

I commented, "Are you sure? It would be great to get home an hour earlier. It's been a very long day." She listened to me and then said, "I can see how getting home an hour earlier would really make a difference for you, but my system is closed for this flight. I can't open it up now."

I accepted my fate at this point and let it go, but the other latecomer started asking the same questions but in a much more complaining tone. After listening to him, her response was, "I know it's the last direct flight out but our departure was already delayed and passengers need to make their connections. I can't hold it any longer."

After he complained again, she said, "It may seem like a straightforward thing to do but you'd have to go back down to Departures, get an override — and there are fees for this kind of last-minute change — and there's just not enough time for that now." The second man finally walked away, grumbling quite loudly that he didn't see "why

> it couldn't be done. It seems so simple." I went off to get a coffee to pass the time until my indirect flight.
>
> The ground service person never gave in to something she couldn't do, and she was never anything less than positive, both in her acknowledgment of our self-justifying, wheedling tactics and in her resistance to our last-minute requests. As I passed by her desk a couple of minutes later with my coffee, she looked up, smiled and said, "Sorry I couldn't help earlier. Too bad you didn't come sooner." I smiled back, acknowledged my fate and thought to myself, "Hey, she couldn't do anything to get me on the plane but she could be pleasant . . . and that's always something."

Situational Requirement Description: "What else can we do? Your mother's coming on Friday."

Sometimes the other person simply needs to be awakened to the larger pressures on both of you to do something they don't want to do. By shifting their attention off you and onto the situation, you can help move them toward an agreement.

The goal is to reach an agreement to change — one that works for you and the other — without beating up yourself or the other person.

Conflict Management: Life Positions[3]

The basic model of interpersonal conflict is built on two questions that seem important to people each time they find themselves in conflict with someone else: (1) "How important is it to me that I get what I want, in this situation?" — the fulfillment or frustration of my goals in this situation — and (2) "How important to me is my relationship with the other person in this situation?" — will the relationship be sustained or be sacrificed to fulfill our goals? The combinations of the answers to these two questions generate five archetypal conflict-management styles (one for each corner of the diagram and one for the center). There relationship to each is shown in the figure on the next page.

Avoiding

Probably the most common approach to conflict management is **avoidance**. Most of us really don't like to confront others in difficult situations. The "avoiding" style is based on our beliefs that achieving our goals is not important at this moment, nor is maintaining a relationship. We just don't want to get involved. This approach comes out of the Passive Defensive orientation and represents either the nurturing Parent or adaptive Child ego state.

As a short-term tactic, avoiding is highly recommended. Stepping away from a potential conflict for even a few minutes can give us (and the involved other) a chance to

Key Conflict Management Styles

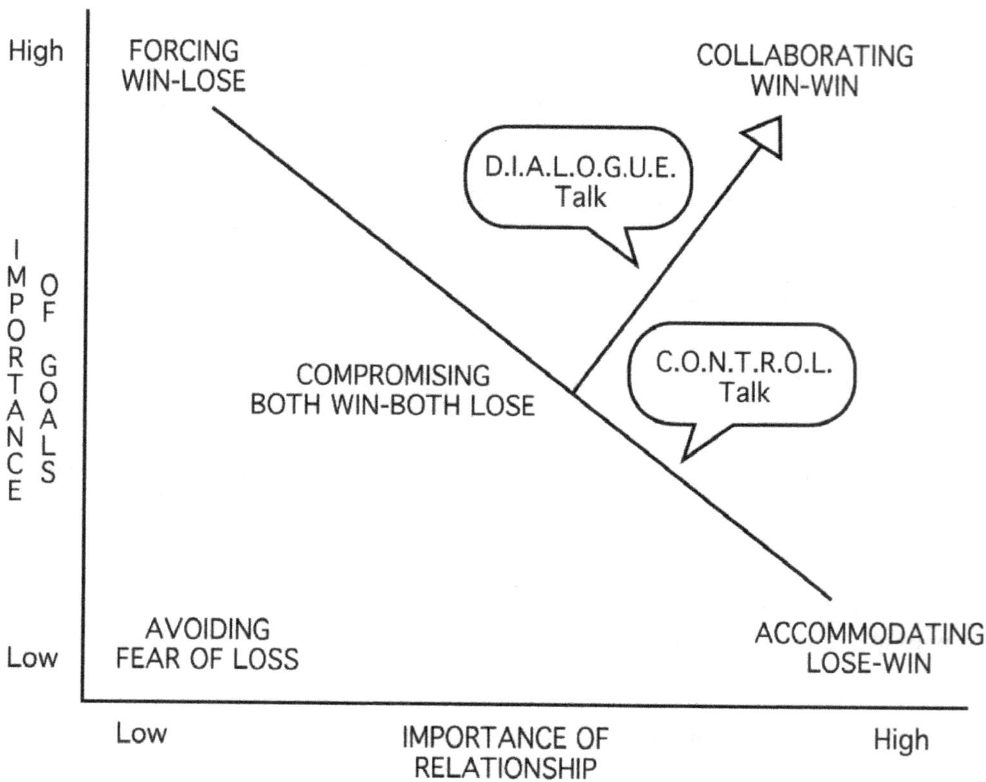

calm down and come down our emotional and cognitive inference ladders. As a basic approach to all conflict, however, avoidance is not a good strategy because we have little chance of satisfying our wants, and the others involved will begin to think of us as uncaring or cowardly, which will diminish our chances of maintaining positive relationships over time.

Forcing

The **forcing** style is in the upper-left corner of the diagram because it is "high" on getting what we want and "low" on considering the relationship to be important. With this style, a person is likely to start a discussion using light persuasive C.O.N.T.R.O.L. talk to get what they want, but if the other resists, they can easily escalate into heavy C.O.N.T.R.O.L. because what matters is getting what they want. They are not concerned for the other person and the relationship between them, so they go for it using all the forms of power, compliance-gaining tactics, and, if necessary, threats to get their way. These are folks who reflexively come at conflict from the Aggressive Defensive orientation.

Not surprisingly, people using this style tend to speak out of their controlling Parent or rebellious Child ego states. What is more surprising, this style can actually generate better outcomes than those reached using the less aggressive Compromise conflict-management style. Sometimes there is a "one best way" as opposed to "a little of this and a little of that."

Accommodating

The opposite style — **accommodation** — focuses on the importance of maintaining the relationship, even if it means giving up on getting our goals fulfilled. This kind of talk comes out of the Passive Defensive orientation and, in TA terms, the adaptive Child ego state. They both use passive light C.O.N.T.R.O.L. talk. However, people can consciously choose to accommodate in specific situations. They choose to give in "this time." They are likely to be using assertive "I-messages" and D.I.A.L.O.G.U.E. and be speaking out of their nurturing Parent ego states.

The difficulty with this style is that it creates and sustains win-lose situations for the person who uses it. In the short run it can help to maintain relationships in difficult situations, but if it is used constantly, others will treat the person like a doormat.

Compromise

The conflict-management styles diagram makes clear that most of the "talk" we do between these two extremes of forcing and accommodation occurs along one dimension (called the "distributive" dimension in some models) and is always a variety of C.O.N.T.R.O.L. talk — heavy to light at the extremes. The **Compromise** conflict-management style is located in the middle of this dimension. Other than **Avoiding** as a first choice, when we have to finally face conflict, **Compromise** is the most common approach to managing it. With this style, we are concerned with both goals and relationships, and try to resolve the conflict through conceding something on the goal side. We give a little and we get a little. Both partners give up something in their pursuit of their goals in order to maintain a workable relationship with each other. This approach comes out of a mixture of psychological orientations with a strong emphasis on the Constructive orientation. The talk involved often begins with competitive light C.O.N.T.R.O.L. and moves to a limited form of D.I.A.L.O.G.U.E. Participants may have started out in the Parent or Child ego states but will eventually move to the Adult ego state, because compromise is a limited form of problem solving.

In many situations, however, we may get less from the resolution than we wanted, and in some situations — for instance, when we try to improve a relationship or make something new and better happen — compromise doesn't work at all. Compromise is, after all, based on competitive light C.O.N.T.R.O.L. talk, where we are trying to get someone else to give us what we want, while not giving up what we already have (in terms of either our goals or the quality of our relationship with the other). And they are doing the same thing. To get a compromise agreement, however, both parties do have to give up something in order to end the struggle. We achieve better outcomes if we use a different approach and a different kind of talk.

Collaboration

A more powerful form of conflict management is **Collaboration**. It works when we are not prepared to sacrifice the relationship just to get what we want *and* we are also not prepared to give up what we want just to maintain the relationship. If we successfully collaborate, we will both win without losing something. True collaborative conflict resolution is, however, like walking a tightrope. It's as if we are high up in the air, with relationship on one side and goals on the other. We don't want to fall off on one side or the other because both are important to us. This requires a much more complex and difficult form of communication.

To accomplish collaboration in conflict situations, we need to use the three fundamental skills of great communication — mindfulness, appreciation, and meta-communication — and speak in a way that enhances the values of openness, supportiveness, and egalitarianism (the humanistic ideals), using D.I.A.L.O.G.U.E. talk.

Collaboration also demands that we move off the distributive dimension — where we are simply trying to divide up "the perceived pie" — to an entirely new way of seeing the conflict (called the "integrative" dimension) — where we try to create a different or bigger pie. What people want in this approach is a "win-win" solution that gives both parties to the conflict what they want *and* still maintains a high quality relationship.

Three Modes, Three Ego States and Key Conflict-Management Styles

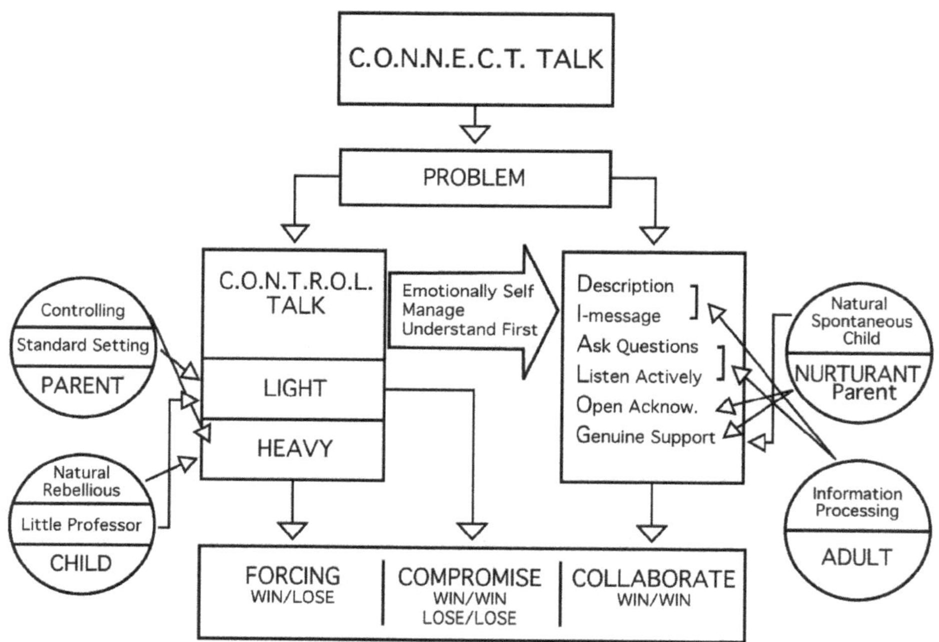

Collaboration requires us to first emotionally self-manage and seek understanding to avoid falling back into C.O.N.T.R.O.L. mode. We need to stay in our Adult Ego state. This enables mindfulness and appreciation and permits us to find the necessary emotional energy to enact the style elements of Assertive D.I.A.L.O.G.U.E. These connections are summarized in the diagram above. It connects all of the concepts we have described for becoming more effective communicators to our "life positions" as conflict resolvers.

To use collaboration as an approach to longer-term conflict resolution, we need to do more than simply speak with firmness, clarity and compassion. We need to begin a structured process of negotiation in order to resolve the issue in a way that will last, by ensuring that both of us gain from the outcome.

Assertive D.IA.L.O.G.U.E. For "Win-Win" Conflict Management

Falikowski[4] states that collaboration can lead to an integrative "win-win" decision, if we follow the steps (outlined by Johnson) of a structured process of constructive conflict resolution:

1) Confront the opposing party
2) Define the conflict together
3) Communicate personal positions and feelings
4) Express cooperative intentions
5) Understand the conflict from the other party's viewpoint
6) Be motivated to resolve the conflict and to negotiate in good faith
7) Reach an agreement

Like all lists of advice, it is logical and linear. It gives the impression that a collaborative conflict-management process might move in a straightforward way from step 1 to step 7. This rarely happens. Although this list identifies *what* we should do in a difficult situation, it doesn't tell us in any detail *how* to do it. However, we have already covered this in our analysis of Assertive D.I.AL.O.G.U.E.

For instance, notice steps one and two on the list. Somehow the other has to be "confronted" in a way that will allow them to stay with us to work on defining "the conflict" together. This is quite a feat and can only be accomplished with the kind of emotional self-management and higher ideals we have described for D.I.AL.O.G.U.E., and in a difficult situation like this, Assertive D.I.A.L.O.G.U.E.

Separate the People from the Problem

Fisher[5] and his colleagues argued that a lasting, positive outcome from negotiation can only be created when we are "hard" on the problem but "soft" on the people involved. *They* aren't the problem (although they may have brought it to the table); the problem is the perceived or real differences between us.

We must let the other person know that a conflict exists rather than escaping into avoidance. How we do this makes all the difference in terms of our future success. We could confront them with C.O.N.T.R.O.L. talk — "There's a problem and it's your fault" or we could use D.I.A.L.O.G.U.E. and start with a short, "mutualizing" **Open acknowledgement** of the conflict.

A mutualizing acknowledgement is a "Descriptive I-message" statement that is framed from the viewpoint of both parties in the situation. "It looks like we're both trying to do the best we can to get what we want here, but we're getting in each other's way. I'd like to resolve this." Then continue with a *brief* statement of your view of the problem, using a few more Descriptive I-messages ("The way I see it, we need to . . ."). Then stop talking. Don't behave as if you're in C.O.N.T.R.O.L. mode by talking too much.

The second step in collaboration is "Define the conflict together." Moving naturally from the first step, after you end your short introductory statement, **Ask** them a question to get their story — "Can you tell me how you see the situation?" Then **Listen actively**, giving them your undivided attention and occasional understanding feedback. You have to get their story before you can reach a mutual agreement on the nature of the conflict.

As they wind down, ask them if you can tell your story. While they've been talking, you've only been listening — no criticism or debating their points — so you need to tell your side. Asking them for permission to talk is a way of demonstrating equality, openness and politeness, and not interrupting their story is your way of modeling the behavior you expect from them when you start to talk. If they attempt to interrupt your story, remind them gently but firmly that you listened to them all the way through and you want them to give you the same respect. When you feel it's appropriate, ask them for some understanding or feedback on your story to make sure they've gotten your message from your point of view.

At this point, the collaboration process should begin to look like an interwoven D.I.A.L.O.G.U.E., not a linear process of logical steps. It becomes a flow of information involving the other steps that Johnson describes. These include

- Descriptions of personal positions and feelings ("This is what I want and when it doesn't happen I feel . . .")
- Repeated expression of cooperative intentions ("I really want to resolve this"), and
- Motivation to resolve ("I don't want this to come between us").

The most important thing here is to stay in your Adult voice no matter how *they* sound and stick to your assertive D.I.A.L.O.G.U.E. mode when *they* try to C.O.N.T.R.O.L. you. With time and positive persistence you will come to a common understanding of the situation. Mutual understanding and agreement on the problem is essential before it can be solved.

We need to be reminded, that none of this can be done if we don't focus on the problem as somehow separate from the person across the table. Without this critical (and dialogical) mind shift, Principled Negotiation and win-win solutions can't happen.

Focus on Interests Not Positions

Johnson's model finally states: "Reach an agreement," and as we've said above, things aren't quite as simple as that. The second and most important element of Fisher's "win-win" negotiation process reveals the complexity beneath Johnson's simple assertion. Among other things, throughout the D.I.A.L.O.G.U.E., we have gained insight into each other's positions and feelings around those positions. The positions we take in situations, however, are the forces that separate us not the ones that connect us.

Our position in a conflict is made up of the fixed solutions, proposals, demands, threats, or pre-determined points of view that we bring into the collaboration process. They are about dis-connection, not connection. So, after all of our discussion, we know more about our positions than we did before, but knowing more, and even understanding more, doesn't necessarily re-connect us. To reconnect, we need to figure out the deeper interests that lie behind our positions.

Our "interests" represent what really matters to each of us — the deeper needs that lie behind our willingness to struggle in this situation. Interests are often shared and hidden within our early, antagonistic positions. If we can ask the right questions and listen effectively, we can discover them. When we know them, we can almost always create solutions that will give both of us a win and re-integrate our relationship.

Divorce Mediation Example

To clarify the differences between positions and interests in conflict, let's use a classic example from divorce mediation. The mediator is dealing with a couple that has successfully agreed to divide up most of their common property but is deadlocked on the issue of their house. In the mediator's office they are making their positions quite clear:

Mediation: Third Party Support for Collaboration

She: I am keeping the house. Forget about selling it.

He: Hey, the only way to divide up a house is to sell it and split the money.

She: I don't care. I'm never going to agree to selling it.

The mediator intervenes with a question to him: "Tell me why it's important for you to sell the house."

He: "I need my half of the equity to continue to invest in my business. It's growing now, but I need a cash infusion if it's really going to be successful."

Then the mediator turns to her: "And why do you want to keep the house?"

She: "I am not tearing up my kids' lives any more than this divorce already has. Their friends and their school are nearby. They need some stability."

The mediator turns back to the husband: "How will investing in your business affect your child-support payments?"

He: "It will insure I can make them. In fact, I could even pay a bit more if my business grows the way I know it will. I love my kids and I am going to get them the money they need to have a decent life. It'll be easier if I can grow my business."

Mediator to both of them: "So it seems that despite your different positions on the house, your real interest is in doing the best you can for your kids."

(To her) "You want to stay in the neighborhood to stabilize your children's lives."

(To him) "And you want to be sure you can provide their support."

(To her) "If we could locate a place of equivalent quality to rent or buy in the neighborhood, could you think about selling the house?"

(To him) "And if we sell the house, can we think about your increasing your support payments by a reasonable amount in the next couple of years, as your business expands?"

In the end they reach an agreement — a "**win-win**" solution — where their real interest — supporting their kids — is fulfilled. Notice that in this situation, the Adult "voice of reason" is that of the third-party intervener — the mediator, who models D.I.A.L.O.G.U.E. by asking good questions, listening actively, and behaving supportively so the couple will stay open and keep talking in a difficult situation.

This example also demonstrates that collaborative conflict management through principled negotiation also speaks to the last two "negotiation process goals" that Fisher and his colleagues argued were critical to achieving "win-win" solutions:

- Invent options for mutual gain, and
- Insist on objective criteria.

As mentioned earlier, collaborative problem solving is not about distributing pieces of the currently "perceived pie" but is about reinventing the pie to include everyone's interests. So inventing options for mutual benefit is a vital part of the process.

Finally, even when people are satisfied with the immediate outcomes of a win-win negotiation, they may feel uncertain about how they and the other will follow through on their promises. An effective win-win outcome must last beyond the negotiation, so it is just as important for people to agree on how to continue to measure their own and the other's commitment to the agreement as it is to come up with something creative the first time.

Collaboration as the Ultimate "Unnatural Act"

What the mediator does for our warring couple is what we have to learn to do for ourselves when we are faced with conflict. We have to become mindful and aware of the situation and "compassionately confront" the other rather than unthinkingly fleeing into avoidance or into a flurry of C.O.N.T.R.O.L. talk, up and down the distributive dimension. This first choice is built on another choice. We have to decide we want to really solve "the problem" rather than escape into the emotional satisfaction of being "right." If we choose to solve, we also must choose to be flexible and open (we are going to hear things we won't like) and to be able to talk about not only the issues we have or problem we are facing, but also about the conversation that's going on right in front of us (meta-communication).

To make these choices we have to manage our *cognitive* responses (staying as close as possible to what's happening in the moment) and our *emotional* responses (cooler feelings), in the face of what we *perceive* to be the other's provoking behavior, so that we can find and stay in our Adult ego state and enact all the elements of D.I.A.L.O.G.U.E.

This series of choices and actions represents the most unnatural state of the human mind — a willingness to manage the contradictory and even paradoxical state of not being prepared to give up what we want just to maintain the relationship *and, at the same time, not being willing to sacrifice our relationship just to get what we want.* If this sounds hard, that's because it is. But it's not impossible. We now know that all of these choices are forms of communication competences that can be learned or improved.

Consider the Alternatives

Consider the alternatives to a more mindful and hard-working communicative style: a life of unthinking, low-level irritation, marked by occasional high-level conflict (often unresolved) where we rarely get exactly what we want but maintain good enough relationships with people to make up for our losses; or a life of intense competition where we almost always get what we want but we learn not to trust anyone or to care deeply.

We have the tools to be truly effective people — not just effective communicators. We simply need go learn how to use them to give ourselves more and better choices. We'll talk more about this in the last chapter.

End Notes

---

[1] *Ury. W.* (2007) The Power of a Positive No: How to Say No and Still Get to Yes. *New York: Bantam.*
[2] Gilbert, D. (2007) *Stumbling on Happiness.* Toronto: Vintage Canada.
[3] Based on Kilman, R. Thomas, K. (1975) "Inter-personal Conflict Handling Behavior as Reflections of Jungian Personality Dimensions" *Psychological Reports, 37,* pp. 971–980.
[4] Johnson, D. as cited in Falikowski, A. (2002). *Mastering Human Relations*, 2nd Edition, Toronto: Pearson Education. Chapter 6.
[5] Fisher, R. Ury, W. (1997) *Getting to Yes: Negotiating Agreement Without Giving In.* New York: Penguin.

CHAPTER THIRTEEN

A LAST WORD ABOUT TALK

The Results of Ineffective Communication

In Chapter 1 we referred to a large survey conducted in the United States that asked people what they thought about the quality of the interpersonal communication in their life. As we mentioned, 62% of respondents felt very comfortable in communicating but only 42% thought they were effective. They weren't sure that other people were getting their message.

It's also important to note that most respondents recognized that a lack of effective communication could create serious problems in their lives. For example, 44% believed that poor communication was a "very frequent" cause for ending a marriage or a long-term relationship. In fact, only poor communication (53%) and money (29%) stood out as "very frequent" causes of marriage breakdown; all other causes were ranked first by fewer than 1 person in 10. Overall, everyone thought communication was very important and wanted *more* of it in their lives.

It's interesting that public perception of poor communication as a cause of **marriage breakdown** fits well with Gottman's's[1] detailed review of the literature on the subject. After outlining the results of a number of large studies from several countries, on people's reasons for dissolving marriages, he states that, "gradually growing apart and losing a sense of closeness, and not feeling loved and appreciated" is reported to be the major cause of divorce. He argues that these results counteract the dominant myth that infidelity causes most divorces.

The real cause of what he calls the "slow slide toward divorce" is the *way* we treat each other in everyday C.O.N.N.E.C.T. talk. When the other turns away from or turns against most of our efforts to bid for positive emotional connection (see Chapter 9) we begin to give up, and as we let go two things happen — we forgive the other less and we use the worst forms of talk more.

We enter into a cycle of criticism and defense (heavy C.O.N.T.R.O.L.) that leads to stonewalling and withdrawal in the other. This becomes the ultimate demonstration of my seventh axiom — when faced with disagreement and disorder we need to feel right. In this cascade of distancing communication, we seem to substitute the feelings of righteous vindication for those of love and connection. Of course, the damage is even worse when this kind of talk happens around children. Not only do they feel what's going on long before their parents consciously admit the problem, but their unconscious minds are always paying attention — watching, learning, internalizing the worst ways to communicate about problems.

Not More but Better

As in the survey noted above, when dealing with communication problems people inevitably yearn for *more* communication. I hope, however, that I have made clear in the previous chapters that we don't necessarily need *more* communication — especially more one-way communication. What we need is *better* communication. And particularly when it matters — when things go sideways in our relationships — when the devils of difference, disagreement and disorder undermine our personal realities in ways that frighten us.

The need for better communication applies in all of our relationships — with spouses, friends, colleagues and bosses. To lead a better life, we need to create and sustain positive emotional connections with people in every part of our lives. The purpose of this to book is to explain how to build such connections and to stay connected even in situations that pull us apart.

Making More Mindful Choices

To do this we need to be clear about what we're doing when we talk. I've made you aware of the simplistic models of talk we all carry around in our heads (talk as a tennis match and as a contest) and how they compare to the layered complexities of face-to-face communication revealed in communication research. My intention has been to help you understand what really happens when we talk; to give you some insight into the causes of ineffective communication; and to suggest how you might "change your mind" about how talk works so you can change the way you respond in difficult situations.

I also hope that you have come to recognize the full engagement of our unconscious mind in every moment of your waking life. It's a **preference machine** and it's instant "like-dislike" choices, driven by **"associative activation"** never stops. It shapes the way we see, feel and think about anyone who enters our personal space. Its emotional reactions, based on deeply learned schema, are essential to our conscious mind's assessment of the quality of *this particular communication moment* and the effects of the other's responses on our conversational "face" — our self-esteem. Our unconscious mind can instantly tell whether the essential questions of "Do I matter?" "Am I competent?" and "Can I influence this situation?" are being answered positively by the words and actions of the other. Our sensitivity to the subtle emotional shifts in our conversations is summarized elegantly by Clifford Nass, a social scientist helping engineers design more "human" reactions into the computers we deal with everyday. As he asserts:

> In every thing you do and every decision you make emotion plays a role. The human brain is so exquisitely attuned to emotion, so obsessed with it and attuned to it and so good at detecting it, that even the slightest markers of emotions can have an enormous impact on how our brain behaves.[2]

The second part of this text is intended to make you aware of how to strengthen your mindful choices about *what to say next* when situations are ambiguous or difficult. In particular, I want you to recognize that often C.O.N.T.R.O.L. talk is an *automatic* response to what your unconscious perceives to be a low-level threat. When differences appear, light C.O.N.T.R.O.L. comes easily but can often lead us into difficulty — to competitive light C.O.N.T.R.O.L. — and compromised decisions, or worse, to standoffs. These, in turn, can create righteous anger in us and in the other with whom we are struggling. This emotion automatically calls up the darker forces of heavy C.O.N.T.R.O.L. When we head down this path, we often don't get what we want or be the "self" we want to be.

Choosing to Be a Better Self: A Conversational Matador

I have detailed a series of skills and forms of speech that we need to learn to be our better selves in difficult situations. I think they can be summed up in one metaphorical ideal — be a conversational matador. Why? Because matadors are trained to do something when the bull charges them that the rest of us haven't learned. They've been trained to consciously control their emotions, calmly step aside, and let the bull, with all its angry energy, go by. Unlike the self-managed matador, when someone's "bull" comes at us, we usually take it straight on. It hits us right in the heart and knocks us over, psychologically speaking. It momentarily stuns our conscious mind, so we automatically react from our fearful unconscious. To avoid this and to become effective in threatening moments, we need to "wake up" and compel the "lazy controller" of our conscious mind to make **mindful choices** to:

1) Emotionally self-manage.

    1a) Slow our reactions — pause, breathe to calm ourselves — let their emotions go by.

    1b) Ask ourselves an "I wonder" question to engage the conscious mind.

2) Be present, honest communicators. **Speak only from our position, not theirs.**

    2a) Use the descriptive I-messages of D.I.A.L.O.G.U.E.

    2b) Say only what we see, think and feel. Never tell others how they should think and feel. No "you are" messages.

3) **Listen from their position, not ours.**

    3a) Ask "descriptive questions" to get them engaged in helping us solve whatever is confronting us.

    3b) Listen to get their story, their meanings, not just to see if they agree with us.

4) **Appreciate others** and their efforts to try.

    4a) Openly acknowledge what we see going on with them, and

    4b) Use genuine support when appropriate to demonstrate our continuing connection to them, even in this difficult situation.

Conversational Matadors Lead Better Lives

When we choose to keep people connected to us even in situations that tear at those connections, we are doing more than simply getting through another tough conversation, we are making vital ethical choices. We make no choices at all when we use C.O.N.T.R.O.L. talk. It comes "naturally" — automatically. We have to consciously *choose* to do D.I.A.L.O.G.U.E. because it's an "unnatural" way to talk. In making that choice we are taking the path of nonviolent communication. We are choosing not to invade the other's psychological space with our superiority, contempt and angry judgments just because we feel challenged. We choose not to diminish them and ourselves in the process.

D.I.A.L.O.G.U.E. is the harder but higher road, because it forces us to take responsibility for our words and ourselves. The very form of this talk compels us to stop using judgment and blame to "get away with" our lives. For at least one moment, we must stop and appreciate the other — recognize their humanity even in the face of disagreement — and talk in ways that show them respect. When we do this we answer the question, "When difficulties arise do we show more respect to a spouse, lover, friend, child or colleague than we would to a head of lettuce?" This sounds ridiculous. It's not. It contains enormous ethical implications, as you will see, in this reflection from the Buddhist Philosopher, Thich Nat Hahn[3]:

No Blame — Just Understanding

When you plant lettuce, if it does not grow well, you don't blame the lettuce. You look for reasons it is not doing well. It may need fertilizer, or more water, or less sun. You never blame the lettuce.

Yet if we have problems with our friends or our family, we blame the other person. But if we know how to take care of them, they will grow well, like the lettuce. Blaming has no positive effect at all, nor does trying to persuade using reason and arguments.

That is my experience.

No blame, no reasoning, no argument, just understanding. If you understand, and you show that you understand, you can love, and the situation will change.

Lead a better life. Choose D.I.A.L.O.G.U.E.!

Please, don't just read this book. Use it!

End Notes

---

[1] Gottman, J., Declaire, J. (1999) *The Marriage Clinic*. New York: W. W. Norton and Company.

[2] Nass, C., as cited in Daviss, B. (2005) "Tell Laura I Love Her," *New Scientist*, (188) 2528: 42–46.

[3] Nat Hahn, T. (2004) *Taming the Tiger Within: Meditations on Transforming Difficult Emotions*. New York: Riverhead.

About The Author

Dr. Dalton Kehoe has been a teacher, communications trainer, organizational change consultant and public speaker for over 41 years. He is a social psychologist with a research background in interpersonal and small group communications. He recently retired from York University in Toronto, Ontario, Canada, as Senior Scholar of Communication Studies.

During his teaching career he was voted one of the top teachers in Ontario by his peers, won York's university-wide teaching award, and was a top rated workshop leader for the Executive Education Center of York's Schulich School of Business. He was also chosen by the province's public television network as one of the best lecturers in the province.

A major research focus during his career concerned the use of communication technology to improve the teaching-learning experience in university classrooms. This work led to his creation of a rich media, learning system that permits him to continue teaching his communication courses online in a format that fully engages his students. His work has been recognized at the national level by both *University Affairs* in Canada and by *The Chronicle of Higher Education* in the United States.

This fifth edition of *Communication in Everyday Life* will serve the needs of his York students, but he has substantially revised the book in the hopes of serving a much larger audience.

In 2009, he was invited to create and deliver a course for the Great Courses Company of Chantilly, Virginia — only the second Canadian academic to do so. Dr. Kehoe's DVD lecture series called *Effective Communication Skills* was their most successful new release in 2011 and continues to sell well, everywhere. His unique approach to interpersonal communication has now found an international audience.

Dr. Kehoe lives with his life partner, the beautiful and very patient Giovanna Di Ciaula, in an elegantly renovated condo apartment in downtown Toronto. From there, he continues to teach and write about the joys and challenges of face-to-face talk.

INDEX

A

B

C

D

E

F

G

H

I

J

K

L

M

N

O

P

Q

R

S

T

U

V

W